BIBLE BLINDSPOTS

Intersectionality and Theology Series

This series is a home for theologies that weave in the strands of gender, race, and class. Because weaving involves stripping the strands, this series makes room for plaiting sub- and minor- strands. Each volume of the series, as such, will exhibit the interwoven and intersectional natures of theology—theology is a weaving or intersection where words, images, schemes, stories, bodies, struggles, cultures, and more, meet and exchange. At this weaving/intersection, traditions, standards and ideals inspire, transpire, and some even expire.

BIBLE BLINDSPOTS

Dispersion and Othering

Edited by Jione Havea and
Monica Jyotsna Melanchthon

PICKWICK *Publications* · Eugene, Oregon

BIBLE BLINDSPOTS
Dispersion and Othering

Pickwick Publications
An Imprint of Wipf and Stock Publishers
199 W. 8th Ave., Suite 3
Eugene, OR 97401

www.wipfandstock.com

PAPERBACK ISBN: 978-1-7252-7676-5
HARDCOVER ISBN: 978-1-7252-7677-2
EBOOK ISBN: 978-1-7252-7678-9

Cataloguing-in-Publication data:

Names: Havea, Jione, editor. | Melanchthon, Monica Jyotsna, editor.

Title: Bible blindspots : dispersion and othering / edited by Jione Havea and Monica Jyotsna Melanchthon.

Description: Eugene, OR: Pickwick Publications, 2021. | Includes bibliographical references and index.

Identifiers: ISBN 978-1-7252-7676-5 (paperback). | ISBN 978-1-7252-7677-2 (hardcover). | ISBN 978-1-7252-7678-9 (ebook).

Subjects: LCSH: Bible—Postcolonial criticism. | Bible—Hermeneutics. | Bible. OT—Criticism, interpretation, etc. | Bible. NT—Criticism, interpretation, etc.

Classification: BS521.86 B51 2021 (print). | BS521.86 (ebook).

11/01/21

Cover art and Figure 1.1—*Untitled* Maria Fe (Peachy) Labayo (2016; acrylic on canvas, 15"x8"). Used with the permission of the artist. Photo courtesy of the artist.

Unless otherwise noted, Scripture quotations are taken from the New Revised Standard Version Bible copyright © 1989 National Council of the Churches of Christ in the United States of America. Used by permission. All rights reserved worldwide.

Scripture quotations marked (JPS) are taken from *Tanakh: The New JPS Translation according to the Traditional Hebrew Text.* Copyright © 1985, 1999 by The Jewish Publication Society with the permission of the publisher.

The work on this book was supported by
the Council for World Mission

Contents

Part 1 | Trials of Dispersion

Part 2 | Politics of Othering

Part 3 | Ceremony

Preface

THE BIBLE HAS BLINDSPOTS; the Bible also blinds and binds readers and devotees. Several of the teachings, values, and cultures that the Bible is said to propagate and protect are not often seen or assessed, mainly due to the respect and authority that readers associate with the Bible as their holy scripture. In similar ways, many of the subjects and ways that the Bible is understood to reject and demonize slip by unexamined. When those—the privileged and the denounced—are not examined, they fade into and hide at, or are tugged into, the blind spots of the Bible.

Alongside the cultures of election and holiness that take cover at the blind spots of the Bible, are cultures of *dispersion* and *othering*. This collection of essays brings some of the subjects that face *dispersion* (Babel builders, Samaritans, Melchizedek, Israel, Egypt, God, slaves, indigenous Australians, Palestinians, *minjungs*) and *othering* (Jezebel and Zuleika, Gomer and battered women, mothers and motherhood, victims of sexual abuse, Earth and Ruth, gays and foreigners) at the *Bible's blindspots* for engagement and repositioning.

After an opening chapter that sets the beat for the collection and locates the chapters in that pulse, the book is divided into three parts: (1) Trials of dispersion, (2) Politics of othering, (3) Ceremony. As a collection, this work stresses the inter- and ex-changes between dispersion and othering: while *dispersion* is physical displacement that constructs ideological biases and stereotypes, *othering* functions at the ideological level and manifests in different forms of displacement. The essays also draw attention to the inter/ex-changes between Bible and context, experiment with alternative modes and bases of interpretation, and flow from post-colonial and gendered studies to social media and the arts, closing with a drama that stages the biblical character of Ruth in between the blind spots of the biblical world and some of the struggles in the modern world.

Five of the essays—by Néstor O. Míguez, Jin Young Choi, Monica Jyotsna Melanchthon, Mothy Varkey, and Johnathan Jodamus—were presented at the 2018 Dare (discernment and radical engagement) forum hosted by the Council for World Mission at Mexico City (May 24–26, 2018). The other nine contributors added their voices and in*sights* to enable this publication to appear in this form, and to all of them, *muchas gracias*: Laura Griffin, Darío Barolín, Chrisida Nithyakalyani Anandan, Sweety Helen Chukka, Bethany Broadstock, Vaitusi Nofoaiga, Brent Pelton, Ellie Elia, and Jione Havea.

Finally, this work benefitted from the support of Collin Cowan and Sudipta Singh of CWM. *Thenk yuh*!

Contributors

Chrisida Nithyakalyani Anandan, Tamil Evangelical Lutheran Church (India), Lutheran School of Theology at Chicago (USA)

Darío Barolín, Waldensian Church (Uruguay), Professor at Red Ecuménica de Educación Teológica (Ecumenical Network for Theological Education), Buenos Aires (Argentina)

Bethany Broadstock, Pilgrim Theological College, University of Divinity (Melbourne, Australia)

Jin Young Choi, Baptist Missionary Training School Professor of New Testament and Christian Origins, Colgate Rochester Crozier Divinity School, New York (USA)

Sweety Helen Chukka, Andhra Evangelical Lutheran Church (India), Lutheran School of Theology at Chicago (USA)

Ellie Elia, Uniting Church in Australia

Laura Griffin, Lecturer at La Trobe Law School (Australia)

Jione Havea, native pastor and research fellow (Trinity Theological College, Aotearoa; Center for Public and Contextual Theology, Charles Sturt University, Australia)

Johnathan Jodamus, Senior Lecturer of New Testament and Gender Studies, University of the Western Cape, Cape Town (South Africa)

Monica Jyotsna Melanchthon, Associate Professor, Old Testament, Pilgrim Theological College, University of Divinity (Melbourne, Australia)

Néstor O. Míguez, Emeritus Professor of Bible and Systematic Theology, Presbyter of the Evangelical Methodist Church in Argentina

Vaitusi Nofoaiga, Principal, Dean and Head of New Testament Studies, Malua Theological College (Samoa)

Brent Pelton, Pilgrim Theological College, University of Divinity (Melbourne, Australia)

Mothy Varkey, New Testament Lecturer, Mar Thoma Theological Seminary, Kottayam (Kerala, India) and Postdoctoral Associate, Murdoch University (Western Australia)

1

Spotlighting the Bible's Blind(ing)spots

Jione Havea and Monica Jyotsna Melanchthon

In the media age, steered by the transmutations of artificial intelligence, "coding" identifies products and genes as well as traces the locations and movements of genetic strands, of tagged bodies (surveillance), and of operations. While tracking is helpful (but not necessarily ethical) in the context of the Covid-19 pandemic—at the genetics level, to track the mutation of the SARS-Cov-2 coronavirus and at the social level, to identify contacts and reduce the chance for spreading infection—surveillance disturbs a lot of people. Tracking devises might be ethical when used with people on parole, but not for "free" persons whether infected or not.

In the media age, in the whitewash of poverty and the rapture of human trafficking, some women and children have become products to be sold and bought, used and discarded like damaged and expired goods. Such situations are exposed and challenged in the "untitled" painting by Maria Fe (Peachy) Labayo on the cover of this book (see Figure 1.1).

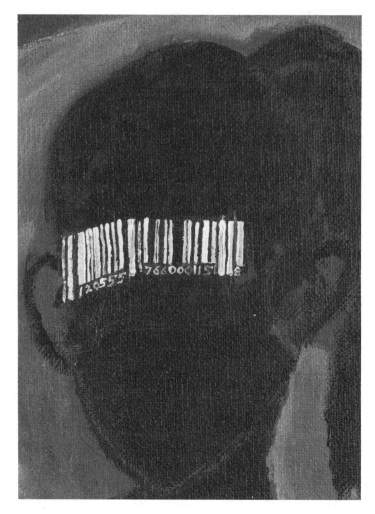

Figure 1.1: Maria Fe (Peachy) Labayo, "Untitled" (2016, detail).
Used with the permission of the artist

The human body is blackened, with no facial features; it is a female body, because of the hair, and she could be a young person. She wears glasses, as if to invite viewers to see her as well as to be seen by her, and her glasses also look like handles on a trophy—she represents the trafficked bodies that have become the prize for the highest bidder. This painting also functions as a mirror, for viewers to see how, when they buy a barcoded product, they might be contributing to human trafficking and to the defacing of those who are trafficked. Human trafficking is not a

SPOTLIGHTING THE BIBLE'S BLIND(ING)SPOTS

phenomenon; human trafficking is a reality, and the blue background behind the blackened head asserts that this is a global reality. Some people
are just barcodes, and the barcode on this subject is a blindfold.

The 2015 movie *Spotlight* directed by Tom McCarthy is about another kind of blindfold: the cover-up of the sexual abuse of young people
and children by priests and church leaders. *Spotlight* focuses on cases in
the USA, but these horrendous behaviors—the abuse and the cover-up—
are global realities. Adults too are sexually abused in church premises,
under the shadows of the cross and the eyes of the bible, and some of
those are also covered-up (or blindfolded), but *Spotlight's* focus is on
the more vulnerable parishioners who are *pushed into the blind spots* of
church leaders and church records.

This collection of essays discusses some of the cases of abuse and
violence at the blind spots of the bible, and it works against the use of the
bible to cover-up abuse and violence in society (in other words, the use of
the bible *to blind* devotees and critics). There are four assumptions that,
in different combinations and grades, the contributors to this collection
share: first, the bible has blind spots; second, the bible is blinding; third,
the bible is used to blind victims and critics; fourth, the bible can (be used
to) expose blind spots and heal blindness. These assumptions play out in
the following essays, divided into three overlapping sections—one focusing on *dispersion*, one dealing with *othering* practices, and one imaging
a space where the dispersed and othered might re-gather and celebrate.

Flows of the Book

The intersections (or, inter- and ex-changes) of dispersion with othering—dispersed subjects are othered, and othered subjects are dispersed
(at least emotionally dispersed if not physically dispersed as well)—make
the *division* of the essays into three sections *fraud*. That said, we also add
that the experience of dispersion and othering proves that *division in
itself is fraud*. Dispersion and othering violate divisions and limits. Mindful of this conundrum, this collection comes upon the assumption that
divisions and limits are *fluid*, and the voices that come through each essay
seek to gather, to congregate, with the help of and in the eyes of readers
who are not blind(ed) but who have both commitments and attitudes.
Put directly, this work is for the eyes of readers who are also (interested

in becoming) activists for and advocates of the dispersed and the othered in the bible and in society.

The division between the three sections is fluid, but there are themes and drives that flow and connect the voices in the essays. The essays in the first section—Trials of dispersion—flow from the dispersion of the builders of the Tower of Babel and the struggles of the indigenous people in Australia (Laura Griffin) to the ground level of Latin American Liberation Theology from where comes a call for solidarity with the dispersed people of Palestine (Darío Barolín), to the call for affirming slaves as siblings (Chrisida Nithyakalyani Anandan), to the call for reconsidering of antagonism toward Egypt and most things Egyptian (Jione Havea), to the call for reconsidering the rejection of Samaritans that biblical and modern empires manufacture (Néstor Míguez), to the call for affirming the fluidity of sacred margins in Hebrews (Mothy Varky), and to the call for embracing the dispersed in Mark and in the Asian diaspora (Jin Young Choi). There are, of course, more to each of these essays, but this reductionist introduction is for the purpose of explaining the fluid limits between the essays and for easing the fraudness of the divide between the three sections.

In the second section—Politics of Othering—the flow is from the othering of foreigners and females (Monica Jyotsna Melanchthon) to the othering of Zuleika in the shadows of Joseph in Gen 39 (Sweety Helen Chukka), to the othering of Gomer in Hosea 2 and battered women in modern settings (Bethany Broadstock), to the othering of a woman in birth pangs in Rev 12 (Vaitusi Nofoaiga), to the othering of women who are not or cannot be mothers in 1 Tim 8 (Johnathan Jodamus), to the othered voice in Ps 4 as a threshold for gay communities (Brent Pelton).

The final section imagines Ruth as a "ceremony site" for dispersed and othered subjects to re-gather and celebrate (Ellie Elia and Jione Havea). This twisting introduction is for the purpose of explaining one of the ways in which the essays flow into each other (more detailed introduction to each essay follows).

Trials of Dispersion

Laura Griffin (chapter 2) sets the tone for this first section with a reading of the dispersion of humanity in Gen 11:1–9. This narrative tells of a united humanity—speaking a common language—attempting to construct a city with a tower to reach to the heavens, a building project that troubled Yhwh. Yhwh responds by confusing the language of the people and scattering them to distant lands, and the remaining half-built city/tower is named Babel.

This narrative is one of the iconic narratives in the Hebrew Bible. It has long captured the attention and imagination of artists, storytellers and communities. Griffin's essay offers an exegetical analysis of this pericope, building upon a brief outline of historical and literary frames for understanding the text. Griffin then propagates views that run counter to dominant theological commentaries, and invites rereading this narrative in "stolen lands," such as the one that has come to be called Australia. The critical drive of this essay is for readers who live on stolen lands (and who doesn't?) to reconsider their readings of the bible's blinding spots.

Darío Barolín (chapter 3) wrestles with the words of Atahualpa Yupanqui (1908–1992), an indigenous poet and musician from Argentina who wrote a song titled *Little questions about God*. The song ends with these lines:

> There is an issue on Earth
> Much more important than God:
> That nobody spits blood
> For others to be at ease.
> Whether God cares for the poor,
> Maybe yes, and maybe no.
> But I am sure he eats
> At the table of the boss.

Barolín's response to the song is in three questions: Is God [still] at the boss's table? What or who put God at the boss's table? How might we move God from the boss's table? Barolín reflects on these questions from his Latin American context, in solidarity with the struggles of the dispersed people of modern Palestine, around the topics of oppression, liberation, exodus, the chosen ones, the native people of the land, the failures of liberation criticism, and the ongoing tasks for biblical interpreters.

Chrisida Nithyakalyani Anandan (chapter 4) analyzes the manumission of the slaves in Deut 15:12–18, drawing upon social identity theory, to determine whether group dynamics and group identity formation played a role in segregating masters from slaves. In the case of debt slavery, people who could not pay their debt become laborers to their neighbors (who are from the same group); this raises critical questions: Should their identity change when their circumstances change? Are they neighbors, laborers or slaves? Do they become neighbors again after they repay their debts? How did these differing identities influence or affect these people who believed in one God and one people? What are the implications of the Deuteronomic writer addressing the laborer as "your brother [and sister]"? For Anandan, it is significant that Deut 15:12–18 reminds landowners that their slaves are siblings.

Anandan answers the above questions in relation to the themes of land as a blessing from God, family ethos of love and kinship, social identity and formation in the slavery law codes—and in conversation with the experiences of bonded and migrant laborers in India.

Jione Havea (chapter 5) appeals to the music hall practice of remixing (or dubbing) to reformulate the image of Egypt, one of the empires in the ancient world. Biblical texts do not demonize Egypt as much as pro-Israelite readers do. Havea steps back from the exodus pandemonium in order to remix the impressions of Egypt. Egypt was house of refuge and of bondage, hated and longed-for, empire and home for refugees including Abram and Sarai, Jacob and his household, Jeremiah and his friends, Mary and Joseph with their child, and more recently the peoples of Gaza, Tunisia and Libya. Refugees continue the exodus to and through Egypt.

Havea turns from Egypt to the empires of today (e.g., USA, England, France, Australia): how might we convince modern empires to open their borders for those who are displaced by crises that are suffocating them? This chapter is committed to those who are drowning in the wilderness due to (the politics of) ecological and political crises. In a way, Havea remixes Psalm 24—*O gates, lift up your heads! Up high, you everlasting doors, so that the drowning may come in.*

Néstor Míguez (chapter 6) turns to the history of the Samaritans, a people who experienced physical and ideological dispersions. Míguez exposes the role of empires (Assyrian, Persian, Roman) in this history, and the imperialist and anti-imperialist power games that run through it, then brings the story to modern days and how those that are despised by the empires and their allied local elites are to be included as part of God's people and reign.

Before being ill-reputed as "the Samaritans," they were part of the elected people of Israel; as a matter of fact, they were the majority (ten tribes). The schism was provoked by the imperialist legacy of Solomon's reign, and the crown's taxing avidity. Scripture witnesses to the corruption of both reigns, and the ensuing prophetic condemnation by God, and its "dis-election." Assyria and Babylon intervene and impose their imperial politics in order to persist in the separation of the people, by fostering prejudice to assure their dominion.

The Samaritans were again "dis-elected" by the returning exiles in the time of Nehemiah. The creation of an "ethics of purity" and the support of the imperial power to the returning elite, over against the "people of the land," and afterwards the intervention of the Roman Empire in order to control the land through the divide and rule empire politics, deepened the separation and discrimination.

Over against the prejudice thus created, and in terms of the coming reign of God, the Samaritans are included again by Jesus through his parable in Luke 10:30–37, and in the story of the cleansed lepers (Luke 17:12–19). The gospel of John witnesses in various ways to the inclusion of the Samaritans among Jesus' followers.

Míguez points out the roll of empires (Assyrian, Persian, Roman) in this history, and the imperialist and anti-imperialist power games that run through it, then brings the story to our days and how those that are despised by the empires and their allied local elites are to be included as part of God's people and reign.

Mothy Varkey (chapter 7), with a postcolonial perspective, re-visits the theological and political agenda of the diaspora (dispersed) Jewish community behind the letter to the Hebrews. The community associates the Old Testament tradition of Melchizedek, who disappears after Gen 14:18–20 and reappears in Ps 110:4, with Jesus as high priest. As a Canaanite king, Melchizedek was a priest of El Eloy, the head of the Canaanite pantheon. Melchizedek combined kingly and priestly roles— when King David conquered Jerusalem (2 Sam 5:6–10), he adopted the local (Canaanite) imperial strategy of combining religion and state so that he can manipulate and perverse religion in such a way that his imperial agenda has religious endorsement and ratifications.

Varkey argues that the letter to the Hebrews customizes David's royal/imperial strategy to explicitly overturn Aaronic and Levitical priestocracy as well as to challenge "immovable" genealogical, ethnic, and purity boundaries. The community that shaped the letter invites its readers to cross the *fixed* "sacred margins" and to embrace the "shame" of those on the margins by going outside the city gates of the holy city, Jerusalem (13:11). By associating this boundary crossing imagery with the believers' anticipated, eschatological city (13:14), the letter reflects how permeable boundaries constitute a defining characteristic of the new community.

Jin Young Choi (chapter 8) weaves diasporic experiences in Mark with the experience of doubly displaced (by dispersion, and by history writers) Asian diaspora communities in the American continent. Choi argues that separation is intrinsic to the concept of diaspora as it means "dispersion from" home. Moreover, the experiences of diaspora comprise of crossing borders that separate physical spaces. Such border crossing results in dislocation and relocation.

However, cultural hybridization is often celebrated in the increasingly globalized world. Asian diaspora is not an exception in this phenomenon. Rather than being idealized or essentialized, these diasporic experiences should be historicized. One may ask: what socio-economic, political, and cultural conditions mark the trajectories of Asian diaspora in these places of the Global South?

Choi takes up the task of historicizing Asian diaspora in Latin America and the Caribbean. This task is accomplished by rereading images of separation prevalent in the Gospel of Mark. The purity law separates people, places, and culture; and the multitude—dispersed *ochlos*—cross borders and are displaced.

Separation is a heuristic tool in interpreting the Gospel of Mark from an Asian diasporic perspective. This interpretation tackles the dominant theological interpretation of the Gospel, which focuses on Christology and discipleship but ignores the presence and role of the multitude as highlighted in Asian minjung hermeneutics. For example, "Mexicans enjoy their pan chino with coffee for breakfast, Peruvians swear on their uniquely named chifa restaurants that they have the best Chinese food in the world, and Cubans love the lottery game they call la charada china."

Choi spotlights displaced minjung against the backdrop of the Roman Empire and revisits the issues of Asian diaspora in Latin America as related to the US exclusionary policies of Asian immigration, as well as European and American imperialism/colonialism. The slavery and indentured laborers of Asian people have conveniently been obliterated in the official history of the US. Historicizing the Asian diaspora in the

Americas through the lens of the dispersed minjung in Mark challenges both the American empire and dominant Western biblical scholarship.

Politics of Othering

Monica Jyotsna Melanchthon (chapter 9) focuses on the complexity of relationship between nationalism, gender and identity, and how those are like grease in the machinery of othering. The foreign woman became a marker to shape differences with the non-Israelite, specifically in the exilic and post-exilic times.

Melanchthon looks at how Israelite publicists broadcast a series of stereotypes through a flurry of redacted and revised texts. These texts compound and conflate images of Israelite masculinity and identity and build negative views about foreign woman through texts such as the Jezebel narrative, the story of victimized and heroic Israelite men such as Elijah—these texts are examples of the domestication of the foreign woman. Israelite authors were troubled by fantasies about possible re-lations between Israelite men and foreign women, as reflected in texts such as 1 Kgs 18–19 and the book of Ruth. These texts draw sharper cleavage between the Israelite and the non-Israelite and underline the elected status of the Israelite. Melanchthon assesses the issues of election and rejection in these texts, drawing inspiration and insight from the socio-political movements of *Shuddhi* and *Sangathan* in the early 1900s in India—powerful movements to consolidate Hindu ranks, and help galvanize the process of the construction of a pan-Indian Hindu com-munity rigidly set apart from the rest.

Sweety Helen Chukka (chapter 10) reads for Zuleika's narrative in Gen 39. The narrator's portrayal of foreign women's use of their sexuality is critical in Chukka's reading. Feminist biblical scholars applaud female subjectivity and yet they are cold toward Zuleika, the unnamed wife of Potiphar, whom they find to be feisty, villainy, willy, and sexually intense due to her foreignness and "outrageous" behavior.

Traditional readings of Gen 39 have focused on the virtues of Jo-seph. While Zuleika is portrayed as a seductress, Joseph is elevated as a wise sage who interprets dreams. Joseph found favor in God's sight, in Potiphar's sight, in Zuleika's sight and in the chief jailer's sight. On the other hand, for many readers Zuleika is a negative temptress. The Qur'an for example allocates an entire Sura to the encounter between Joseph and Zuleika. Though Sura 12 depicts a crafty Zuleika, it also records her remorse for her behavior. The Midrash too explains Zuleika's acts, but the negativity ascribed to Zuleika in the biblical text supersedes both the Qur'an and the Midrash.

Chukka is vigilant to the narration of Zuleika's story in Gen 39. Her vigilant reading unmasks the power dynamics prevalent in the text that demeans and subjugates the voice of Zuleika in order to elevate the status of Joseph, and in the process, she deconstructs the narrator's understanding of the sexuality of foreign women.

Bethany Broadstock (chapter 11) offers a contextual reading of the prophetic metaphor in Hosea 2, where the brokenness of the relation between Yahweh and Israel is represented by a narrative of unfaithfulness in the context of Hosea's marriage to Gomer. The way in which this unfaithfulness is described and addressed in the metaphor, echoing the disproportionate power and dominance which so often escalates into violence and characterizes abusive relationships and situations, is compared to narratives of domestic violence in the contemporary Australian context where high levels of often fatal violence pose a stark and serious socio-political challenge.

Hosea 2 becomes a challenge, related but not limited to the use of the female body as the arena in which dynamics of divine judgment play out. Gomer is doubly othered, by her gender and her representation of the community. Those realities often go unrecognized by readers of the text, or only recognized subconsciously, by readers who assume that one must read from the male perspective in order to understand the text's structure and message.

Broadstock is concerned with two key issues: first, that the words ascribed to God via Hosea's prophetic metaphor imply that violence hovers as a threat over God's way with God's people in the context of the covenant; and second, that if a reader in the contemporary world understands this to be justified, the text may leave itself vulnerable to exploitation by those who seek to theologically legitimate certain forms of violence in the context of marriage or other intimate settings. Broadstock accordingly explores how to renegotiate Hosea's metaphor so as to critically engage with its gendered violence and its theological implications, while maintaining its significance as a commentary on divine judgement and compassion.

Vaitusi Nofoaiga (chapter 12) reads Rev 12 from his Samoan context, drawing attention to the use of the image of a woman crying out in birth pangs to define the pain encountered in following Jesus. In Rev 12 a pregnant woman cries out in the agony of giving birth. Nofoaiga reads her cry as a revelation about discipleship: "The pregnant woman after giving birth to a son fled to the wilderness but is pursued by a dragon. And the earth came to the help of the woman."

Nofoaiga appeals to a Samoan wisdom saying—*Tagi e le fatu ma le eleele* (The rock and earth weep)—to explain the interconnectedness of humans to *eleele* (earth), an interconnectedness that occurs because of the inter-*tautua* (inter-serving of each other). Nofoaiga interprets Rev 12 from the inter-*tautua* perspective and explores the cosmic textures of Rev 12 as apocalyptic literature where both the woman and earth may be understood as "disciples" *(tautua mo le Atua)*.

Johnathan Jodamus (chapter 13) queers the portrayal of childbearing as constitutive of punitive femininity in the discourse of 1 Tim 2:8–15, a text that has been used to regulate women's roles within and beyond the church in matters ranging from women's ordination to women's reproductive choices. The concomitant result has been the concretizing of stereotypical gendered normativities that script bodies to perform according to heteronormative sex and gender assumptions. As such the text of 1 Timothy has received much feminist scholarly attention, but this attention has been limited methodologically and sometimes re-inscribes mothering as constitutive of femininity.

A recent turn in the literature on motherhood gives attention to the embodied and philosophical experience of "mothering," as opposed to the conventional focus on the institution of motherhood. Appealing to Butler's notion of gender as constitutive Jodamus engages in a reading that problematizes heterosexual gender normativities, and thus reads 1 Tim 2:8–15 for the "dis-elected" others. In this turn, Jodamus suggests the possibility of fathers as (m)others.

Blending sociorhetorical interpretation (SRI) and gender-critical interpretive strategies applied to the text of 1 Timothy, Jodamus demonstrates that mothering can be viewed beyond the essentialist feminine identity, and that when viewed in this way the notion of mothering as salvific in this text is not as oppressive as some feminist scholars have argued. This reading opens up new possibilities for soteriology beyond gender confinements, offers potential to queer this text beyond the feminine and masculine binary, and responds to calls from theologians advocating more redemptive masculinities.

Brent Pelton (chapter 14) finds in Psalm 4 the perspective of one who struggles with the anxiety of being symbolically attacked for her or his behavior or beliefs, and who turns to God for support in facing the psychological harm that has taken place. Pelton makes use of contextual hermeneutics, drawing on historical and literary works on the psalm, as well as insights from the social sciences. Through these approaches, one may read Psalm 4 as a narrative from the perspective of a contemporary gay male.

Pelton uses Psalm 4 as a model for speaking into a contemporary community's concerns. Through the work of contextual theology and contemporary translation, Psalm 4, thus, can be a template for addressing the contemporary concerns of a particular community in light of a Christian faith perspective. While Pelton's focus is on Psalm 4 and the gay community, his approach may also be applied to other texts for the purpose of empowering more othered communities.

Ceremony

Ellie Elia and Jione Havea (chapter 15) wind up the collection with a script of a drama that circles around the story of Ruth, a foreign woman taken into diaspora (dispersion). In this instance, Judah is the diaspora where Ruth is othered in several ways: as a Moabite; as a daughter-in-law; as booty in an inheritance; as a mother whose new-born was taken and given to someone else, and etcetera. In this drama, Ruth is the gathering site (similar to the ceremonial sites of native communities) for dispersed and othered subjects, in other words, this drama involves Ruth et alia (and others).

The mention of her name, Ruth, raises various reactions from subjects such as raped victims, transgender subjects, trafficked workers, refugees, et alia. From the mention of her name, the drama unfolds and invites praise. antipathy. disbelief. indifference. uncertainty. annoyance. dispersion. dis-person. regathering. embrace. ceremony.

Bodies

The final tasks for bringing the essays together for this publication took place in the first half of 2020, as Covid-19 was mutating, building its potency and spreading its dominion. Time will tell the full story of Covid-19, but it is already obvious that certain bodies receive less protection and far less opportunities than others. Black, brown and ethnic minorities have been infected in greater proportion as compared to the white bodies in communities both in the global south and in the global north. This comes as no surprise, for such is the way things were in the "old normal." Prior to the advent of Covid-19, black, brown and ethnic minorities were more likely to be dispersed and othered. They were and are more likely to be buried in the blind spots of politics and societies.

One of the responses from more powerful governments, such as USA and Australia, to the economic crisis that Covid-19 brought was to wind back policies that offer environmental protection (e.g., Endangered Species Act and the National Environmental Policy Act in the USA). Those governments gave "executive orders" that removed environmental checks from major infrastructure projects—such as building roads and expanding the mining industry—deemed "essential" for fast-tracking economic recovery. The impacts and threats of climate change were put aside in the name of the economy and national security, and the blame fell upon Covid-19. We on the other hand cannot put climate change aside. In the midst of the Covid-19 pandemic, between April 1–11, category 5 cyclone Harold upturned settlements in Papua New Guinea, Solomon Islands, Vanuatu, Fiji and Tonga. As these black and brown island nations were closing their borders in the hope to keep Covid-19 out, the impacts of climate change were destructive and economically costly. We in fact expect that the economic cost of climate change will far exceed the economic cost of Covid-19. This comparison is to make the point that it is not appropriate to put climate change aside, rather than in order to suggest that one crisis is worse than the other. Climate change is the consequence of the old normal, and it has contributed to the dispersion and othering of many bodies. Climate change is not only threatening black and brown lives, but all bodies. Climate change is not threatening only humans. It is a threat to all living creatures, on land and in the sea.

In the first half of 2020 also, the Black Lives Matter (#BLM) movements was reignited by the death of George Floyd (25 May 2020) in the hands of Minneapolis police officers. Racism and police brutality are also part of the old normal, and so is the demise of dispersed and othered bodies under the authorities of so-called civil societies. In the midst of the #BLM uproar, the then president of the USA took a bible for a photo op at St. John's Church (Washington DC, June 1). Donald Trump was appealing to American voters for whom the bible is scripture and authoritative.

In light of these global events—Covid-19, climate change, #BLM—this collection of essays comes as an invitation for students and readers of the bible to reassess how and what we read in the bible, as well as how and why we see the bible as authoritative. This invitation comes through the readings of texts involving dispersed and othered subjects in the bible. Those subjects represent many other bodies at the blindspots of the bible, as well as many bodies at the blindspots of readers. Those bodies are more than barcodes (see Figure 1.1). They too have names.

In response to the global events of Covid-19, climate change and #BLM, reading for dispersed and othered bodies is unfinished business.

Part 1

Trials of Dispersion

2

Dispersal, Defense, and Dispossession

Rereading Genesis 11:1–9 from Stolen Land

Laura Griffin

So the Lord scattered them abroad from there
over the face of all the earth,
and they left off building the city.
(GEN 11:8)[1]

These words of ours are from the old days before we were born . . .
The words come from our ceremonies
to teach us about places and relationships.
· (GULA LALARA, WARNUNGWAMADADA ELDER AND
STORYTELLER)[2]

---

1. Unless otherwise indicated, all biblical translations are from the NRSV.
2. Rademaker, "Language and Australian Aboriginal History," 222.

Wendy, it's been over 10 minutes and you keep talking to everybody

and you're not moving on.

500 metres from here is your move on.

(WESTERN AUSTRALIAN POLICE OFFICER TO ABORIGINAL
ROUGH SLEEPER, 11 APRIL 2020)[3]

The iconic passage of Gen 11:1–9 recounts the story of a united humanity, speaking one common language, attempting to construct a city with a
tower to reach to the heavens. Yhwh is troubled by this plan and responds
by confusing the language of the people and scattering them to distant
lands. The half-built city/tower is named Babel. This narrative has long
captured the attention and imagination of artists, storytellers and communities.[4] Traditional readings have applied a moralistic frame, identifying prideful or sinful behavior and consequent punishment by Yhwh.
Alternative readings share this view in some respects, by interpreting the
narrative as an anti-Babylonian or more generally anti-imperial polemic.

This essay adds a different postcolonial reading—one offered from
stolen land. Several tasks are necessary in order to make such a reading
possible, especially since this is a well-known passage that has long been
laden with moralistic interpretations. Taking stock of existing interpretations allows us to identify how the various methods used by commentators have shaped views of the morality and theology of this text. We can
also then contrast these interpretations with what appears—or does not
appear—on the text's surface.

This allows us to engage critically with aspects of the narrative not
usually attended to—in particular, Yhwh's defensive strategy of dispersal,
and its use to rupture a unified language, land, and humanity. This geopolitical strategy and its catastrophic impacts are recognizable as a form
of colonial violence, opening the way to an account of dispersal's ongoing
role and impacts on the stolen land from which I write. A comparison
between the Babel narrative and the historical and ongoing violence
endured by Indigenous peoples in what is now called Australia, reveals
several commonalities. In both cases, we see dispersal being used as a

---

3. Hirini, "Homeless Aboriginal People in Perth."

4. Written exegesis of the passage varies greatly, dating back to the time of Josephus. See Feinman, *Jerusalem Throne Games*, 104–7.

strategy to disempower and dispossess, silencing speech and irreparably breaking a nexus between land, language and community.

Historical Observations

There is little common ground when it comes to historical critical analysis of Gen 11:1–9. Scholars typically ascribe the passage to the Yahwist source (J). With regards to literary parallels in the ancient Near East, there are only few.[5] Different theories about authorship and timing relate to different views of the story's nature as either "Yahwistic primeval history"[6] "about the dawn of human civilization [. . .] or whether it can be situated in some specific historical context."[7] For instance, Gnuse sides with arguments of "late sixth-century-BCE Chaldean Babylon as the setting for this story, and the work of Nabonidus in particular."[8]

Ultimately, issues of authorship and dating are inextricably tied to questions of the story's purpose. Some scholars—like Westermann— prioritize the tale's etiological nature, with its "focus on how the present emerged from the distant past."[9] They also trace the multiplicity of narrative units or etiological concerns, particularly "the two etiologies of geographical dispersion and linguistic confusion," although this raises further questions about the narrative role of the tower in tying the two units together.[10] Alternatively, some have read the tower narrative itself as etiological: "An old theory suggests that the story recalls some particular ruined ziggurat observed by Semitic nomads in their wanderings, and they wove a tale to explain its ruined condition."[11] More generally, there are certainly plenty of historical parallels with regard to tower-building, as various Mesopotamian kings built significant ziggurats:

> The Ziggurat was a structure that was built to support the stairway (simmiltu) which was believed to be used by the gods to

5. See Gnuse, *Misunderstood Stories*, 248–9.

6. Carr, "Genesis," 25.

7. Feinman, *Jerusalem Throne Games*, 12.

8. Gnuse, *Misunderstood Stories*, 252.

9. Feinman, *Jerusalem Throne Games*, 115.

10. Tongue, "The Babel Complex," 164; See also Feinman, *Jerusalem Throne Games*, 116; LaCocque, "Whatever Happened in the Valley of Shinar?"

11. Gnuse, *Misunderstood Stories*, 251.

travel from one realm to the other. [. . .] The stairway led at the
top to the gate of the gods, the entrance to the divine abode.[12]

Building on historical parallels, some have focused on particular
events likely to involve ziggurats. Seely, for example, suggests that the
story "refers to the disruption of Sumerian culture by the Akkadian empire under Sargon."[13] Thus it is possible to read in the text an experience
shared by the authors (or redactors), namely the scattering of diverse
peoples in relation to a failed attempt at an imperial construction project:

> When Babylon fell to the Persians, and subsequently the Per-
> sians allowed exiled people to return home, the allusion in Gen-
> esis 11 to the scattered peoples might refer to the return of so
> many exiles, including Judeans, to their homes.[14]

The description of multi-lingual context can also be seen as based in the
experience of exiled Israelites.[15]

Differences in historical placements of the text also turn on whether
scholars equate the city referred to in Gen 11:4 with the historical city
of Babylon—with some asserting or simply assuming an obvious direct connection,[16] and others disputing any such correlation.[17] There is
a linguistic fit, particularly as "the Babylonians understood 'Babel' to
mean 'gate of the god.'"[18] Thus "the Hebrew . . . (balal) is seen by some
interpreters as a pun on the Akkadian bab-ilu, a 'gate of/to God' that is
constructed."[19] Notably, those who read "Babel" as "Babylon" tend to assume the tale's function as anti-Babylonian polemic.[20]

The passage's location in the wider text does not offer many clues
regarding authorship or timing, as Gen 11:1–9 stands in quite stark contrast both to the preceding Table of Nations (in Gen 10) and the subsequent genealogy found in Gen 11:10–32. Dillmann "is particularly struck
by the absence of any reference to the three sons of Noah who had figured

12. Feinman, *Jerusalem Throne Games*, 128.

13. Gnuse, *Misunderstood Stories*, 251.

14. Gnuse, *Misunderstood Stories*, 250.

15. Gnuse, *Misunderstood Stories*, 249–54.

16. Like Provan, *Discovering Genesis*, 63.

17. See Feinman, *Jerusalem Throne Games*, 115–6.

18. Provan, *Discovering Genesis*, 128; See also Carr, "Genesis," 25; Ilan Stavans, "On
the Tower of Babel," 78.

19. Tongue, "The Babel Complex," 157.

20. See Provan, *Discovering Genesis*, 128–30; Brueggemann, *Genesis*, 97.

so prominently in the two preceding chapters. Instead humanity is still a unity here."[21] Thus the narrative in 11:1–9 can be read as quite a separate unit. Overall, based on the range of views summarized, we can say that the interweaving or layering of primeval etiology with historical detail— particularly the naming of the city and its specified location in Shinar— most likely indicates "different stages of growth" for the passage.[22]

Intertextual links

Gen 11:1–9 easily reads as a stand-alone narrative. Nonetheless, readers have looked to its positioning when analyzing the pericope and its moral and theological messages. Reading Gen 11:1–9 in its literary context, Brueggemann characterized the story as the "last narrative of the pre-history,"[23] occupying a "hinge-like position."[24] Thus scholars commonly contextualize the narrative within a broader arc or cycle spreading from early Genesis (typically chapter 3),[25] and contrast it to the Abraham narrative which defines Genesis from 11:27 onwards.[26] As Stavans summarizes, "no matter how one looks at it, the episode of the Tower of Babel is a turning point."[27]

Some draw intertextual contrasts or connections based on language. Provan, who notes that by the end of the Babel narrative, which features a theme of naming, "[t]he peoples of the ancient world have now been assigned their proper places; we await the entrance of Abraham, descendant of Shem, which in Hebrew actually means 'name.'"[28] Likewise, Campbell

---

21. Feinman, *Jerusalem Throne Games*, 111.

22. Feinman, *Jerusalem Throne Games*, 115.

23. Brueggemann, *Genesis*, 97.

24. Fernandez, *God's Reign and the End of Empires*, 64.

25. For example, Carr, "Genesis," 25: "The LORD's scattering of humanity and confusing of language is the final step in creation of civilized humanity, with its multiple territorial and linguistic groups. The movement toward cultural maturity begun in chapter 3 is complete. Each step toward this end has been fraught with conflict and loss." Also see LaCocque, "Whatever Happened in the Valley of Shinar?" Alternatively, Ellen van Wolde considers the narrative's connections with Gen 1, and its function as a culmination of the broader creation story offered across Gen 1–11 (see van Wolde, "The Earth Story").

26. See Feinman, *Jerusalem Throne Games*, 121; see also Provan, *Discovering Genesis*, 130.

27. Stavans, "On the Tower of Babel," 78.

28. Provan, *Discovering Genesis*, 130.

notes that in the following chapter, "it is God who will make a great name for Abraham."[29] Word-plays in the narrative have also been attended to by scholars seeking to define the passage as historical or polemical, and to locate its authorship in time.[30]

Some scholars are keen to smoothen the beginning of the tower narrative with the preceding Table of Nations. Delitzsch thus "takes the perspective that the immediate descendants of Noah still would have been one family with one language."[31] In contrast, Campbell has asserted that the Babel story is

> "Out of place" because it is a story of a time when the earth "had one language and the same words" (Gen 11:1), but in the preceding chapter the progeny of the three sons of Noah had spread across the earth by lands, languages, families and nations (see Gen 10:5, 20, 31). In the context, one language for the whole earth is out of the question.[32]

Along the same lines, some exegetes accept the connection with Nimrod asserted at Gen 10:9–10: "He was a mighty hunter before the LORD; therefore it is said 'Like Nimrod a mighty hunter before the LORD.' The beginning of his kingdom was Babel, Erech, and Accad, all of them in the land of Shinar."[33] They therefore take Nimrod to be the builder of the tower.[34] But there is a clear absence of any leader or individual being named in Gen 11:1–9 itself. Rather, consistent with the form of the story as primeval and etiological (as discussed above), the human actors are simply referred to as a single collective. Inter-textual readings have also informed theological interpretations of the tower narrative, as explored below.

29. Campbell, *Making Sense of the Bible*, 75.

30. For a summary of analyses of the narrative structure, and the connections (or not) with historical critical approaches, see Baden, "The Tower of Babel."

31. As summarised in Feinman, *Jerusalem Throne Games*, 110. See also Provan, *Discovering Genesis*, 127.

32. Campbell, *Making Sense of the Bible*, 75.

33. There is even a tradition, as cited in Josephus, that Nimrod "initiated the building of a tower with the specific purpose of negating the power of God to destroy humanity again through a flood" (Feinman, *Jerusalem Throne Games*, 104; see also Kugel, *Traditions of the Bible*, 231–2). However, such a reading is problematic given that Yhwh had already expressly promised never to do so again.

34. Feinman, *Jerusalem Throne Games*, 107.

Narrative observations

Having canvassed various approaches to this text, we now turn to a close reading of the passage and its language. This language is shown to support various interpretations of the text, as we elaborate further in the next section.

Genesis 11:1–9 opens with "Now" (NRSV) which on the surface connects to the previous chapter, but this is subject to opposing interpretations. The meaning of "the same words" (11:1) repeats the same idea of a universal language among humankind. Various scholars have discussed what this "one language" was, and whether it was Hebrew.[35] The explicit pointing out of a universal language prefigures the situation to come (and presumably that of the intended audience), where different languages exist between social groupings. At this point, the common language is accompanied by (or reflects) a shared identity, and the community moves and operates (in 11:2) as a single entity.

Eastward movement is significant in 11:2 and it is commonly read as the continuation of the movement out of the garden of Eden, as mandated by Yhwh in 3:23–24. As is true of much of the Pentateuch, nomadism and settlement occupy ambiguous positions in this narrative. On the one hand, the table of nations provided in Gen 10 would imply settlement of different clans in particular areas. On the other hand, settlement can be read as a failure to follow Yhwh's instructions (in Gen 1:28; 9:1; and 9:7) to "be fruitful and multiply, and fill the earth." These instructions have been attributed to the Priestly tradition,[36] whereas the Babel narrative is generally accepted as coming from the Yahwist source.

The migrants start to build in 11:3. The choice of building materials is meaningful, as bricks and mortar are "Babylonian construction materials."[37] This would tend to support readings which interpret the city in question as Babylon.

In 11:4, the settlement is envisioned as an urban one. Recall the earlier discussion of towers (ziggurats) reaching to the heavens or the divine sphere: the intention may have been to create a kind of bridge between the divine and earthly realms, perhaps for the descent of a deity rather than (as commonly assumed) for humans to ascend to the heavens. Kugel

---

35. Kugel, *Traditions of the Bible*, 235–7.
36. Carr, "Genesis," 25.
37. Feinman, *Jerusalem Throne Games*, 113.

even goes so far as to say that they "tried to storm heaven."[38] Others, such as Ellen van Wolde and Theodore Hiebert, resist the implication of any goal to access or bridge to the divine realm.[39] Towers, of course, were also monuments of royal or imperial power. Regardless of any intention to connect with the divine realm, towers were also political projects and statements:

> A Tower at the heart of a city not only offers a totalizing view out to the plains or up into the heavens but is also a symbol of power, asserting itself on both the visual and imaginative horizon. Such a Tower is meant to be seen.[40]

In this regard, "make a name for ourselves" (11:4) is significant and possibly misleading in its translation given current colloquial usage:

> It is easy today to think of making a name for oneself as acquiring fame or by being a celebrity braggart. To understand the meaning of this verse in ancient times, we need to recognize that the process of making a name for oneself was a physical one and generally reserved to kings who built canals, walls, palaces, temples, and occasionally, new cities.[41]

Provan likewise points out that "Biblically speaking, of course, it is only God who makes a name for himself (cf. Isa. 63:11–14)."[42] However, Gen 6:4 does refer to the "men of renown," or "men of the name."[43] There are also other parallels with 6:1–4, as noted below.

The reference to scattering, like the point about a common language in 11:1, again seems pre-emptive—of the coming scattering by Yhwh, and/or of the implied audience's known world (again, with potential connections to the exilic or postexilic experiences).

The Lord notices the building project and comes down to check it out (11:5). This humanized view of Yhwh as coming down, and seeing, fits the Yahwist's references to similar actions by Yhwh throughout Genesis up to this point, such as walking and directly addressing humans (at the garden, 3:8).

---

38. Kugel, *Traditions of the Bible*, 228.
39. van Wolde, "The Earth Story," 150; Hiebert, "The Tower of Babel," 37–8.
40. Tongue, "The Babel Complex," 168.
41. Feinman, *Jerusalem Throne Games*, 112.
42. Provan, *Discovering*, 128.
43. Provan, *Discovering*, 128.

Yhwh speaks up (11:6), but to whom? This language appears to echo the polytheistic traditions of the Ancient Near East. Alternatively, some scholars have theorized that Yhwh is speaking to the angels, who were ordered to descend (either with Yhwh or in Yhwh's place).[44] As discussed further below, Yhwh's response here is not an emotive one. Rather, Yhwh is simply commenting on what has been observed of the current actions, and an assessment of its implications or possible consequences. As Hiebert has argued, this verse offers "a simple observation about what the people have done," which has been unnecessarily "embellished by translators to imply that the people have sinister plans."[45]

Yhwh's speech—"Come, let us . . ." (11:7)—echoes that of the humans in preceding verses. Another word-play is visible here too: "The verb expressing God's plans . . . "let us mix (their languages)," echoes, with both alliteration and assonance, the verbs expressing the people's plans—"let us make bricks" (v. 3), and "let us build" (v. 4)."[46]

"So the Lord scattered them abroad from there over the face of all the earth, and they left off building the city" (11:8. NRSV). How exactly the scattering is achieved is not spelled out—were people forcibly expelled, or did their movements simply arise from the confusion created by a sudden loss of common language? This relates to the question of how two (or more) etiological narratives may have been interwoven. It also points to the connection between language, community and settlement as noted above, which has now been ruptured by Yhwh.

As Brueggemann notes, "The narrative is as symmetrically structured as any since chapter 1 of Genesis. Its beginning with "whole earth" and "one language" (v. 1) is neatly balanced in v. 9 with "all the earth" and "the language of all the earth."[47] However, while in 11:1 "the whole earth" refers to the whole of humanity—a population—here it seemingly refers to humanity *and* (or *within*) a particular geographical space. These repeated phrases also reflect the connections between space, identity and language—whether unified (as in vv. 1 and 3) or fractured (as in vv. 8–9).

Confusion and scattering are aligned side-by-side, possibly indicating twin narrative sources. To a modern reader, the logical connection between the two is not necessarily clear: "even people who speak the same

44. Kugel, *Traditions of the Bible*, 241–2.

45. Hiebert, "The Tower of Babel," 44.

46. Hiebert, "The Tower of Babel," 47. For a discussion of the use of the cohortative in the primeval history, see Strong, "Shattering the Image of God," 628.

47. Brueggemann, *Genesis*, 98.

language are expert at speaking past each other without listening to or understanding the words of the other."[48] Likewise, cooperation does not always arise from a shared language; nor is conflict confined to clashes between linguistic groups.[49] However, it is possible that in the temporal and geopolitical context of the implied author/audience, conflict was understood as occurring between rival nations/empires with different languages and territories.

Theological observations

There are clear parallels between the tower of Babel narrative and other units within Genesis that involve "the theme of preservation of the divine-human boundary. The threat to that boundary, self-reflective speech by the Lord, and act of divine prevention all parallel 3.22–24 and 6.1–4."[50] In almost all cases, scholarly exegetes (particularly those reading through the lens of the Christian New Testament) have imputed the story with a moral content, particularly concerning sin and judgment/punishment.[51] For instance, Brueggemann is quick to assert that the tale "suggests that all human language has become a language of disobedience."[52] Likewise, scholars such as Feinman merge Priestly and non-Priestly texts to draw a contrast framed as defiance:

> The concept of human dominion over the earth means humanity remaining settled in one city is an act of defiance which warrants punishment. This punishment then generates the exact action God decreed in the first place: dispersal over the earth.[53]

Occasionally commentators[54] even read a sin of idol worship into the story, despite no mention or implication of such practice at all in the text. Noting the tendency to moralize the Babel story, Tongue asks:

48. Feinman, *Jerusalem Throne Games*, 103.

49. "Speakers of the same language frequently don't get along either, and some of the cruelest wars in history, as we know, have been fought between them" (Stavans, "On the Tower of Babel," 78).

50. Carr, "Genesis," 25. See also Campbell, *Making Sense of the Bible*, 75.

51. For a summary and critique of such "pride-and-punishment" readings, see Hiebert, "The Tower of Babel."

52. Brueggemann, *Genesis*, 97.

53. Feinman, *Jerusalem Throne Games*, 111.

54. For example, Li, "Confusion at the Tower," 117.

"How, then, does the tower come to be linked with punishment when the biblical text is so reticent in assigning a singular motivation to the builders' project?"[55] Tracing historical exegesis, he finds that "The notion that Babel signifies a militaristic rebellion against a sovereign Yhwh has deep roots."[56]

However, as noted by Pippin, "in Genesis 11 there is no mention of perversion."[57] If we attend closely to the text, we see that there is no particular attack or malice directed toward Yhwh, nor any explicit hubris ascribed to the builders of the city/tower. Their actions are framed as self-defensive (so as not to be scattered), and they are even arguably in search of greater connection with the divine, if the planned tower is taken to be similar to a ziggurat. On the divine side, Yhwh's response is not framed as angry, or disapproving, or reproachful—particularly when contrasted with earlier passages with which parallels have been drawn. As Hiebert helpfully points out, the narrative does not include any cursing, moralizing or explicit framing as punishment, accompanying Yhwh's actions.[58] Indeed, if any emotion could be implied by Yhwh's observations and exclamations, it is anxiety or fear—that "nothing that [humans] propose to do will now be impossible for them" (11:6). Such a view is mentioned in passing by Stavans:

> Halkin replied: "I've never read the Tower of Babel story as being one of punishment. God makes men speak different languages not to punish them, but simply to prevent them from ganging up on Him; it's a divide and conquer maneuver."[59]

Thus, Yhwh's response to the tower can be seen as self-defensive—just as were the actions of the builders. Yhwh experiences the encroaching capabilities of humanity as a threat—if not to Yhwh, then at least to the created order and arguably to the divine-human boundary. The response is no curse (cf. Gen 3:14–19), but instead a strategic, geopolitical response to contain the threat, by limiting the capabilities arising from human communication, cooperation and closeness.[60] Yhwh's solu-

---

55. Tongue, "The Babel Complex," 161.

56. Tongue, "The Babel Complex," 161–4.

57. Pippin, *Apocalyptic Bodies*, 57 (cited in Tongue, "The Babel Complex," 161).

58. Hiebert, "The Tower of Babel."

59. Stavans, "On the Tower of Babel," 77.

60. This geopolitical interpretation is also supported by the terminology for scattering found in Gen 11:4, as wording that "can be used in military parlance for the

tion is that distance must be maintained—it is distance between humans (geographically, linguistically and socially) that enables appropriate distance between the human and divine realms to be preserved.

The reality of Yhwh's actions—with dispersal as a self-defensive political strategy—is typically missed by those who read the narrative as an anti-imperial polemic. Such interpretations, favored by liberation and postcolonial scholars, share a surprising amount of common ground with the traditional readings focused on pride/sin and punishment. As Hiebert observes:

> According to this approach, the story is [still] about pride and punishment, yet now the pride about which it speaks is the hubris of imperial domination, and the punishment it describes is God's judgment on the empires, in particular Babylon (Babel), that oppressed Israel and Judah. The emphasis on one language at the beginning of the story represents the imperial suppression of local languages and cultures, and God's punishment brings down the empire with its monolithic aims, setting free the local languages and cultures to flourish.[61]

In both traditional and existing postcolonial interpretations, then, Yhwh's actions in this narrative continue to be viewed favorably, and the significance of dispersal as a geopolitical and colonial strategy is missed.

We therefore see a shared reluctance to view or analyze Yhwh critically in this passage. Regardless of their interpretations of the builders' actions (as negative, neutral or even positive), scholars tend to share a positive view of Yhwh's response.[62] Even existing postcolonial or anti-imperial readings locate empire in the deeds of the builders, rather than those of Yhwh. Either way, scholars arguably miss the significance of Yhwh's act of dispersal and confusion *as an act of violence*, and thereby foreclose any possibility to recognize or grieve what has been lost as a result. This goes hand-in-hand, then, with the failure to attend meaningfully

---

sorry fate of the enemy (Num 10:35; 1 Sam 11:11; Ps 68:2)" (LaCocque, "Whatever Happened in the Valley of Shinar?" 35).

61. Hiebert, "The Tower of Babel," 30. Hiebert critiques such interpretations, relying on literary analyses of the text, e.g., Croatto, "A Reading of the Story of the Tower of Babel"; Fewell, "Building Babel"; Oduyoye, *The Sons of Gods and the Daughters of Men*. Notably, interpretations of the tower as symbolic of empire and imperial violence are not limited to biblical scholarship—see, for instance, Derrida, "Des Tours De Babel."

62. This even includes those seeking to pursue a resistant or alternative reading—such as Bell, "Interpreting the Bible on Language."

with the recurring theme that is so apparent on the text's face, namely the close nexus between language, community/identity and land.

Both these limitations can, I suggest, be addressed through applying a postcolonial lens somewhat differently. In particular, we can draw a parallel between the language/community/land connection in Gen 11:1–9 and the epistemologies and ontologies of Indigenous peoples, as described by them. Likewise, we can recognize the violence involved in rupturing a community's common language and forcibly dispersing them from their land, as a particularly *colonial* form of violence that has been resisted and endured throughout many lands and times. Attending to the voices and experiences of Indigenous people(s) can thus foster new ways of relating to this biblical passage—ways that may offer us new forms of personal and political responses.

Stolen land

In the remainder of this essay I offer a postcolonial reading of this passage—in which I read from my own place, as a settler in what is now called Australia, living on Wurundjeri land and writing in a foreign, colonial language. Specifically, I attend to the significance of dispersal as a form of colonial violence which was used to dispossess the First peoples of this land and their languages, and which can be seen in patterns of colonial violence continuing to this day. The effectiveness, and effects, of this strategy can only be understood by taking seriously the connections between community, land and language as experienced by First peoples.

As Rademaker has summarized, "From an Aboriginal perspective, land and language are inseparable; they were formed together."[63] This view is captured in the words of Gula Lalara: "These words of ours are from the old days before we were born [. . .] The words come from our ceremonies to teach us about places and relationships."[64] Given the role of language in ceremony, language not only comes from the land, but it is a key way in which the land is also related to and sustained.[65] In an Indigenous epistemology and lived experience, then, there is an inextricable nexus between

63. Rademaker, "The Great Australian Silencing," 222.

64. As quoted in Rademaker, "Language and Australian Aboriginal History Anindilyakwa and English on Groote Eylandt."

65. See the voices of Indigenous contributors in House of Representatives Standing Committee on Aboriginal and Torres Strait Islander Affairs, "Our Land Our Languages," particularly in chapter 2.

land, language and identity/community. With this in mind, we can begin
to understand how separation from land and destruction of language are
connected, in both the forms and impacts of colonial violence.

From the time of early frontier wars in colonial Australia, dispersal of Aboriginal communities was an explicit strategy by the invading
Europeans. Indeed, massacres of Aboriginal families and communities
were routinely recorded literally as "dispersals," and were often aimed at
removing Aboriginal people from areas of land which colonizers wanted
to take over.[66] The brutality and widespread nature of these massacres is
difficult to overstate. Importantly, such violence was not simply the actions of aberrant individuals: agents of the state (military, police, or other
government officials) were involved in at least half of these massacres.[67]
They are therefore best understood within the broader context of colonial
dispossession of land, as the opening of land to colonizers was both a
cause and effect of such violence: "[Even when] the government may not
specifically be involved with, say, police and soldiers [. . .] they [were] also
opening up the crown lands to enable settlers to carry out the massacres
themselves."[68]

Beyond the frontier wars, dispersal was sustained as an important
strategy for dispossessing and disempowering Aboriginal families and
communities throughout the colonial era. Where Aboriginal communities gathered of their own accord (or were already gathered), colonial
authorities intervened to disperse them "elsewhere," including to designated missions and reserves, which were in turn subject to closure. This
involved a cycle of dispersal and relocation extending into the twentieth
century, as for instance traced by Peter Read regarding the Wiradjuri:

> Several techniques to reduce the reserve populations were
> evolved after 1909. Amongst the most commonly used were the
> expulsion orders, by which men and women, unemployed or
> "non-Aborigines" were prohibited from remaining on or enter-
> ing one or more reserves. Over a decade more than a thousand
> people were so proscribed: one notification of 1915 contained
> the names of eighty-eight people. Another technique was the

66. Evershed, "Frontier Massacres." The naming of Mount Dispersion on the Mur-
ray River reflects such usage of this term, as the site was named by Major Mitchell
following a massacre by his men in May 1836. For further details of this and other
massacres in the frontier wars, see Ryan et al., "Colonial Frontier Massacres."

67. Ryan et al., "Colonial Frontier Massacres."

68. Ryan, cited in "Frontier Massacres."

revocation of thinly populated reserves by refusing entrance to all prospective residents, so that through natural wastage it was within a few years possible for the Board to revoke them as "uninhabited." The closure of the more populous reserves was more complicated. Natural wastage had to be supplemented by expulsions and threats; often the more obstinate residents had to be forcibly removed from their homes.[69]

These expulsions must also be understood alongside the other key colonial strategy of dispersal—namely the breaking up of Aboriginal families through removal of children.[70] The systematic removal of so-called mixed-race children from their Aboriginal mothers/families well into the twentieth century has now been well documented, as the creation of Stolen Generations.[71] Systematic removal of children to "elsewhere" also worked in tandem with the dispersal of Aboriginal communities from reserves and missions: many families left reserves in order to avoid having their children taken from them, sometimes even in response to explicit threats by authorities to do so.[72] Both strategies of dispersal and removal are best understood as reflecting the "logic of elimination" which underlies settler-colonial discourses and governance, and which is inextricably linked to the dispossession of Aboriginal communities and the taking of their lands.[73]

The impacts of this dispersal—of ongoing cycles of expulsion and relocation, and removal of children—have been absolutely apocalyptic for Indigenous communities. Cycles of intergeneration trauma, abuse, violence and incarceration are ongoing. The impact on connection to land has in most places been devastating, and significantly for our purposes here, so has the impact on language: "Of the 250 or so languages spoken here when colonisation began, less than half are still spoken.

---

69. Read, "'A Rape of the Soul So Profound,'" 26.

70. Read refers to these as "two principal techniques of dissociation" (see "'Breaking up These Camps Entirely,'" 45.

71. Government of Australia and Wilkie, "Bringing Them Home"; Wolfe, "Nation and Miscegenation."

72. See, for example, Read, "'Breaking up These Camps Entirely,'" 47–8.

73. One way in which dispersal and the struggle for land continue is that historical acts of dispersal continue to undermine attempts by Aboriginal communities to claim "native title" to their traditional lands, given that such title depends on proving an uninterrupted connection to land. See Wolfe, "Nation and Miscegenation," 122.

Only 13 could be considered 'strong'—that is, they are still being spoken by children."[74] Indigenous languages have been

> silenced by the death, forced relocation or removal of their
> speakers [. . . as well as] efforts to delegitimise Aboriginal ways
> of communicating. [. . .] For Aboriginal people, their languages
> were irreplaceable. Their words were embedded in their land in
> a way that English could never be.[75]

Recalling our analysis of Gen 11:1–9 above, we can identify a number of parallels. Yhwh's act of confusing the builders at Babel leads to their dispersal—what was an intimate and communal connection between language and land, is interrupted by the violent intervention of an external force. In both the biblical passage and the lived realities of Indigenous peoples on these lands, then, dispersal and loss of language are inseparable, each precipitating the other. And in both cases the impacts of this violence are, effectively, earth-shattering.

It is important to recognize that dispersal, as a form of colonial dispossession and violence, persists. Despite the Stolen Generations having been formally recognized through reports and official apologies, more Aboriginal children are being removed from their families than ever before, now under the guise of child protection.[76] Various projects aim to protect and revive Aboriginal languages.[77] Given the nexus between land, language and community, these struggles are connected to Aboriginal presence on country:

> To the extent that the Australian settler state was, and remains,
> based on the acquisition and total control of land, Aboriginal
> people, with a prior claim not only to ownership of, but also
> sovereignty over, the land, pose a threat to settler hegemony and
> legitimacy. For settler colonialism, therefore, a continuing Ab-
> original presence in Australia represents a persistent claim that
> could never be fully resolved within its structures.[78]

---

74. Rademaker, "The Great Australian Silencing." See also Jalata, "The Impacts of English Colonial Terrorism and Genocide."

75. Rademaker, "The Great Australian Silencing."

76. See Krakouer, "The Stolen Generations Never Ended."

77. See Korff, "Aboriginal Language Preservation & Revival."

78. Silverstein, "Indirect Rule in Australia," 100–101.

As likewise observed by Deborah Bird Rose, in the context of settler-colonial violence, Aboriginal people "got in the way just by staying at home."[79]

A recent incident in Perth illustrates well the anxieties experienced by the settler-colonial state in the face of Aboriginal people's ongoing presence and their gathering, and the use of dispersal as a response. In April 2020, police officers approached a group of homeless Aboriginal people who had been sleeping rough in make-shift camps several blocks from the city's main train station.[80] In an all-too-familiar display of the over-policing of Indigenous communities, police questioned everyone, disposed of their belongings in a council rubbish truck that had been sent specifically for this purpose, and issued "move on" notices to disperse the group.[81] One woman, Wendy, had a broken arm and had been using her good arm to fill a trolley with her possessions:

> "Wendy, it's been over 10 minutes and you keep talking to everybody and you're not moving on, 500 metres from here is your move on," one officer said to her.
>
> "If you don't move on, you will be arrested and taken to the station," another says to her as she tried to pull her loaded trolley with her one arm.
>
> As the people moved out from their temporary home with what they could carry, the rangers moved in.
>
> After an hour, the police left and both of the camps had been completely cleared.
>
> Everything had been loaded into the [rubbish] truck and there was no evidence that less than 90 minutes earlier this place was home to around a dozen people.[82]

Conclusion

This chapter has analyzed the Babel narrative found in Gen 11:1–9 and offered an alternative, postcolonial reading of this passage. It began with a summary of historical-critical analyses, demonstrating that matters of literary form and social function (such as etiology) are in practice inseparable from questions of authorship and dating. Literary matters

79. Rose, *Hidden Histories*, 46.
80. Hirini, "Homeless Aboriginal People in Perth."
81. Hirini, "Homeless Aboriginal People in Perth."
82. Hirini, "Homeless Aboriginal People in Perth."

were expanded upon as we saw how the passage's place in the book of Genesis informs its themes and understandings of the language found within it. The essay then reflected on theological messages which have been ascribed to the text and argued that these have often been imported unnecessarily. Instead, a closer attention to the text itself was advocated, with different theological implications. Rather than reading the impulse or desire of humankind to reach beyond—to know or access the divine— as sinful, a less moralistic interpretation is possible. We can then also see Yhwh's response differently, and specifically as a self-defensive, geopolitical strategy of dispersal. This strategy succeeded in rupturing the close nexus between community/identity, land and language that was shown to feature so prominently in the language of this passage.

Focusing on this nexus, as well as the strategy of dispersal, enables a new kind of postcolonial reading: one which resists interpretations of this passage as an anti-imperial polemic. Offering a reading from stolen land, then, the final section outlined how strategies of dispersal in colonial Australia have repeatedly and systematically interrupted the nexus between land, language and community/identity among Indigenous peoples—the same nexus that can be discerned in the pre-dispersal condition of "all the earth" in Gen 11:1. From the perspective of Indigenous communities who have been subjected to cycles of dispersals—expulsions, removals and silencing of their languages—Yhwh's strategy in this narrative rings familiar as a form of colonial violence, rather than appearing as an anti-imperial resolution. This alternative reading allows us to view Yhwh's actions in a new and more critical light, and makes possible a greater appreciation of the profound loss experienced by the community that once inhabited Babel. Conversely, reading biblical texts from our own lived positions may also open up new ways of appreciating and questioning the forms of violence shaping our own lives, lands and communities.

Bibliography

Baden, Joel S. "The Tower of Babel: A Case Study in the Competing Methods of Historical and Modern Literary Criticism." *Journal of Biblical Literature* 128 (2009) 209–24.

Bell, Allan. "Interpreting the Bible on Language: Babel and Ricoeur's Interpretive Arc." In *Ears That Hear: Explorations in Theological Interpretation of the Bible*, edited by Joel B. Green and Tim Meadowcroft, 70–93. Sheffield: Sheffield Phoenix, 2013.

Brueggemann, Walter. *Genesis*. Interpretation. Atlanta: John Knox, 1982.

Campbell, Antony F. *Making Sense of the Bible: Difficult Texts and Modern Faith*. New York: Paulist, 2010.

Carr, David M. "Genesis." In *The New Oxford Annotated Bible with Apocrypha: New Revised Standard Version*. Oxford: Oxford University Press, 2010.

Croatto, Severino. "A Reading of the Story of the Tower of Babel from a Perspective of Non-Identity." In *Teaching the Bible: The Discourses and Politics of Biblical Pedagogy*, edited by Fernando F. Segovia and Mary Ann Tolbert, 203–23. Maryknoll, NY: Orbis, 2009.

Derrida, Jacques. "Des Tours de Babel." Translated by Joseph F. Graham. In *Difference in Translation*, edited by Joseph F. Graham, 165–207. Ithaca, NY: Cornell University Press, 1985.

Dillmann, A. *Genesis, Critically and Exegetically Expounded*. Translated by W. M. B. Stevenson. Edinburgh: T. & T. Clark, 1897.

Evershed, Nick. "Frontier Massacres: Role of Australia's Colonial Government Forces Revealed—Datablog." *Guardian*, 5 Mar 2019. https://www.theguardian.com/australia-news/ng-interactive/2019/mar/05/frontier-massacres-role-of-australias-colonial-government-forces-revealed-datablog

Feinman, Peter. *Jerusalem Throne Games: The Battle of Bible Stories after the Death of David*. Oxford: Oxbow, 2017.

Fewell, Danna Nolan. "Building Babel." In *Postmodern Interpretations of the Bible: A Reader*, edited by A. K. M. Adam, 1–15. St. Louis: Chalice, 2001.

Gnuse, Robert. *Misunderstood Stories: Theological Commentary on Genesis 1–11*. Eugene, OR: Cascade Books, 2014.

Gonzalez, Fernandez, Antonio. *God's Reign and the End of Empires*. Translated by Joseph V. Owens, SJ. Miami: Convivium, 2012.

Government of Australia and Meredith Wilkie. "Bringing Them Home: Report of the National Inquiry into the Separation of Aboriginal and Torres Strait Islander Children from Their Families." Sydney: Human Rights and Equal Opportunity Commission, 1997.

Gunkel, Hermann. *Genesis*. Handkommentar zum Alten Testament 1. Göttingen: Vandenhoeck & Ruprecht, 1901.

Hiebert, Theodore. "The Tower of Babel and the Origin of the World's Cultures." *Journal of Biblical Literature* 126 (2007) 29–58.

Hirini, Rangi. "Homeless Aboriginal People in Perth Given Move on Notices by WA Police." *NITV News*, 11 Apr 2020.

House of Representatives Standing Committee on Aboriginal and Torres Strait Islander Affairs. "Our Land Our Languages." Canberra: Commonwealth of Australia, 2012.

Jalata, Asafa. "The Impacts of English Colonial Terrorism and Genocide on Indigenous/Black Australians." *Sage Open* 3/3 (2013) 1–12.

Korff, Jens. "Aboriginal Language Preservation & Revival." Creative Spirits. https://www.creativespirits.info/aboriginalculture/language/aboriginal-language-preservation.

Krakouer, Jacynta. "The Stolen Generations Never Ended—They Just Morphed into Child Protection." *Guardian*, 17 Oct 2019. https://www.theguardian.com/commentisfree/2019/oct/17/the-stolen-generations-never-ended-they-just-morphed-into-child-protection

Kugel, James L. *Traditions of the Bible: A Guide to the Bible as It Was at the Start of the Common Era*. Cambridge: Harvard University Press, 1998.

LaCocque, André. "Whatever Happened in the Valley of Shinar? A Response to Theodore Hiebert." *Journal of Biblical Literature* 128 (2009) 29–41.

Li, Loretta F. "Confusion at the Tower." *Journal of Research on Christian Education* 23 (2014) 108–25.

Oduyoye, Modupe. *The Sons of Gods and the Daughters of Men: An Afro-Asiatic Interpretation of Genesis 1–11*. Maryknoll, NY: Orbis, 1984.

Pippin, Tina. *Apocalyptic Bodies: The Biblical End of the World in Text and Image*. London: Routledge, 1999.

Provan, Iain. *Discovering Genesis: Content, Interpretation, Reception*. Grand Rapids: Eerdmans, 2015.

Rademaker, Laura. "The Great Australian Silencing: The Elimination of Aboriginal Languages and the Legacy of Colonisation." *ABC Religion and Ethics*, 21 Jan 2019.

———. "Language and Australian Aboriginal History Anindilyakwa and English on Groote Eylandt." *History Australia* 11 (2014) 222–39.

Read, Peter. "'Breaking up These Camps Entirely': The Dispersal Policy in Wiradjuri Country 1909–1929." *Aboriginal History* 8 (1984) 45–55.

———. "'A Rape of the Soul So Profound': Some Reflections on the Dispersal Policy in New South Wales." *Aboriginal History* 7 (1983) 23–33.

Rose, Deborah Bird. *Hidden Histories: Black Stories from Victoria River Downs, Humbert River and Wave Hill Stations*. Canberra: Aboriginal Studies, 1991.

Ryan, Lyndall et al. "Colonial Frontier Massacres in Australia, 1788–1930." The University of Newcastle, 2019. https://c21ch.newcastle.edu.au/colonialmassacres/.

Silverstein, Ben. "Indirect Rule in Australia: A Case Study in Settler Colonial Difference." In *Studies in Settler Colonialism: Politics, Identity and Culture*, edited by Fiona Bateman and Lionel Pilkington, 90–105. London: Palgrave Macmillan, 2011.

Stavans, Ilan. "On the Tower of Babel." In *Reading Genesis: Beginnings*, edited by Beth Kissileff, 75–82. London: Bloomsbury, 2016.

Strong, John T. "Shattering the Image of God: A Response to Theodore Hiebert's Interpretation of the Story of the Tower of Babel." *Journal of Biblical Literature* 127 (2008) 625–34.

Tongue, Samuel. "The Babel Complex: Taking a Turn around the Tower and the City." In *Looking through a Glass Bible: Postdisciplinary Biblical Interpretations from the Glasgow School*, edited by A. K. M. Adam and Samuel Tongue, 153–74. Biblical Interpretation Series 125. Leiden: Brill, 2014.

Van Wolde, Ellen. "The Earth Story as Presented by the Tower of Babel Narrative." In *Earth Story in Genesis*, edited by Norman C. Habel and Shirley Wurst, 147–57. Earth Bible 2. London: Bloomsbury, 2000.

Wolfe, Patrick. "Nation and Miscegenation: Discursive Continuity in the Post-Mabo Era." *Social Analysis: The International Journal of Social and Cultural Practice* 36 (1994) 93–152.

3

Is God at the Boss's Table?

DARÍO BAROLÍN

WRITING THIS REFLECTION HAS been a long, difficult and enriching process. I have always felt close to the suffering of the Palestinian people and the unbearable injustice they are suffering. My solidarity, prayers and concern were and are with the people living in Palestine, an occupied land. My heart is clear and without doubt that the occupation of Palestinian land by the modern State of Israel is just not right.

However, whilst I was concerned, this did not represent a challenge to me in my theological work. It was not until recently that I got engaged in the task of scrutinizing my own field of research, Old Testament Studies. The result has been devastating and upsetting.

I became aware of the consequences that Christian Zionist interpretations[1] have brought to the Palestinian people.[2] God's promises to an oppressed people that brought them freedom and justice have been used through history to justify oppression. The following considerations

1. Christian Zionism should not be considered as "literal interpretation" of the biblical text. Not only because to interpret "literally" is impossible, but also because Christian Zionism imposes upon the text a theological assumption. Dispensationalism becomes the text and the biblical text is just support material.

2. See Masalha, *The Bible & Zionism*, 85–132.

37

reflect solidarity with the Palestinian people and the conviction that it is necessary to be in accompaniment with the people living in the occupied Palestine territory to build an inhabitable land that welcomes everyone.

From the southern cone of Latin America, I bring some of the experiences, insights and failures of my work as a Waldensian pastor engaged with Liberation Theology (LT). I approach this engagement with Palestinian people with the urgency to learn from their struggle to build a place of hospitality for locals and foreigners, a place to practice justice and live in peace. I also recognize that the Palestinian people have to find their own way to approach the Bible in an empowering, liberating and transformative way. Knowing this, I offer some ideas that may be helpful to engage in a constructive dialogue.

Latin American Context

First, I bring to the table the specific context of Latin American Liberation Theology. When Christopher Columbus and the Spanish arrived at the American continent in the late 15th century, they transformed it into their "promised land." The inhabitants of the continent were the "Canaanites" to be conquered. The conquest "was killing, robbing, enslavement, stealing their goods and lands and dominion."[3] This was at the same time the primary encounter of the indigenous people of our continent with Christian faith.[4] Certainly, there were exceptions like Bartolomé de las Casas (1484–1566), Antonio Montesinos (1475–1540), Francisco de Vitoria (1483–1546), Toribio de Benavente (1482–1569) and José de Acosta (1540–1600). But mostly our Native American people discovered Christianity as oppression and the Bible as a book to justify their suffering and the conquerors' privileges.[5]

This understanding of God was not only confined to the fifteenth century but is present even now. Atahualpa Yupanqui (1908–1992), an indigenous poet and musician from Argentina wrote a song titled *Little questions about God* from which the following lines have been extracted (my translation):

3. De Las Casas, *Historia de las Indias,* 94.

4. Rev. Obed Vizcaíno from Venezuela wrote a poem for October 12 that includes these lines: "they brought a bloodthirsty 'god', hungry for blood, plunderer."

5. See Pagán, *A Violent Evangelism,* 1992.

One day I asked:
Grandpa, where is God?
My grandpa got sad
And responded nothing.
. . .
Later, I asked:
Father, what do you know about God?
My father got serious
And responded nothing.
. . .
There is an issue on Earth
Much more important than God:
. . .
Whether God cares for the poor,
Maybe yes, and maybe no.
But I am sure he eats
At the table of the boss

The realities summarized in this poem point to the context from which liberation theologies needed to think in Latin America. And the first element that LT brought up from the biblical text was the certainty that God was *not* dining at the boss's table. Rather, in line with Jesus' table practices as portrayed in the gospel narratives, God sits at the table of the excluded and outcasts.

In fact, Carlos Mesters and Francisco Orofino find out that the most revolutionary move of LT is the certainty that we are called to walk with the poor and the excluded in the certainty that there we meet God. In their own words:

> The poor find out the major discovery of all: If God was in that time with that people in the past [the people of Israel enslaved in Egypt], then, He also will be with us in this struggle for liberation. He listens to our clamor too! (Ex 2, 24; 3, 7). In this way a new experience of God and life, imperceptibly, comes to life, it becomes the most decisive criteria of the popular reading and the one that less appears in their explanations and interpretations.[6]

Atahualpa Yupanqui described the reality of oppression suffered by his people and the place of God justifying that oppression. To the contrary, LT does not expect God to be at the table of the boss. Religion discourse done by those in power puts God there. However, as Jesus's

6. Mesters and Orofino, "Sobre la lectura popular de la Biblia," 1.

ministry shows, God walks with the outcast and excluded. God is in the midst of those working in the field, the mine, or the prison, between "sweat, malaria and snakes." Even more important, God does care for the poor, God listens to their clamor expressed with "flute and drums" and inspire liberation.

The second element, equally important, was to deconstruct an understanding of God that was linked exclusively to spiritual matters or the afterlife. This is where the exodus narratives about the liberation of a concrete people from their enslavement under an abusive master order came in. In them LT could make its point that "God is understood as savior because he acts in human history, and not, in the first place, in a meta-history."[7]

These two elements, the presence of God with the suffering and exploited people and God's liberating, justice-oriented action within human history, are from my point of view the central elements of Latin American liberation theology. These elements did not emerge in a vacuum. As Atahualpa Yupanqui's poem so vividly conveys, LT came to dispute a prior comprehension of God as an ally of those in power and as a justification of oppression.[8]

Liberation and Oppression

Second, I would like to remember the place this specific reality has in Liberation Theology and how the exodus's event was interpreted in this context.

> [Liberation Theology] came as an answer to the necessity to understand the revolutionary political situation that Latin America was facing and to find out what was the place and the engagement God was calling his [sic] people to adopt in this particular historical situation. The primary emphasis is not on the academic knowledge but on the present situation of the readers. What is relevant for PRB [Popular Reading of the Bible] is the sense of the text in the present situation and how it challenges

7. Croatto, *Exodus*, 27.

8. Jaime Rynés has shown, the exodus has been long present as a theological trope in Latin America. It was used to explain the situation of oppression of indigenous and African people brought as slaves but also celebrated by the conquerors. They both, oppressed and oppressor found themselves in the exodus narrative, but always identifying himself with the Israelites. Cf. Rynés, "La Biblia de los conquistadores."

the present reader. Because of that, the point of departure is not Biblical academic investigation, although it has a place, but a careful listening to the concrete praxis of those participating in the process of PRB.[9]

In the particular Latin American context, the exodus has been one of the fundamental texts to call people to a process of liberation. However, Native American, African and Palestinian theologians, among others, have experienced the opposite with this narrative. Or, to be more precise, it was the affiliated accounts of the conquest of Canaan understood as a necessary complement of the exodus texts that have been used again and again to justify the expulsion and genocide of native populations and the occupation of their land.

The critique of the exodus paradigm is too serious to be ignored. Robert Warrior and Edward Said,[10] among others, have been clear and specific. Robert Warrior cautions us: "As long as people believe in the Yahweh of deliverance, the world will not be safe from Yahweh the conqueror."[11] His warning challenges the exodus reading practiced in Latin American liberation theology and in the following considerations I would like to address some of these concerns.

Is Any Text without Sin?

I believe that we need to recognize that almost every Biblical text can be used (and a lot are indeed used) to justify oppression or to go against God's will. The conflict between Jeremiah and Hananiah in Jer 28:1–16 and the temptation of Satan in Matt 4:1–11 are two examples for this phenomenon from within the Bible itself. Hananiah based his prophecy on what God has done in the former invasion from Assyria (701) and the theological tradition of Zion (Psalms 46–48, 76). In the case of Matt 4:1–11, not only Jesus quotes Scripture to affirm himself in God's will but also the Devil quotes Ps 91:11–12 to tempt Jesus.

To add a few more examples, after emperor Constantine's conversion in the fourth century the Bible as a whole was used to support the Roman Empire, the same Empire that killed Jesus and prosecuted the earlier Christian communities. Further down the road, Noah's cursing of Ham

9. Darolín, "Popular Reading of the Bible in Revolutionary and Imperial Times," 35.

10. Said, "Michael Walzer's Exodus and Revolution."

11. Warrior, "Canaanites, Cowboys, and Indians," 264.

in Gen 9:20–27 became the justification for enslaving African people in North America, and of Apartheid in South Africa. John's conflict with his fellow-Jews expressed in John 8:44, alongside the complex, contentious negotiation between the early Christian movement and Judaism as reflected in New Testament texts like Matt 27:25, was turned into a Christian legitimation of anti-Jewish pogroms and finally the Holocaust. The Genesis narrative of Creation and Fall in Gen 1–3 was read as support of patriarchy and ecocide. The list could be extended to many more texts, including the book of Joshua that gives divine and sacred character to the conquest and large-scale disposal of native populations from their land.

The mere fact that a text has been read in an oppressive way does not mean that this is the only way to read it.[12] I therefore make a distinction between texts that have been interpreted in an oppressive way but can be read also in a liberating way, and those texts we find in themselves to be oppressive. As Nancy Cardoso Pereira points out:

> For women it is fundamental to recognize that in the Bible there are texts that are not normative but merely circumstantial. A patriarchal text that justifies discrimination against women cannot be normative because it is contrary to the liberating spirit of the Gospel. Neither the oppressive aspects of the cultural tradition and those who interpret the text can be projected as normative points of the texts.[13]

Evidently, texts regarding the violent occupation of the land, mainly in the book of Joshua, are functioning in a way like the Trojan horse, bringing the enemy inside. Nonetheless, as Old Testament scholarship reminds us, those texts full of gruesome bloodshed were written a long time after the events they narrate; they construct a story more oriented to support and differentiate themselves in the context of the Persian, Greek and Roman empires than to reflect historical happenings.[14]

---

12. A classic text on this aspect of hermeneutic is Segundo, *The Liberation of Theology*. Segundo understands the hermeneutic process as a circle with four moments: "*Firstly*, there is our way of experiencing reality, which leads us to ideological suspicion. *Secondly*, there is the application of our ideological suspicion to the whole ideological superstructure in general and to theology in particular. *Thirdly*, there comes a new way of experiencing theological reality that leads us to exegetical suspicion, that is, to the suspicion that the prevailing interpretation of the Bible has not taken important pieces of data into account. *Fourthly*, we have our new hermeneutic, that is, our new way of interpreting the fountainhead of our faith (i.e., Scripture) with the new elements at our disposal" (9).

13. Pereira, "Pautas para una hermenéutica feminista de la liberación," 9.

14. If readers want to remain in a literary mode, the existence of the book of Judges

This historical argument is not meant to ignore the problem of the "conquest texts" on the literary or theological level, or to justify them. But we have to understand that they are born out of the impossibility to transform the essence of the biblical message into a reality, i.e. they are written from a position of powerlessness and defeat under foreign empires (after the exile in 586 BCE erased all hopes of an independent existence in line with the laws of God). What has happened now is that these texts are read from a position of power and with the capacity to put into reality what used to be the fiction of the overpowered and defeated. That is what happened with the Christian conquerors in America and the Israelite occupation now in Palestine.

Exodus, Deeper Meaning

As I mentioned above, the identity of God as savior of the oppressed is central to LT and this comprehension of God has been strongly based on the exodus story. However, it is necessary to be more precise about how some biblical scholars understood those texts. Croatto makes a distinction:

> It is not the "outside" aspect of the "exodus" that makes this motif and the biblical texts that mention or re-read it relevant. The return from the Babylonian captivity or the return of the Jews to Israel had that nature; but most of the processes than have been nourished from the message of Exodus were not "departures" from places of captivity to "go" to a free place, but acts of liberation in their own places where people suffered internal or external domination.[15]

In this distinction the relevance of exodus for Latin American Liberation Theology (LLT) is not in the external aspect but its deeper meaning: "it is not the external fact of the archetypical event that lives on, but its deeper *meaning*, its capacity to activate the human reserves of hope in new processes of liberation."[16] According to this reading, the continuum and ongoing importance of the exodus in LLT is not in the conquest and the extermination of the inhabitants of Canaan but in the prophetic discourse against the monarchies of Israel that became as oppressive as

---

shows that Joshua is improbable. Dreher, "Josué," 49–68.

15. Croatto, "La relevancia sociohistórica y hermenéutica del éxodo," 155.

16. Croatto, "La relevancia sociohistórica y hermenéutica del éxodo," 156.

the pharaoh.[17] Taking the example of the prophet Amos, he mentions the exodus and the people's presence in the land to make a critical statement against the lack of justice in Israel itself (Amos 2:1–3:2; 4:10; 9:7). Due to the specific context of LLT, the exodus event is understood as a sociopolitical event and from a social and class perspective, rather than as a national conflict.[18]

Readers and Options

LLT emerged at a time when the historical methods of biblical interpretation were at their peak and the historical context or production of the texts were of key importance. Nowadays, literary methods and reader response criticism play a much more crucial role in the interpretation of the texts. Nonetheless, it is not possible to put aside all the research done with regard to the complex process of composition of the texts and the conflicting theologies we find in the Hebrew Bible and the New Testament.

It is not responsible to just take books, or a composition of books like the Torah or even the entire Hebrew Bible and suppose that they express a coherent and harmonic voice. In fact, the Bible is a text where different and conflicting trajectories representing contradictory models of social and religious organization competing with one another are found.[19] Therefore, choosing between options and taking sides are inevitable hermeneutical requirements. We as readers have to decide if we accept a particular trajectory, or the other one, or even if we understand both of them together as an invitation to find a third one. The multivocal canon of the Hebrew Bible and the New Testament in the way it is constructed requires this critical discernment, i.e. partisan readings. LLT chose to give voice to the exodus event of liberation, the prophetic call for justice, Jesus' ministry and Paul's counter-imperial theology. And because of that it needs to deconstruct conquest narratives, royal theologies, the patriarchal motifs, and so forth.[20]

---

17. See the parallelism of vocabulary between 1 Kgs 12 and Exod 1.

18. Segovia, "Engaging the Palestinian," 29–80.

19. See Brueggemann, "Trajectories in Old Testament Literature," 307–33.

20. I am not suggesting a simple dualistic separation or choice of good versus bad texts. A more complex and careful reading is needed of every text, that prioritizes specifically the potential consequences of my reading to others, in particular the "little ones" (Mat18:6), and that stays suspicious about my own choices.

This seems an adequate approach if we accept our active role as readers, readers that have taken side in favor of the oppressed. Because our basic theological foundation rests in the encounter with the poor and excluded, it is there that we find God. However, there is also a dangerous risk if we absolutize our reading. I believe that, as the canon requires us to take side, it also demands respect, confrontation and dialogue with competing readings. It is necessary to be explicit about our moves and diligently work to deconstruct our own reading as well, not just the reading of the "others."[21]

Native Inhabitants

Fourth, Mitri Raheb proposes the need to incorporate the land and the native people of the land as fifth and sixth gospels.[22] His suggestion brought to my mind the experience of reading the Bible with indigenous people in the northern part of Argentina and how they understood their relationship and belonging to the land.

One of the key elements in reading the Old Testament is the issue of land. We worked together to get a deeper understanding of this topic and of how Qom's people[23] might find a way to recuperate some of their land that were stolen and occupied. As we read Exod 13:17—14:31, one of the participants called "uncle" Daniel tells with a calm voice how during the times of military dictatorship some people wanted to expel the Qom community from the area of El Colchón, located in an impenetrable, northern part of Chaco, Argentina. At the beginning, I did not understand why he "broke in." More out of respect than comprehension, I shut up and listened: "We told them that they could not throw us out from there, because that was our land, and we belong to that place. There, our ancestors are buried. After that the intruders left and did not bother us anymore." The land is important because of the ancestors, and this highlights a minor detail in the text we were studying. Moses went out of Egypt with Joseph's bones (Exod 13:6). The land to where they were going

21. De Witt has worked on this issue, see *Through the Eyes of Another.*

22. Raheb, "Toward a New Hermeneutics of Liberation," 11–28.

23. Qom's people is an indigenous group located today in the Northern part of Argentina, especially in the province of Chaco and Formosa. The Qom were originally nomadic hunters and gatherers living in a wide area named Gran Chaco (Argentina, Bolivia, and Paraguay).

is not a new and unknown land, it is not only the land of God's promise but also the land where the ancestors are buried.

Certainly, in the final form of the Pentateuch the land of Canaan is the Promised Land to Abraham in Gen 12, a promise that was later ratified by covenant in Gen 15 and 17 and repeated to representatives of his linage. However, there is an entire chapter (Gen 23) to ensure that Abraham legally bought a piece of land in Machpelah to bury Sarah there. Not only a chapter is dedicated to this issue but also the literary strategy of "showing" (instead of "telling") is used to increase the dramatic aspect and heighten the relevance of the story.

The importance of the ancestors' burial place is also demonstrated in the fact that this issue comes up with most of the ancestors. Abraham, Isaac, Rebecca, Leah and Jacob are buried in the same place as Sarah (Gen 25:9–10; 49:29–32; 50:13). Especially important is the effort it took to bring Jacob's body from Egypt. Only the Egyptian technique of embalming would have allowed his family to fulfill their promise. Rachel is buried in a different place, in Bethlehem (Gen 53:19). Joseph is buried in the same place that Jacob legally bought from "the children of Hamor" (Gen 33:18–20; Jos 24:32).

The point made by uncle Daniel and the Qom people is close to the point made in the Genesis narratives. The relationship and belonging to a specific land and territory is based upon the burial place of the ancestors. This is true for the relationship of the native Palestinian people to their land as well. It does not matter if they are Christian, Jewish or Muslim. The native Palestinian people belong to Palestine, and their claim must be respected. This claim requires us to approach the topic of land with a different perspective. It is not an issue of ownership and property but of belonging to the land.[24]

Idea of Election

Finally, the issue of election needs reconsideration. This has come up in the discussions among Latin American liberation theologians on the occasion of the 500th anniversary of the European arrival to the Americas.

---

24. How important for our discussion is the sense of scarcity in Isaac's promise to Jacob and his denial to promise land for Esau? Was there really not enough space for both sons?

The phrase "occupied text" connects "our" conquest five hundred years ago with the settler imperialism of present-day Israel. When the state of Israel chose to call itself "Israel" it not only occupied a land but the Hebrew Bible as well. Claiming its identity as the Biblical Israel it automatically became the inheritor of God's promise, the only one. Certainly, contemporary Jews may consider part of that people, and part of that promise, but they are not the only one. There is a much-needed task of deconstructing this equation.

Elsa Tamez's article on Rom 9–11, titled "The Election as Guarantee of Inclusion,"[25] presents important findings about election. She understands that election is part of a prior salvific plan of God to give salvation to all of humanity. It was precisely because of that universal scope that God chose Israel as the least, the excluded, the oppressed people. For in order "to accomplish the merciful plan of God in its plentitude, not letting anyone outside of God's saving plan, God has to opt for those excluded of the society."[26] Tamez also shows how many times in history the chosen ones mistook the election based on God's grace as their own merit *and as permission to be superior to others.* Because of that, Paul's letter to the Romans in chapters 9–11 puts so much emphasis on a correct understanding of election. Paul wrote to Christians who were quarreling and boasting themselves over and against each other. There were Christian Jews that considered themselves more important than non-Jewish Christians, and non-Jewish Christians who felt far above Christian Jews and Judaism in general. This attitude of superiority for Tamez is the point where the "chosen ones" may lose their status as they depart from God's plan of salvation for all. At this point, God has the sovereignty to "break off" some and to "graft in" others (cf. Rom 11:17–24).

Furthermore, the concept of "election" is used, or not used, differently throughout various texts and traditions of the Hebrew Bible. In each case its varying theological or pastoral meaning is derived from concrete contexts. In the Deuteronomistic theology "election" meant a call to the people to walk according to God's will (Deut 14:2), and there is a stern warning about understanding it as a result of their own merit (Deut 7:6–8). Or, to give another example, in the book of Isaiah "election" was used in the context of Diaspora hopelessness in order to ensure the

25. Tamez, "La elección como garantía de la inclusión."
26. Tamez, "La elección como garantía de la inclusión," 164. See also 1 Cor 1:27–28.

people of God's saving presence (Isa 41:8–9; 43:10; 44:1–2). For Tamez, this means that

> being elected, as act of solidarity of God, transforms the exclud-
> ed in someone with dignity, included in God's liberation plan.
> Becoming aware of being chosen, selected by God, re-creates:
> strengthens to face hostilities of which one is the object; hope
> while confronting an uncertain future, and the conscience of the
> praxis to carry on God's liberation plan.[27]

This invitation to understand election from the perspective of the oppressed, based on God's plan of salvation for all, and, at the same time, on the sovereignty of God to "break off" and "graft in" opens a new, liberating way to understand this biblical concept.

Conclusion

In this reflection I traced some issues addressed by LLT that might be relevant for a Palestinian or contextual theology. Understanding the exodus as God's election of the oppressed makes this contested narrative a powerful text to keep working on/with. It certainly has its limitations, as any other biblical text, and especially if we remain in an "external" and nationalistic mode of reading.

It is crucial to keep in mind the complex character of the Bible and the intentional tension between texts. In light of this, the active role and discernment of the reader are an unescapable task. It requires us to reflect consciously and critically both about our own reading choices as well as the readings of others. Indispensable in this endeavor, however, is to always keep the excluded and oppressed at the center, because this is a way to bring "Good News" to all.

The biblical narratives of Genesis, I believe, are opportunities to affirm the relationship of the native inhabitants with their land and, at the same time, to challenge the fictional conquest stories. From a Christian point of view, the concept of election cannot ignore how the New Testament reads it. Despite nuances, it is affirmed as an inclusive trajectory that we already find in the Hebrew Bible.

Regarding the construct of the scriptural canon, both Jews and Christians can find a rich tapestry of conflicting, contrasting and

---

27. Tamez, "La elección como garantía de la inclusión," 165.

complementary texts in it. I believe this is an invitation to open a hermeneutic space so that we may find place for all.

Bibliography

Barolín, Darío. "Popular Reading of the Bible in Revolutionary and Imperial Times." *Exchange* 44 (2015) 27–44.

Brueggemann, Walter. "Trajectories in Old Testament Literature and the Sociology of Ancient Israel." In *The Bible and Liberation: Political and Social Hermeneutics*, edited by Norman Gottwald, 307–33. Maryknoll, NY: Orbis, 1983.

Craotto, José Severino. "La relevancia sociohistórica y hermenéutica del éxodo." *Concilium* 209 (1987) 155–64.

Croatto, J. Severino. *Exodus: A Hermeneutics of Freedom*. Maryknoll, NY: Orbis, 1981.

de Witt, Hans, et al., eds. *Through The Eyes of Another: Intercultural Reading of The Bible*. Elkhart, IN: Institute of Mennonite Studies, 2005.

Dreher, Así Carlos A. "Josué: ¿modelo de conquistador?" *RIBLA* 12 (1992) 49–68.

Las Casas, Bartolomé de. *Historia de las Indias*. Caracas: Fundación Biblioteca Ayacucho, 1956.

Masalha, Nur. *The Bible & Zionism. Invented Traditions: Archaeology and Post-Colonialism in Israel-Palestine*. London: Zed, 2007.

Mesters, Carlos, and Francisco Orofino, "Sobre la lectura popular de la Biblia." *Pasos* 130 (2007).

Pagán, Luis Rivera. *A Violent Evangelism: The Political and Religious Conquest of the Americas*. Louisville: Westminster John Knox, 1992.

Pereira, Nancy Cardoso. "Pautas para una hermenéutica feminista de la liberación." *Revista de interpretación bíblica latinoamericana* 25 (1997) 5–10.

Raheb, Mitri. "Toward a New Hermeneutics of Liberation: A Palestinian Christian Perspective." In *The Biblical Text in the Context of Occupation*, edited by Mitri Raheb, 11–28. Bethlehem: Diyar, 2012.

Rynés, Jaime. "La Biblia de los conquistadores y de los vencidos." *RIBLA* 12 (1992) 27–48.

Said, Edward W. "Michael Walzer's Exodus and Revolution: A Canaanite Reading." In *Blaming the Victims: Spurious Scholarship and the Palestinian Question*, edited by Edward W. Said and Christopher Hitchens, 161–78. New York: Verso 1988.

Segovia, Fernando F. "Engaging the Palestinian Theological-Critical Project of Liberation: A Critical Dialogue." In *The Biblical Text in the Context of Occupation. Towards a New Hermeneutic of Liberation*, edited by Mitri Raheb, 29–80. Bethlehem, Diyar, 2012.

Segundo, Juan Luis. *The Liberation of Theology*. Translated by John Drury. Maryknoll, NY: Orbis, 1976.

Tamez, Elsa. "La elección como garantía de la inclusión." *RIBLA* 12 (1992) 153–66.

Warrior, Robert. "Canaanites, Cowboys, and Indians: Deliverance, Conquest, and Liberation Theology Today." *Christianity and Crisis* 49/12 (1989) 261–65.

4

That Slave Is Your Sibling

A Reading of Deuteronomy 15:12–18

CHRISIDA NITHYAKALYANI ANANDAN

THE LAW ON MANUMISSION of slaves is found in the Covenant code (CC), Holiness code (HC), Deuteronomic code (DC), and in ANE law codes such as Laws of Hammurabi (LH). Even though they talk about the same issue, there are significant differences. This essay will focus on the manumission of the slaves in Deut 15:12–18 (DC) using social identity theory to find whether the group dynamics and group identity formation played any role in segregating masters versus slaves. In debt slavery, did the identity of people who became laborers change? How did these differing identities influence or affect a people who believed in one God and one people? What is behind the Deuteronomic writer's address of a slave-laborer as "your brother"? Was it in order to encourage a community of siblinghood?

In light of social identity theory, the text will be compared with the Exodus slavery law and the concept of love that runs through Deuteronomy. I will employ social scientific criticism, in particular social identity theory,[1] to find out the inter and intra group dynamics. Here, social

1. Social Identity Theory was pioneered by Henri Tajfel, born of Polish Jewish heritage. According to Tajfel, social identity is defined as the "aspects of an individual's self-image that derive from the social categories to which he perceives himself as

identity theory is an "academic inquiry into the relation between the individual and society and the development of an individual's personal and social identities."[2]

Slavery Laws

Comparing Exodus 21:1–11 with Deuteronomy 15:12–18

The Covenant Code begins with a set of laws in which the slavery law (Exod 21:1–11) comes first. Verses 2–6 are about male debt-slave and vv. 7–11 are about female debt-slave. These are casuistic laws in which each section begins with conditional clause and conjunction כי (in v.2) followed by four subordinate conjunction אם (in vv. 3a, 3b, 4 and 5); the same format is repeated in v. 7 followed by vv. 8, 9, 10, and 11. It is interesting to note that law on male debt-slave begins with his freedom and ends with his permanent enslavement. In contrast, the law for female begins with her permanent servitude and ends with her freedom.[3] The law in the covenant code is detailed and talks about the marriage of the Hebrew slave in which, if he gets his wife from his master, he will have to leave them when he goes free whereas if he comes with his wife while he entered servitude, his wife and children can also leave with him. This detail is missing in Deuteronomy—where, if he loves his master and his wife and children, he can choose to stay by setting an awl, whereas Exodus specifies that it happens before God.

With the comparison of Exod 21:2 and Deut 15:12, it is striking that the sentence in Exod 21:2 is the only one in personal form and also uses the rare phrase, "Hebrew slave"; there is probably an influence from Deut 15:12. The rest is then kept in third person in Exod 21:3–11 while in Deut 15:12–18 this is framed as an address to the speaker. That is to say that the form of Exod. 21:2 is not usual in CC.

While it seems likely that Exod 21 already refers to debt slavery in its original context and so does Deut 15 more explicitly, this is even more the case in the slavery legislation of H in Lev 25. It extends the rules for handling debt-slavery. With regard to the composition of H, the outline in Lev 25:39–46 differs from CC and D. As the Deuteronomic code uses the word "your brother" as a reference to the equality of community members on humanitarian grounds, it denotes that the person who has

---

belonging" (Tajfel, *Human Groups and Social Categories*, 224–25).

2. Baker, "Social Identity Theory and Biblical Interpretation," 129–38.

3. Wright, *Inventing God's Law*, 123.

turned out to be a slave is your brother (fictive kinship). In the same way, the HC also uses "your brother" and the author clearly distinguishes between slave and hired laborer indicating that he needs to be treated as hired and not as a slave (Lev 25:39–40). The motivation for this law is that the debt-slavery is highlighted in H, with a recurse to the Exodus motif. The community self-identifies as the ones whom Yahweh brought out from the land of Egypt and, consequently, they should not be treated harshly for the sake of their shared history as slaves, that is, for fear towards Yahweh. Hence, the HC stresses the humanitarian concern not to treat community members as slaves that are not to be sold.[4] H also uses the six-seven-year scheme similar to Deuteronomy. Nevertheless, LH stipulates that a debt slave would work only for three years and should be released in the fourth year.

Among the slave category, in modern categories, there are chattel slaves who are captives or slaves from foreign countries and debt-slaves who are ethnically Hebrews. The question that arises is whether biblical laws and the laws in ANE make a clear distinction between chattel and debt slaves. In LH, this distinction is evident as the word *wardum* is not used to denote debt-slaves. Urbach distinguishes between two types of Hebrew slaves enslaved to fellow-Jews. The first type is a thief sold to a victim to pay for the loss he created, and the second type is a freeborn Jew who sold himself into slavery.[5]

In the covenant code, Exod 21:2 mentions the slave as Hebrew slave (עבד עברי) thus making a clear-cut indication that it addresses debt-slave. On the contrary, when the word "slave" (עבד) is used without being qualified by "Hebrew" (עברי) it indicates both chattel-slave and debt-slave.[6] "A chattel slave may be distinguished by his or her status as property, over whom a master has right of disposal."[7] It is common that the household heads had significant rights over even the dependents who were free citizens and at the same time, the slaves had human rights limiting the power of the masters over them.

In Deuteronomy, the word "slave" is replaced with "your brother," reiterating the understanding that he or she is not an outsider, neither a person of different identity or group, but one among the community. This

---

4. Van Seters, "Law of the Hebrew Slave," 537.

5. Urbach, *The Laws Regarding Slavery*, 9.

6. Chirichigno, *Debt-Slavery in Israel and the Ancient Near East*, 182–83.

7. Baker, *Tight Fists or Open Hands?*, 112.

encourages and affirms the kinship concept of love and oneness. Houston argues that the text in Deut 15:12–18 admits that the selling of family members in bondage to pay back the debts would, of course, continue to happen, which can be seen with respect to the usage of the verb "sell" (מכר). He confers that the law for the release of bondservants after their six years' service has taken three different alterations in Deuteronomy. In the first instance, DC applies it equally to women in vv. 12, 17b, in contrast to Exod 21:7–11, denoting that women (העבריה) are part of this community when "brothers" are addressed. Second, DC leaves the idea that the master can have control over the personal life of the bondservant giving him a wife and her staying back when the bondservant leaves. Third, Deuteronomy stresses that when the bondservant is free, he should not be sent empty-handed but given generously from the master's share of property and wealth.[8]

Exodus deals with marital status and how it affects the release of the debt slave. His staying back is connected to his desire to stay together with his wife and children and in turn, the release of his wife and children is dependent on whether the wife was given by the master or he was married when he became debt-slave. This puts a hold on the debt-slave from going out freely after his sixth year. The masters can take this as an advantage to keep the slave with him forever. In contrast, Deuteronomy does not give any specifics about whether the slave is married or not, or whether the wife was given by the master or not, but the option of going out free solely rests on his opinion and decision.

In Exod 21:2, the protasis is in second person ("When you buy a Hebrew slave . . .") and the apodosis is in third person ("he shall go out"). In Deut 15:12, the protasis is in third person (When your brother, a Hebrew man and Hebrew woman, is sold to you) and the apodosis is in second person (you shall send him free) directly addressing to the owner or master. Moreover, Deut 15 starts with the exposition placing the labor's six-year term first. This points out that the command is not primarily about the obligation to serve, but it is about his right to be released from serving. In its very form, Deuteronomy expresses the rights of the slave. Another significant indication for this tendency is that Deuteronomy mentions the rights of the handmaid in addition to the slave. The handmaid is treated in the same way as that of the male slave.

---

8. Houston, "You Shall Open your Hand to Your Needy Brother," 310.

Social Understanding of Slavery

Baker mentions that a class structure that distinguished three ideal typi-
cal main social classes was prominent in the Old Babylonian period and
in neighboring countries. The first group comprises of the elite or free
citizens (*awilu*), which would include priests, nobles, officials, merchants
and landowners. The second group are the subordinate or semi-free citizens or serfs (*muskenu*), that includes the craftsmen, shepherds, laborers and tenant farmers, the ones who do not own the land but work for
the state or for private landowners. The third group are the chattel slaves
(*wardu,* male; *amtu* female). They are considered to be the property of
the owners and this group includes foreign captives and slaves bought in
markets or the children of the slaves born in the master's house.[9] However, free citizens face the risk of falling into the category of semi-free
citizens when they lose their land or means of production. From an economic point of view, these social demarcations arise when free citizens
lose their means of production and depend on the landowners and merchants for their resources which would lead to procure loans with high
interests. If crop fails or if they did not get the expected result, farmers
would come under pressure to return their loan and this may lead them
to sell their dependents into debt-slavery. In contrast, in the case of chattel slaves (see LH 170–171), the children of a house-born slave would
become legitimate and could get their freedom after the master dies. So,
there is a mobility in the statuses, where there was a possibility for a free
citizen to become a debt-slave and a chattel slave to reach the status of
free or semi-free citizen, yet a chattel slave is clearly distinguished from
the former one.[10]

Despite these structures, the terms "free" and "slave" are relative
in meaning. No one had complete freedom, and at the same time some
slaves possessed substantial power and wealth. It is difficult to define the
term "slave," for even a king would be described as a slave with reference
to a hierarchically higher person, such as the emperor or god and any
inferior person in a hierarchy could be included in this term.[11] This term
designates a relationship and is relative in its use.

During the settlement period, Israelites were free, and each tribe,
clan and family had land of their own except the priests and levites who

9. Baker, *Tight Fists or Open Hands?*, 111.

10. Chirichigno, *Debt-Slavery in Israel and the Ancient Near East*, 102–4.

11. Baker, *Tight Fists or Open Hands,* 111.

were compensated with other privileges. Unlike the Akkadian word *wardu*, which means "the one who has come down in social position," the Hebrew word commonly used for slave (עֶבֶד; *ʿebed*) literally means a worker. However, the people such as chattel slaves, temporary slaves and bonded laborers, concubines, widows and orphans, and ethnic minorities were at the margins forming a lower class.[12] While we may suppose that Israelite society also knew of slaves and their overlords as a hierarchical model of the society, the Hebrew Bible chooses to address the differences between slaves and overlords and presupposes an idealized community of brothers.

Nicholson views Israel, in Deuteronomy, as a depoliticized society. He asserts that they exhibit their identity in a collective manner as "brotherhood" and in a cultural manner as "the people of Yahweh."[13] Israel's identity as a community has its own distinctive features such as its identification with Yahweh, the exclusive worship of Yahweh and the way they act in relation to Yahweh. These features make it different from other cultures.[14] One of the unique things about the rendition of the slavery laws in Deuteronomy is the inclusion of the terms "Hebrew woman" (העבריה) and "your brother" (אחיך) the latter being used extensively throughout Deuteronomy. Even though it explicitly refers to Israel, scholars differ in their view of which social class the references to Hebrew man and woman in Deut 15:12 indicate. Scholars such as Horst, Merendino, Cholewiński, and Cardellini suggest that עברי refers to a lower social class of Israelites who were forced to sell themselves.[15] Some suggest that they are landless Israelites.[16] The terms העברי and העבריה qualify the "your brother," indicating that the whole nation should relate and treat each other as kin. "Your brother," as Wright suggests,[17] is broader in its meaning and is not just about blood-related kin but also refers to the fictive kinship that Israel was concerned about. The term יִמָּכֵר in Deut 15:12a render the sale

---

12. Baker, *Tight Fists or Open Hands*, 112.

13. Nicholson, *Deuteronomy and the Judean Diaspora*, 50–53.

14. Crouch, *The Making of Israel*, 115–16.

15. The term was used to refer to people descended from Eber and would define an ethnic group. The slavery laws make the point of *not* treating Hebrew slaves the same way as they would treat non-Israelites. The key term in the debate is "ibri." The slavery laws are a complicated piece in the ethnography and self-identity of the Israelites.

16. Chirichigno, *Debt-Slavery in Israel and the Ancient Near East*, 275–77.

17. Wright, "What Happened Every Seven Years in Israel?," 196–97.

in a Niph'al form[18] and it could be translated either in passive or reflexive form as "is sold" or "sells himself" respectively. I have translated it in the passive form as the reflexive form would put the emphasis on the slave. The words in v. 12b stresses the responsibility of the master, whether he was sold by someone or his debts made him to sell himself.

We could notice, in both CC and DC, this law deals with 6/7 release formula and most of the scholars identify it as connected to the sabbatical release in vv. 1–3 and compare the seven-year release with the fifty-year release in Leviticus. Otto uses this comparable concept to relate the Sabbath law to the 6/7 laws about slavery. These laws of release bookend the collection of Exod 21–23 (21:1–11/23:10–12) as their relevance as a social principle is engrained in legal tradition. The CC puts this law first and this influenced Deuteronomy but with some modifications. In Exod 21:2b, the verb used is יֵצֵא in which the slave is the subject that shall go whereas Deut 15:12b uses the verb תְּשַׁלְּחֶנּוּ meaning "you shall send him free," in which the responsibility is given to the master in freeing him and also, is obliged to provide him liberally.[19]

Carmichael suggests that Deuteronomy is concerned about two separate issues—the release of the person from slavery and, on the other side, the material resources for his living as he goes out. He insists that these are two issues prevalent in the Exodus story.[20] Deut 15:13 gives a mandate to the masters not to send out the laborer empty into freedom. The word employed is רֵיקָם which occurs in other passages such as Gen 31:42 and Exod 3:21 in the context of release after servitude. The master is directed not to send the male or female labor empty, but also to provide liberally from flock, threshing floor and wine vat with which God has blessed him. Here, the Deuteronomist insists that the property and land is a blessing from God and so the master should willingly share the gift that he has received.

Deuteronomy 15:13–15 is a religious call to the master to be reminded that the prosperity he enjoys is divine blessing (v.14) and, the master should remember that he was a slave in Egypt and Yhwh redeemed (v.15)

---

18. The Niphal is related to the Qal: (a) reflexive of the Qal, (b) in a reciprocal sense, (c) passive. From the passive meaning is derived the sense of 'to allow something to be done to someone'" (Waltke and O'Connor, 379).

19. Chirichigno, *Debt-Slavery in Israel and the Ancient Near East*, 283.

20. Carmichael, "The three Laws on the Release of Slaves," 520.

him—these imply that a division on the basis of class is not relevant as everyone was a slave now freed owing the liberty and prosperity to God.[21]

Deuteronomy 15:16–17 is a sub-counter case to the release of the debt-slave where he/she is given an option of entering into permanent servitude. The laborer is given an option to choose whether he needs to work with his master forever. There are several reasons to highlight this. First, in v. 16, the phrase כִּי־יֹאמַר אֵלֶיךָ uses a conditional clause in which the labor may decide that he does not want to go out, which makes a difference. Second and most importantly, unlike Exodus, the Deuteronomic code does not put any hold on the laborer with regards to his marriage. In Exod 21 it seems advantageous for the master to withhold his wife and children if he has given him a wife in marriage, which, consequently, would be a driving force for the slave to stay and to enter into permanent slavery. Deuteronomy, by making the law equal for both men and women, releases the male and female debt-slaves without any condition of their spouse or children being enslaved with the master which shows a humanitarian concern towards the slave.

Ethical Basis for the Law of Siblingship

The Deuteronomic law code on the manumission of slaves provides ethical grounds to encourage siblinghood and love towards one another in a positive manner dealing with the concerns of the people at the margins compared to the way Exodus deals with it. I highlight some of the ethical concerns here.

Siblinghood

In Mesopotamia and other ancient Near Eastern city-states, the tribal and rural populations were socially organized based on kinship. This was either real or fictitious kinship, often called by anthropologists as lineage systems which could be distinguished as three stages of kinship—minimal lineage (nuclear family), lineage proper (clan), and maximal lineage (tribe).[22]

Deuteronomy, on the whole, reiterates the importance of relationship throughout, as it was considered by the writer to fix the people as

21. Houston, "You Shall Open Your Hand to Your Needy Brother," 311.

22. Chirichigno, *Debt-Slavery in Israel and the Ancient Near East*, 32.

one community of siblings which is evident through the repetitive usage of the phrase "your brother." It was essential for them because kinship was not just understood as blood relation, but it was meant to be understood as being one community of God. Deuteronomy uses Yahweh, the people of Israel, worship and social justice as the main theological tenets that run throughout the book.

Here, the "slave" is a brother, or in other words, one of your brothers has been made a slave. Houston suggests that in a community where all are brothers, there is no master or slave. The contract that is made here is not about slavery, but about the sale of one's labor for a specified and limited time.[23] The phrase "your brother" occurs several times and has this programmatic undertone in Deuteronomy, often referring to the entire community as fictive kinship strategy (Deut 15:3, 7, 9, 11, 12; 17:15; 22:1–4; 23:8, 20, 21; 24:14; 25:3; 32:50).

Memory

The overarching conceptual framework of slavery law in Deuteronomy exhorts the people to remember their collective past as slaves in Egypt. Throughout Deuteronomy God reiterates that they need to remember their past and teach their children how Yahweh brought them out of slavery (Deut 4:9; 5:6; 6:12, 25). "Deuteronomy warns against begrudging the gifts of freedom and stake to begin a new life."[24]

This command is also a reminder to the people not to treat the disadvantaged of the society with contempt. Repeatedly, God commands the people to take care of the orphans, widows and poor (Exod. 22:22–23, etc.). This call to remember reminds the people that they are from same slave status and there is no different group dynamics. The Exodus motif present here relates to the Decalogue in Exod 5:15: "Remember that you were a slave in the land of Egypt, and the Lord your God brought you out from there with a mighty hand and an outstretched arm; therefore the Lord your God commanded you to keep the sabbath day" (NRSV).

Every society establishes sub-groups with respect to their differences and creates in-group and out-group that can turn against each other. The Deuteronomic author reminds the people that all of them come, originally, from the same shared experience of being slaves and,

23. Houston, "You Shall Open Your Hand to Your Needy Brother," 311.
24. Green, *Deuteronomy*.

consequently, demands mutual solidarity. Thereby, it exhorts the people to treat their laborers with love and kinship.

Land as a Blessing

The instruction that the laborers should not go empty-handed is an important motive to stop the laborer falling into debt immediately after going out from slavery. The landowners are asked to provide liberally out of the flock, threshing floor and wine press. This instruction is followed by a clause "which the Lord has blessed you." It adds stress to the fact that all the riches, land, flock and property are a gift and blessing from God. Whatever the people have belongs to God, and was a gracious divine provision which makes the landowner obliged to share from his property. This has a similarity with the provisions provided by Egyptians, when they released Hebrews from slavery with the only difference that it is not jewelry but the land and flock.

Love and Kinship

Deut 15:16–17 has a conditional clause, "if the slave shall say that he loves you." The concept of love is predominant in Deuteronomy, revealed in several places through programmatically de-routing the people of Israel to move towards love and kinship. The willingness of the laborer to stay with the master is totally dependent on his love toward his master and his household which in turn also depends on the way the master treats or relates with the laborer. In a legal sense, the term love refers to mutual benevolence in which both parties exhibit love towards each other. The love that exists between these two different groups is a motivation to enter a family relationship of being one people and one family. The laborer's decision to work permanently leads to becoming one family which echoes siblinghood—the person who works is not a slave but a sibling. Only out of love, this relationship is possible. Only if love exists between the owner and laborer, the relationship would be mutual, and this kinship service could continue. Or else, the laborer should be set free. The Deuteronomic author discourages this hierarchical relationship which could turn to malevolence if it continues to be oppressive or unloving. Through love and kinship model, he encourages mutual benevolence between these two groups.

Social Identity and Formation

The people of Israel, while they were in Egypt, were slaves working in hard labor for Pharaoh. All were in the same situation and they were identified as one group of slaves over against their masters, the Egyptians. When they reached the promised land, these slaves claim a different self-identity as free people. Nevertheless, intra- and inter-groups were formed—that is, insiders and outsiders in the same group. Tajfel explains this in his social identity theory: "Social and economic conditions leading to rivalry between groups for various kinds of objective benefits are associated with a diffusion of certain derogatory notions about the outgroup. These notions, which are related to attitudes and behavior establishing various forms of social distance between groups can hardly be conceived as originating directly from a situation of objective struggle for a distribution of resource."[25] We can find a similar social situation in Neh 5:1–13 in which it is told to Nehemiah that many people are in debt and have sold their daughters and sons in slavery for repayment of debts. The key problem here is that they have demanded and taken interest from their "brothers" which is a serious violation of Deuteronomic and Holiness codes.

As a community with varied groups of people with different economic backgrounds, the community of Israel have different groups which considered one as outsider over against themselves. In this situation the Deuteronomist stresses the fact that they are one community of siblings who were all considered as slaves whom Yahweh brought out of the land of slavery irrespective of their present status.

Modern-Day Slavery

Even though slavery has been abolished by many countries, it manifests itself in various forms. In the context of differentiating social groups as "us" and "they," there are issues that greatly hinder living with justice and equality. All over the world, issues such as racism, casteism, poverty, and so on exclude one or more groups as "others" and discriminate on a larger basis. The issue of bonded labor could be seen all over the world and especially, at a larger rate, in Southeast Asia. The migrant and bonded laborer, voluntary or involuntary, is hired or bought on several layers of oppression including caste, economic deprivation, sexual abuse and so on.

25. Tajfel, *Human Groups and Social Categories*, 224–25.

A 2013 Tamil movie based on the English novel *Red Tea* by Paul Harris Daniel published in Chennai (Higginbothams, 1969), deals with tea plantation workers in the Madras Presidency[26] during the British Raj touching on several issues such as poverty, migration, unemployment, and caste in the context of colonization. This is not the story of the past alone. In the modern era, in and outside of India, some poor people are forced into labor taking advantage of their illiteracy, ignorance, economic status, and caste.

The ethical basis found in Deut 15 which stresses on the relationship with the labor as sibling and not as a slave is relevant even today, globally. Deuteronomy 15 motivates us to relate to everyone as siblings, remembering that this earth is a blessing from God that we share with all.

Conclusion

Deuteronomy 15:12–18 moves forward on how to treat a laborer and talks about the manumission of the labor. Compared to Exodus, Deuteronomy is ahead in terms of humanitarian and gender concerns. Deuteronomy develops further certain areas in which Exodus falls short. Comparing the two texts shows development in terms of the right of the labor in choosing his/her freedom and also about the equal treatment of the handmaid. The usage of "your brother" instead of slave is one of the topmost changes that Deuteronomy makes to discourage from slavery and to ensure treating as a brother any Israelite debt "slave." The DC offers an ideal ethos of siblinghood and love through its motivation of kinship irrespective of blood relations, its exhortation to remember the past that they were slaves, its recognition of land as a blessing from God, and its emphasis on the importance of family ethos. This ethos is expected to have as its consequence a comprehensive blessing, "Yahweh your God will bless you in all that you do."

Bibliography

Baker, Coleman A. "Social Identity Theory and Biblical Interpretation." *Biblical Theology Bulletin* 42 (2012) 129–38.

26. Included much of southern India—the present-day State of Tamil Nadu, the Malabar region of North Kerala, Lakshadweep Islands, the Coastal Andhra and Rayalaseema regions of Andhra Pradesh, Brahmapur and Ganjam districts of Orissa and the Bellary, Dakshina Kannada, and Udupi.

Baker, David L. *Tight Fists or Open Hands? Wealth and Poverty in Old Testament Law*. Grand Rapids: Eerdmans, 2009.

Carmichael, Calum. "The Three Laws on the Release of Slaves." *Zeitschrift für die alttestamentliche Wissenschaft* 112 (2000) 509–25.

Chirichigno, Gregory. *Debt-Slavery in Israel and the Ancient Near East*. Journal for the Study of the Old Testament Supplements 141. Sheffield: Sheffield Academic, 1993.

Crouch, C. L. *The Making of Israel: Cultural Diversity in the Southern Levant and the Formation of Ethnic Identity in Deuteronomy*. Leiden: Brill, 2014.

Driver, S. R. *A Critical and Exegetical Commentary of Deuteronomy*. International Critical Commentary. Edinburgh: T. & T. Clark, 1902.

Green, Stephen G. *Deuteronomy: A Commentary in the Wesleyan Tradition Account*. Kansas City: Nazarene, 2015.

Houston, Walter. "'You Shall Open Your Hand to Your Needy Brother': Ideology and Moral Formation in Deut. 15:1–18." In *The Bible in Ethics: The Second Sheffield Colloquium*, edited by J. W. Rogerson, Margaret Davies, and M. Daniel Carroll R., 296–314. Journal for the Study of the Old Testament Supplements 207. Sheffield: Sheffield Academic, 1995.

Nicholson, E. W. *Deuteronomy and the Judean Diaspora*. Oxford: Oxford University Press, 2014.

Tajfel, Henri. *Human Groups and Social Categories: Studies in Social Psychology*. Cambridge: Cambridge University Press, 1981.

Tsevat, Matitiahu. "The Hebrew Slave according to Deuteronomy 15:12–18: His Lot and the Value of His Work, with Special Attention to the Meaning of מִשְׁנֶה." *Journal of Biblical Literature* 113 (1994) 587–95.

Urbach, E. E. *The Laws Regarding Slavery*. New York: Arno, 1979.

Van Seters, John. "Law of the Hebrew Slave." *Zeitschrift für die alttestamentliche Wissenschaft* 108 (1996) 534–46.

Waltke, Bruce K., and M. O'Connor. *An Introduction to Biblical Hebrew Syntax*. Winona Lake, IN: Eisenbrauns, 1999.

Wright, C. J. H. "What Happened Every Seven Years in Israel? Old Testament Sabbatical Institutions for Land, Debts and Slaves, Part I & II." *Evangelical Quarterly* 56 (1984) 129–38, 193–201.

Wright, David P. *Inventing God's Law: How the Covenant Code of the Bible Used and Revised the Laws of Hammurabi*. Oxford: Oxford University Press, 2009.

5

Remixing Egypt

Jione Havea

Remixing (in the modern form) arrived in Oceania on the waves of reggae and hip-hop music, including the popular and controversial multi-volume FOB (*Fresh off the boat*) CDs at the turn of the century. Remixing is now a crucial part of the lives of diaspora-born Pacific Islanders,[1] several of whom challenged me—that i[2] should consider "remixing" as one of the metaphors for diasporic island hermeneutics. This chapter honors that direction.

The arts of remixing music go back to Jamaica's dance halls in the late 1960s, when DJs compose alternate versions of songs to give new lives to

1. The label continues to evolve, with "siren jam" as the recent mutation in the Pa-sifika diaspora. This is the beat that Jawsh 685 (Joshua Stylah, a young Samoan-Cook Islander who grew up in South Auckland) remixed as "Laxed (Siren Beat)" and shared on YouTube in 2019; this beat "inspired" a duo with Jason Derulo (Black American)—"Savage Love"—which topped the TikTok and iTunes charts in early 2020 and drew choreographers and dancers (including Jennifer Lopez, Lizzo and Jimmy Fallon). The reincarnation of "Laxed (Siren Beat)" in "Savage Love" is an example of how remixing works, mutating across cultures to make voices, minds and bodies dance.

2. I use the lowercase with the first person when i am the subject, in the same way that i use the lowercase with "we," "you," "she," "he," "it," "they" and "others." There is no justification for privileging (by capitalizing) the first person individual (a leaning of English grammar) who *is* in relation to other subjects.

those in clubs and on the radio.³ Remixing is not a recording or editing of an old song, but the stripping down then rebuilding the song, remixing it, with new hooks, echo, reverberation and delay, flirting in the process with copyright laws, to suit the audience. It gives the old song a new twist, tricking listeners' memory of the old song, as Chris Potash explains:

> Because it's often applied to an already-familiar song or rhythm track, dub [i.e., remix] has a uniquely poignant quality: memories are revived, but rather than being simply duplicated (as when we hear a "golden oldie" from our youth on the radio) they are given subtle twists. Memory is teased rather than dragged up, and is thereby heightened.⁴

Robert Beckford defines remixing or dubbing as a form of deconstruction and signification and highlights the intimate connection between dub technique and the spoken word in dub poetry:

> For instance, in the dub poem "Liesense fi kill," Linton Kwesi Johnson, "plays" with the word "licence." Removing the letter "c" and adding "s" after the first "e" he communicates a sense of corruption and disreputable activity in the police. It now means to "cover-up" that is "lie" "sense." Similarly, Birmingham based dub poet *Kukumo* plays with the word "diaspora," re-interpreting the word in light of Caribbean economic struggle in Britain to coin the term "die-as-poor-ya."⁵

From a particular position and perspective, the remixer and dub poet reconstruct the old into a new form thereby recreating the way that listeners hear, understand and appreciate the old song, word or phrase. We should not confuse remixing or dubbing with translation, which is hung up on getting the correct message across languages and cultures. Rather, the remixer and dub poet create alternate structures of meaning that signify in new ways. In this regard, the remixer and dub poet shuttle in the shadows of Jeremiah—who was commissioned to pluck up and pull down, and also to build and to plant (Jer 1:10)—and of Jesus: "When 'Jesus dubs,' those on the margins are enabled to tear down the walls that

---

3. "Remixing" and "dubbing" are synonymous, but i favor "remixing" because that is the term preferred by the native Pasifika islanders with whom i mix. My Caribbean friends, on the other hand, prefer "dubbing."

4. Potash, *Reggae, Rasta Revolution*, 146, cited in Beckford, *Jesus Dub*, 75.

5. Beckford, *Jesus Dub*, 77.

exclude and rebuild and refashion things so that all people are free from the ravages of oppression."[6]

Whereas Beckford focuses on how *Jesus dubs,* i look toward Egypt, a land, nation and people that have received a bad rap from interpreters and thinkers, especially the ones who revel in pro-Israelite spirits. This remixing of Egypt also seeks to account for recent ecological crises and the politics of climate change,[7] aiming to alter the signification of Egypt from being the hated house of bondage *only* to being house of refuge *also.* This double sense is not new, for they are rooted in the biblical account. This attempt to remix Egypt need to strip the biases that demonize Egypt and Egyptian peoples and cultures. I will do that in a later section but turn at this juncture to locate remixing within biblical traditions (the hub for this reflection) and Pasifika cultures (which conditioned my perspectives).

Remixing Is Biblical and Local

The practices of remixing are not foreign to the biblical account. The many instances of legal revision involve remixing.[8] The Decalogue, best known and most hallowed of the biblical law codes, is a telling case. Whereas the Exodus version of the fourth commandment (Exod 20:8–11) links the observance of the Sabbath to the Priestly account of the creation (especially Gen 2:1–3), the Deuteronomic version (Deut 5:12–15) roots it in the bloody liberation from Egypt. Which of the versions was earlier does not matter to me here. What is more interesting is that juxtaposing the two versions suggests that legal revision, which is what happens in remixing, has taken place. Whether one reads the two versions historically or socio-politically, from the Exodus version to the Deuteronomic version or vice versa, one cannot help noticing that remixing has taken place. On the broader scale, the rewriting of history in 1–2 Chronicles and in Second Temple Literature testify that remixing (rewriting, revision) was an ancient art of appropriation.[9]

---

6. Beckford, *Jesus Dub,* 80.

7. Cf. Havea, "The politics of climate change."

8. Cf. Levinson, *Legal Revision,* 22–45, 89–94.

9. Cf. Crawford, *Rewriting Scripture in Second Temple Times,* esp. 39–83; cf. Levinson, *Legal Revision,* 95–181.

Remixing (qua borrowing and appropriating) happened in Oceania even before hip hop and reggae cultures arrived there. Take as an example one of the popular songs in Fiji (*Isa Lei*) and Tonga (*'Ise'isa viola lose hina*), both are three verses each plus a chorus, sung to the same rhythm, fervor, longing and affection. As *Waltzing Matilda* is on the same bar as the national anthem in Australia, so is *Isa Lei* in Fiji and *'Ise'isa viola lose hina* for many Tongans. One song presupposes but it does not translate the other song. There are enough differences between the two songs that they are distinct to these neighboring island groups; there are enough echoes in both songs that when natives from one group hear the song from the other group, their hearts jump as if they are hearing their won.

As one would expect, Tongans claim that Fijians borrowed *Isa Lei* from the Tongan song, and Fijians argue that the Tongans stole the Fijian song and remixed it as theirs. Because of the oral roots of both island nations, and the repeated crossing of the fluid borders between them even before contact with the West, it would be difficult to determine which was the original song. In this case also, it does not bother me that we cannot be certain about the origin (an obsession of modernity) of the songs. The two songs share common thoughts (e.g., begging to be remembered), but there are enough differences to suggest that one is a remixing of the other. For my purposes, this is sufficient to show that remixing was common among my forbearers.

Remixing and Oratory

I divert here to a Pasifika practice in which remixing takes place, oratory (Samoan and Tuvaluan *tulafale*; Tongan *fakamalanga*).[10] Oratory is a component of Pasifika's oral cultures, which i have presented under the umbrella of "talanoa" (a Pasifika term that refers to three overflowing events—story, telling, storyweaving) in earlier works.[11] If orality (talanoa) is understood as the culture, then oratory (tulafale, fakamalanga) may be seen as one of the practices that gives expression to the oral culture. Orality intersects the telling (by orators) and storyweaving (which requires the involvement of an audience) events of talanoa.

Oratory is the Pasifika art of persuasion which takes place in public places such as at maraes and meeting halls (iKiribati *maneaba*). Orators

---

10. See Tamasese, *O Le Tulafale.*

11. See Havea, "The politics of climate change."

sit up (a few stand) to speak seeking to convince their audience to believe their claim (of a case, supported with their interpretations of customs and traditions), some of which may have been fabricated. Other orators would talk back with their counterclaims and counterinterpretations. The aim of the exchange is not to establish the truth, but to persuade and convince the audience. I stress that the event is not about the truth or facts, but about the presentation of claims as (if they are) truths and facts. Put another way, oratory refers to events where claims and interpretations are approved (authorized, similar to events where scriptures were canonized).

For the purpose of this reflection, oratory is the space where words dance and remix. I read similar attempts in the works of biblical prophets and sages, and in the parables of Jesus and the interpretations of his disciples and followers. To illustrate, i briefly turn to the conclusion of the Matthean sermon on the mount. Jesus, as a Mediterranean orator, used the image of building a house on rock as a metaphor for the one who "hears these words of mine and acts on them" (Matt 7:24). Words are the "rock" upon/with which to build one's house (life, family, community). At the end of the event, "the crowds were astounded at his teaching, for he taught them as one having authority" (Matt 7:28b–29a) and they dispersed with his words, his breath, his interpretation, his claim, his oratory, his tulafale and fakamalanga.

Jesus remixed and convinced his audience to the authority (reliability, stability) of his words; but those words (rock) have been moving since. Scribes, translators, interpreters, orators, preachers and many others have built on those words (supposed to be a rock platform) over the ages—and their building continue to move, to roll.

Jesus's rock (words) continues to roll. Moving. Mobile. Migrating. In this brief talanoa, Jesus's remix presents him as a skilled Mediterranean orator.

Remixing and Deconstruction

Remixing is an opportunity to cross boundaries, between cultures and tongues, and across law codes and memories. Remixing is transgressive. But it is also constructive and emancipative, insofar as the remixer and dub artist create new systems of signification. In this regard, Beckford defines "dub hermeneutics," which applies to "remixing reading" also, as follows:

"To dub" is to deconstruct. Deconstruction is a transformative
process involving dismantling and reconstructing. Deconstructive activity involves taking things apart. However, rather than
ending up with nothing, deconstruction seeks to rebuild. Rebuilding is guided by an emancipation ethic, which seeks out
redemptive themes in history, culture and society that can be
the focus for transforming the original thesis. However, emancipation calls for action; therefore, "to dub" is to engage with the
social world through prophetic action. In short, dub is a three-
part process: *deconstruction* guided by the *emancipation ethic* to
produce a dub or a *new praxis*.[12]

To remix Egypt, i come into a groove whose routes go in many direc-
tions, to the dance halls of Jamaica, to the biblical traditions of rewriting, to
serenading locals and orators in Pasifika and the Mediterranean. I step into
a well-journeyed stream, and it is necessary to strip some of the blinding
perceptions over Egypt so that dubbing, remixing and signifying can take
place.

Stripping the Exodus Frame

There are voices in the wilderness narrative that positively long for the
land of Egypt (e.g., Exod 14:10–14; 16:3; 17:3). Of course, how one reads
those urgings depends on how one understands the exodus story. The
dominant view is that the longings for Egypt indicate rebellion on the
part of a people who were impatient and ungrateful. This is the view behind George W. Coats' *Rebellion in the wilderness*. The people of Israel are
damned for wanting to return to the fleshpots and provisions in Egypt
rather than trusting in their leader and on G*d. Even though G*d and
Moses first led the people to bitter water (Exod 15:22–25a) and provided
manna and quail only after the people murmured, rightfully, i must add,
the biblical narrator portrays the people as a problematic lot.

Diana Lipton has a different take in *Longing for Egypt and Other Unexpected Biblical Tales*. With "non-traditional and even quirky" readings,[13]
Lipton targets readers who are alienated by simplistic interpretations that
are blind to the Bible's complexity. The upshot is a series of readings that
attend to the intricate details of biblical texts, traces textual and ideological links between texts within and beyond biblical limits, and shows how

12. Beckford, *Jesus Dub*, 91–92.

13. Lipton, *Longing for Egypt*, 3.

"the Hebrew Bible can never lose its capacity to surprise, excite, and even unsettle."[14] In chapter 1 ("'The Heart Enticed': The Exodus from Egypt as a Response to the Threat of Assimilation"), Lipton presents Egypt as "the apex of the seductive other."[15] The exodus was therefore the rescue of Israel from assimilation and loss of identity, more so than because of persecution under the Egyptian empire.[16] Unlike Joseph, who assimilated into Egyptian society, Moses led Israel out of Egypt to avoid assimilation.[17] Exodus thus "provides an inspiring model of resistance, but offers little or nothing in the way of guidance for those who find themselves wanting to sleep with the enemy."[18]

Though encouraged by rich rabbinic insights, Lipton comes under the same shade with Coats. Egypt and Egyptian cultures are not acceptable, so assimilation is discouraged (Lipton) and wanting to return to Egypt is sign of rebellion against G*d (Coats). Both positions make me nervous because, where i live, crossing between cultures is unavoidable and G*d is not always dependable. Assimilation is problematic but, where i live, negotiation of cultures is unavoidable and has more to do with survival than with preferences.[19] On the other matter, thinking and acting against G*d and the biblical narrator, whether one calls it rebellion, impiety, foolishness or courage, is not a problem in my remixing-reading-eyes.

For my purpose in this essay, i track in the footsteps of the Filipino-American reader Eleazar S. Fernandez, who identifies with the views and struggles of Palestinians and Native Americans for whom the *exodus-from-Egypt-conquest narrative* is a narrative of terror. Fernandez opts to read for an *exodus-toward-Egypt-liberation narrative,* which he finds more appropriate for Filipino Americans, who entered USA "as a colonial people and have gone on to experience life as second-class citizens."[20]

> It [exodus-toward-Egypt-liberation narrative] is a narrative that conveys not a singular notion of liberation and the euphoria that goes with it but an ambiguous nexus of captivity and liberation, of closure and promise, of blessings and alienation.

14. Lipton, *Longing for Egypt*, 11.

15. Lipton, *Longing for Egypt*, 14.

16. Lipton, *Longing for Egypt*, 23.

17. Lipton, *Longing for Egypt*, 43.

18. Lipton, *Longing for Egypt*, 48.

19. Human rights and the right to choose are not universal realities.

20. Fernandez, "Exodus-toward-Egypt," 243. Fernandez has recently returned to the Philippines.

Within such a framework, the term *exodus* carries not only its ordinary meaning of "flight" or "migration" but also its positive biblical connotations of "release" and "liberation." For Filipino Americans, exodus from their homeland has meant release from poverty and fatalism—an exodus toward a land of wealth and opportunity. The irony, however, is that this exodus has as its destination the homeland of their colonial masters, where they are able to share in the cornucopia of their masters' blessings but also remain colonized in brazen as well as subtle ways every day of their lives.[21]

Fernandez draws attention away from the Moses-led exodus to the "promised land" narrative, back to the Jacob and Joseph emigration from the famine of Canaan toward the storehouses of Egypt. The struggle of Filipinos and Filipinas "to make it" in America (seen as "a presence as huge as God") and "to be American," i.e., to be white, donning Fanon's proverbial white masks,[22] brings to mind the struggles of Jacob and his family in Egypt. Fernandez sees this wanting to be American/white to be the "fall" of Filipino Americans. "Dealing with Filipinoness," writes Luis Francia, "is to deal with this condition, with a fall from grace, when the twin-headed snake of Spain and America seduced us with the promise of boundless knowledge—we too could be white Gods!—even as we reposed in an unimaginably beautiful garden."[23]

The desire to be white often turns Filipinos and Filipinas against Blacks, thinking that their fairer skin makes them closer to being Whites.[24] But the white G*d they encounter in America rejects them, and so Filipinos and Filipinas need to experience G*d in their ethnicity. "We encounter God in the context of who we are, not outside of who we are. A God who is encountered outside of who we are and who thus calls us to betray our ethnic identity is a God who works for foreign masters."[25]

The G*d who affirms Filipinos, Filipinas and Blacks is a color-loving G*d who, as Alice Walker puts it, would be "pissed off" if we "pass by the color purple in the field somewhere and don't notice it."[26] The mixed

21. Fernandez, "Exodus-toward-Egypt," 244.

22. Fanon, *Black Skin, White Masks*; see also Havea, "Going public with postcolonial hermeneutics."

23. Fernandez, "Exodus-toward-Egypt," 249.

24. Fernandez, "Exodus-toward-Egypt," 250.

25. Fernandez, "Exodus-toward-Egypt," 252.

26. Cited in Fernandez, "Exodus-toward-Egypt," 253; see also Reddie, *Is God*

blessings experience of Filipino and Filipina Americans is a microcosm of the experience of peoples of color within and beyond American borders. Fernandez concludes:

> The task is not only to understand America . . . but also to make America a just society. This is to realize the America of one's heart. The America that Filipino Americans desire in their hearts can only become a reality through a historical project—a project of breaking silence, of naming the pains, of articulating a colorful society, of acting on dreams so that the promised land may be realized in Egypt.[27]

I affirm Fernandez's complexifying reading and identification of Egypt with America, both are empires but in different times. I will return to this in another section below, but at this juncture of my remixing reading it is necessary to strip the exodus frame from Egypt. I acknowledge that Egypt was an empire but i quickly add that it was not an evil empire *only*. To make this point, i move further back, i re-track/tract, to the Abraham narrative. I make this move not in search of some elusive original view concerning Egypt, but in order to shuffle away from the exodus frame (or blockade) that has laid siege over the wilderness narrative.[28]

Flight to Egypt

Egypt is first named in the biblical account in Gen 12, when Abram left Canaan in search of food because a severe famine had visited the land that G*d promised him, a land on which, Abram discovered upon arrival, Canaanites were already living (Gen 12:6). Because of the famine, Abram took his family to Egypt. Initially, in the biblical memory, Egypt was a land of refuge (Gen 12:10).

As they approached Egypt, a land that symbolized fertility and rich resources (Gen 13:10), the narrator presents the shady side of Abram. He asked his wife Sarai to say that she was his sister, for he feared that the Egyptians would kill him if they knew that she was his wife. If she identified herself as his sister, Abram believed that the Egyptians would spare him, and things would go well for him, on her account (Gen

---

Colour-blind?, 3–17.

27. Fernandez, "Exodus-toward-Egypt," 255.

28. This is the subject of a forthcoming essay, "Hinterland Is Intersection: Talking Back to the Exodus Blockade."

12:11–13). Abram is completely self-interested. He paints a nasty picture of the Egyptians, but that is unfounded, unless one reads back from the memory of the exodus narrative.

The King James Version blackens the image of Egypt by rendering the attractiveness of Sarai as having to do with being a "fair" woman rather than being "beautiful" as in most English translations (Gen 12:11, 14). She won the praise of Pharaoh's officials and, as most heterosexual readers might expect, was taken into the palace to be Pharaoh's wife (Gen 12:19). At this instance Abram, instead of enabling blessings upon Egypt (cf. Gen 12:3), caused Yhwh to afflict Pharaoh and his house with great plagues (Gen 12:17).

Whereas the KJV (unintentionally?) debases Egypt, the narrator gives a different picture. Pharaoh was just. He was favorable to Abram on account of Sarai, and he confronted Abram once he worked out that Sarai was Abram's wife. Whether Pharaoh thought of Sarai as Abram's property or as someone (with agency) for whom Abram was obliged, is not clear from the text. Ambiguity here gives room for both senses. In returning Sarai to Abram the Pharaoh seeks to put a stop to the plagues, and Abram departed a richer man (Gen 13:2) than when he arrived. Abram, Sarai and Lot departed, and Egypt is remembered as a well-watered land, like the region of Jordan and the garden of G*d (Gen 13:10). The initial memory of Egypt is that it is fertile and a place of refuge.

At this early stage of the Abram narrative, the Pharaoh and the people of Egypt are neither ruthless nor immoral. The narrator remembers them for being favorable to Abram, who returned to Canaan and discovered that the people of Canaan were still there. They, the people of the land of Canaan, had survived the famine. In fact, whenever there is a famine, the descendants of Abram get up and leave; when they return, the indigenous people are still there. This is not a new insight. It is not unusual that indigenous people find ways to survive crises. The fact that Abram took his family and fled to Egypt is indication that he is not indigenous to Canaan. If he was indigenous, he would have found a way to survive the famine.

In light of Fernandez's reading, this was the first exodus-toward-Egypt event. The problem that made this exodus necessary is in three parts: first, there was a famine; second, Abram did not have the local indigenous knowledge to survive the famine in Canaan; and third, G*d did not help Abram out. The outcome of the exodus to Egypt is survival and wealth for Abram and his family, and Sarai experienced delight in the palace of Pharaoh.

Egypt returns to the Abram story in the body and story of Hagar, Sarai's Egyptian slave-girl (Gen 16:1–2). Sarai brings her in because of a famine of a different kind. Sarai was barren (Gen 11:30) and the promise of a great nation and great name for Abram (Gen 12:1–2) had not done anything to change her barrenness.

Hagar has caught the attention of many readers, the majority of whom bear feminist and womanist commitments, but what appeals to me here is her Egyptian roots. Yhwh promised, Sarai acted, Abram entered, and Hagar the Egyptian conceived and delivered. There are discomforting elements in the story such as one woman (Sarai) standing over another (Hagar)—so that her husband would take her—and then dealing harshly with her (subaltern, surrogate) to the extent that she runs away (Gen 16:3–6); as well as the angel of Yhwh telling the runaway woman to return and submit to her mistress (Gen 16:9), to be properly discarded later with Yhwh's blessing after Sarai bore a son of her own (Gen 21:8–14). Hagar's son Ishmael had received the covenantal cut of circumcision (Gen 17:23), a rite that initiated him together with other slaves into the covenant between Abram and Yhwh. Circumcision (an Egyptian practice also) would also be an Egyptian marker on the body of Ishmael, and others in the household of Abram. In receiving an Egyptian wife from his mother (Gen 21:21), Ishmael embraced his Egyptian roots through the body of another woman.

In the story of Hagar, we see Egypt's fertility in a different form. Whereas Abram used Sarai for his benefit when they came to Egypt in Gen 12 (fertility of the land), here Sarai uses an Egyptian woman for her own benefit (fertility of the body), and Abram did not object. The narrator had previously announced that Sarai was barren so when Hagar became pregnant with a child, we know that the old man still had potency. The backlash is that we now know that the reason why the promise of offspring has not been fulfilled is because of the old lady. As the land of Egypt was fertile, so was Hagar, who exposed how this old man can still rise and that his seeds can still sprout. There is no reason to be antagonist towards Egypt in these two events. Egypt is a sign of fertility and plenty.

The land of Egypt was outside of the borders of the land that Yhwh promised Abram (Gen 15:18). Sarai and Hagar provide links between land and the bodies of women. But there is a difference. The women and land of Abram are famine-ridden, while the land and women of Egypt are fertile. Throughout the story of Abram, Egypt is fertile land of refuge and of plenty.

In the story of Isaac, dislike toward Egypt develops. The aversion however should not be attributed to Hagar, Ishmael or Egypt, but to discomfort from the side of Abram and Isaac. It was they who distanced themselves from Hagar, Ishmael and Egypt.

There was another famine, as in the time of Abram, and Yhwh gave clear instructions to Isaac: "Do not go down to Egypt, settle in the land [Gerar] that I shall show you" (Gen 26:2). Isaac stayed in Gerar under King Abimelech of the Philistines and repeated the "she is my sister" approach (Gen 26:1–11) that his father made earlier with Pharaoh (Gen 12:10–20) and again with Abimelech (Gen 20:1–18). Like father, like son. The location of the scam shifted from Egypt to Gerar, and the sister/wife moves shifted from being taken as a wife to a foreign king (Gen 12:19) to being taken but not touched (Gen 20:3–7), and to being fondled by her own husband (Gen 26:8).

Abram was more defensive in Gerar than Isaac was, and Abimelech stands in more favorable light than Pharaoh. The narrator also shifts from Egypt, but a remixing reader can't shift so easily. If at the urging of the narrator we praise Abimelech for his high standards and generosity, why don't we do the same for Pharaoh also?

The story of Joseph takes readers back to Egypt, to where Ishmaelite/Midianite traders (Gen 37:25–28) took him, thus saving him from his brothers and saving his brothers from murdering him. Joseph ends up in the house of Potiphar, then to prison and back to Pharaoh's court, where he took on a new name and an Egyptian wife, and "gained authority over the land of Egypt" (Gen 41:45). Lo and behold, another famine devastated Canaan, and the house of Jacob survived by getting food from Egypt. Joseph took advantage of the favor he gained from Pharaoh to bring his family to Egypt, giving them the opportunity to come under his authority.

Joseph became the chief in charge of the house of Potiphar first, then of Pharaoh and Egypt as a whole. It was because of Joseph that Jacob brought his family to Egypt, for survival and for refuge. It is helpful to here reiterate that Joseph is responsible for bringing Jacob and his family to Egypt, rather than Pharaoh and the Egyptians. Of course, the famine was the ultimate reason. Three generations after Abram, the family that originated in Ur of Chaldea (Gen 11:31–32) still had not learned how to live like the indigenous people in the land of Canaan.

In this brief recollection, we see that Egypt and Egyptians were not so wicked. On several occasions, Egypt was a place of refuge. Why then do readers hold ill-feelings toward Egypt?

Signifying Egypt

One of the (partial) successes of bible traditions and of biblical interpretations is the demonization of Egypt and of almost everything Egyptian. The nail on the coffin is the suggestion that a king of Egypt did not know/ remember Joseph (Exod 1:8), permitting him to oppress the children of Israel. The memory of Joseph is lost, and loss of memory is a serious and painful charge in oral cultures. How disrespectful of this king to forget Joseph, the one who engineered Egypt's survival and brought his family (and possibly other families from other lands also) to serve Egypt? How is it possible to lose memory of Joseph, who helped build the Egyptian empire? Loss of memory is tantamount to loss of roots, loss of place, loss of identity and loss of belonging. In presenting the Pharaoh as one who lost the memory of Joseph, the narrator portrays him as an uncaring ruler. Or should the question be, how disrespectful of the narrator to present the Pharaoh as having lost his memory (or lost his mind)?

From the Egyptian side of things, i imagine that it is not so much the loss of memory that hurts but the fabrication of the loss of memory. Lacking from Egypt's detailed records is any account of a significant Israelite population in Egypt who experienced the extent of oppression that readers find in the opening chapters of Exodus. So i am suspicious of the portrayal of Egypt in the exodus account, not for historical but for ideological reasons, seeing that the exodus tradition tends to control how Egypt is perceived by (especially, pro-Israel, in the ancient and modern worlds) bible readers. Whose interests are served by demonizing Egypt and Egyptians in the exodus account? The stories of Sarai in Egypt (Gen 12:10–20) and of Hagar the Egyptian (Gen 16 and 21) make the demonizing of Egypt and Egyptians ridiculous.[29] Pharaoh did not mistreat Sarai while she was in his house, and Hagar proved that Abraham was fertile and could fulfill the promise of G*d. How might one release Egypt from the grasp of the exodus narrator? As Rastafarian cultures change the perception of Babylon by celebrating their location *as* Babylon, seeing

---

29. The story of Potiphar's wife does not help my reading at this point. I touch upon that story in another reflection (Havea, "Mothering").

themselves as living in die-as-poor-ya (diaspora) at home, so do i invite readers back to Egypt, into the shadows of another biblical empire.

My invitation could have been to Assyria or Persia, but i choose Egypt for this essay because it is a place to which (potential) victims and refugees flee. Since Abram and Sarai, Jacob and his family, Jeremiah and his friends, Joseph, Mary and their baby, and, more recently, Palestinians from Gaza, and political refugees from Tunisia, Libya and the surrounding areas, Egypt is a sanctuary for political and environmental refugees.[30] I opt for return to Egypt also in response to the growing need in our current time to open up borders so that we welcome refugees and victims of wars and ecological crises. There are definitely political and contextual agendas behind my call for return to Egypt.

For this to happen we need, first of all, a "return to Egypt" and to reconsider how we read the exodus story. So i propose a remixing reading that is children-oriented: The story of children in the book of Exodus involves two midwives who were willing to break the law of the land. They had to break the law because the Hebrew women were strong and productive, with husbands who were not tired enough from their labors. The midwives were named—Shiphrah and Puah—but they were not racialized. They could have been Egyptian women, among the daughters of the land, thereby making them rebels against their master. The narrative is interested in one instance where the midwives spared the life of a particular child, Moses, but nothing in the narrative prevents readers from assuming that they also spared the lives of other male babies. The narrator encourages readers to sympathize with the children who are innocent victims in the early part of the story, and that obliging feeling of solidarity could have inspired the midwives to collaborate with other mothers in saving their babies, boys and girls alike.

Later on in the story, when Israel was poised to leave Egypt, we again read about sons who are innocent victims of Yhwh's plagues. Yhwh now places the role of a forgetful pharaoh. This time, the victims are the firstborns of Egypt, from the house of Pharaoh to the house of the prisoner in the dungeon, as well as the firstborn of animals (Exod 12:29). The firstborns of Egypt are innocent victims of Yhwh's war, and they lost the opportunity to rejoice the gift of being "young and free." I identify with the firstborns of Egypt in part because they remind me of the first peoples, the firstborns, of Australia. I am drawn to the firstborns

30. For recent attention to migration and asylum as context and locus of theology see Melanchthon, "The Flight to Egypt."

of Egypt also because some of my friends in prison told me to, for they have experienced how life could disappear, overnight. My solidarity with the firstborns of Egypt is therefore political and personal.

The return to Egypt that i am proposing here requires metaphorically again crossing the wilderness, the dry ocean of sand and rocks, across the sea of reeds, and the bodies of Pharaoh and his army, back to the house of slavery. This is not a journey toward a promised land, where one displaces the people of the land, but backtracking to the place of bondage. This child-ish reading may be naïve, but not apolitical.

And we need, second, to respect and favor Egypt and things-Egyptian when we read biblical texts. This invites us, for instance, to celebrate the times when the people of Israel wanted to return to Egypt (e.g., Exod 16:2–3). Egypt was their home, the only place they knew as home; and longing for home is healthy and normal. Egypt was the place where they were fed and were satisfied. How can they sing the Lord's song away from home and on empty stomachs? I join their longing, calling for the return to Egypt, even if that is seen as rebellion.[31]

This is not a new invitation, for African and African American scholars have drawn attention to Africa for many years now.[32] Theirs was based on obvious historical, geographical, biological and cultural connections and heritage. Out of Africa they were shipped, with chains, lashes and locks. Into the cold Atlantic passage, many of them were thrown but Jah did not lift a finger to part the waters. I draw my eyes toward Egypt also because it is both the house of bondage and the home of refuge, the sanctuary for refugees. Two critical questions arise. Return to do what, for whom? Where is the "Egypt" of the bible today?

The exodus story is quiet and silencing about the first question, thus leaving it open for some remixing. Return for food and nourishment; return to get out of the wilderness; return to find shelter; return to be in solidarity with those who are still under the empire; return to join the revolution; return to rebel against the empire; return to be remembered; return to heal the perception of Egypt; return for the sake of returning; and so forth.

The exodus story is dodgy with the second question, because "the Egypt" it represents does not remember "the Israel" it favors. In this

---

31. Cf. Coats, *Rebellion in the wilderness*.
32. Cf. Felder, *Troubling Biblical Waters*.

regard, the return could also be in order to expose a biblical lie: Egypt is not that bad. The Egypt that the exodus blockade demonize is fake news.

From then to now, finally, seeing that many of us live in the shadows of Egypt, the more critical question is, Will we open our borders to those who are coming out of the wilderness? In other words, how may we be hospitable to refugees of wars, to victims of the Covid-19 pandemic, and of the environment?

Calling Every Nation

Whereas the Yothu Yindi song "Calling Every Nation" arose out of "mixed emotions at the 2000 [Olympic] games" and challenges listeners with the obliging question "What does it take to win for a nation," this chapter is less patriotic. My concern is not for winning on behalf of any nation, but toward calling winning nations to account for victims and displaced peoples. This call comes at a time when health and ecological crises are more frequent and more devastating, with annoying debates about the extent of human responsibility for climate change, Tsunamis, earthquakes, droughts, rising seas, oil spills, pandemics, and so forth.

The Bible is littered with accounts of ecological crises, from the announcement that Earth will yield only thorns and thistles to the labor of Ha-'adam, the devastating flood for which G*d repented, visitation by several famines, droughts and scorching east winds, the destruction due to wars and exiles, and so forth. Responses to crises vary, but the one that appeals to me here is the exodus to Egypt. Egypt is the place to which (potential) victims flee.

Leaping from the biblical world to the contemporary world, following the lead by Fernandez, the call for exodus to Egypt is directed at present-day empires. Whereas America is the empire for Fernandez, for those of us in Pasifika, the shadows of the empire stretch from the USA to France, Indonesia and Chile (occupiers of islands in Pasifika). There are two sides to my call: first, it is a call for people in the midst of crises to seek refuge in the empire, bearing in mind the warning by Fernandez that this is a double edge sword. And second, i call upon citizens of the empire to receive and welcome refugees.[33] This will require being involved in public

33. "The act of sharing one's land, one's home, one's bread and one's water resources with a migrant is an act of salvation because in that act for the well-being of that other, one encounters God, works alongside God and becomes one with the suffering migrant and with God" (Melanchthon, "The Flight to Egypt," 168).

and political spheres. Whereas Abram, Sarai, Jacob and Joseph used Egypt for their advantage, and for the advantage of their families, my call is for favor toward others who are from outside one's nations and households.[34]

Bibliography

Beckford, Robert. *Jesus Dub: Theology, Music and Social Change*. London: Routledge, 2006.

Coats, George W. *Rebellion in the Wilderness: The Murmuring Motif in the Wilderness Traditions of the Old Testament*. Nashville: Abingdon, 1968.

Crawford, Sidnie White. *Rewriting Scripture in Second Temple Times*. Grand Rapids: Eerdmans, 2008.

Fanon, Frantz. *Black Skin, White Masks*. Translated by Charles Lam Markmann. New York: Grove, 1967.

Felder, Cain Hope. *Troubling Biblical Waters: Race, Class, and Family*. Maryknoll, NY: Orbis. 1992.

Fernandez, Eleazar S. "Exodus-toward-Egypt: Filipino-Americans' Struggle to Realize the Promised Land in America." In *Voices from the Margin: Interpreting the Bible in the Third World*, edited by R. S. Sugirtharajah, 242–57. Maryknoll, NY: Orbis 2006.

Havea, Jione. "Going Public with Postcolonial Hermeneutics." *Gurukul Journal of Theological Studies* 21/2 (2010) 38–46.

———. "Hinterland Is Intersection: Talking Back to the Exodus Blockade." In *Intersections and Fractures: (re)Visions of the Feminist Theologies*, edited by Stephen Burns and Rebecca Prior. Lanham, MD: Lexington, forthcoming.

———. "Mothering: Eve, Hagar and Mistress of Joseph." In *Mission and Ministry V: Women in the Bible and Theological Education*, edited by Richard E. A. Rodgers, 76–98. New Delhi: ISPCK, 2010.

———. "The Politics of Climate Change, a talanoa from Oceania." *International Journal of Public Theology* 4 (2010) 345–55.

Levinson, Bernard M. *Legal Revision and Religious Renewal in Ancient Israel*. Cambridge: Cambridge University Press, 2008.

Lipton, Diana. *Longing for Egypt and Other Unexpected Biblical Tales*. Hebrew Bible Monographs 15. Sheffield: Sheffield Phoenix, 2008.

Melanchthon, Monica Jyotsna. "The Flight to Egypt: A Migrant Reading—Implications for a Lutheran Understanding of Salvation." In *To All the Nations: Lutheran Hermeneutics and the Gospel of Matthew*, edited by Kenneth Mtata and Craig Koester, 153–68. Leipzig: Evangelische Verlangsanstalt, 2015.

Potash, Chris. *Reggae, Rasta Revolution, Jamaican Music from Ska to Dub*. London: Books with Attitude, 1997.

Reddie, Anthony G. *Is God Colour-blind? Insights from Black Theology for Christian Ministry*. London: SPCK, 2009.

Tamasese, Tusi. *O Le Tulafale* (The Orator). Sydney: Transmissions, 2011.

Yothu Yindi. "Calling Every Nation." *Garma*. Phantom 1091333, compact disc, 2007.

---

34. This call comes at the early days of the covid-19 pandemic. The curves are still rising from the West and the Pharaohs of the modern time are lining up for geopolitical sparring. Time will tell, what becomes of the Egypts of the new normal.

6

Samaritans and Empires

Election, Exclusion and Inclusion

Néstor O. Míguez

Su condición inherente [de la relación hegemónica] es que una fuerza social *particular* asuma la representación de una *totalidad* que es radicalmente inconmensurable con ella

—ERNESTO LACLAU AND CHANTAL MOUFFE

(A hegemonic articulation occurs when a particular element assumes, at a certain time, the representation of a totality that is completely immeasurable in itself.[1])

When We Don't Remember

The historical account is one of the great builders of prejudice and exclusion. In the words of a popular Argentine rock song: "If history is written

1. Laclau and Mouffe, *Hegemonía y estrategia socialista*, 10. The English quotation (which differs slightly from the original) is taken from Biglieri and Guille, "The Deconstructivist Laclau."

by the victors, it means that there is another history: the true story. Let anyone who wants to hear, listen."[2] Among the stories of exclusion, hate and prejudice in the Biblical account, the reference to the Samaritans deserves particular attention because it shows the process of gender exclusion and the disparage of a people and a class at the hands of the dominant sectors.

Today the majority of Bible scholars agree that the so-called canonical text of the Hebrew Bible was largely written, or at least collected, revised and composed in the postexilic period, under the Persian administration. And while a close scrutiny shows both the existence of diverse and older strata, as well as various currents and political projects in its composition, it is interesting to note that, with the exception of some passages especially in Ezekiel and Isaiah, the Hebrew Bible as a whole suggests that the tribe of Judah assumed the total Abrahamic heritage. The reduction goes pace by pace: The promise to Abram is first limited from the totality of his heirs to Israel alone, and then from Israel to the remnant of the tribes of Judah and Benjamin.

Certainly, there are resistances and registration of the leftovers of "another story" to which Nito Nebbia alludes. But finally, the official account is imposed: Judah is "all Israel," the Jews are the only true Israelites and those who enjoy the right to all of the promises of the chosen nation. This remains so up to today, and it is part of the justification of the Jewish right-wing government of the State of Israel, of the construction of the anti-Palestinian prejudice, becoming a model construction for other exclusions. With the support of the American Empire, which holds

---

2. Nebbia, "Quien quiera oír que oiga." The full text goes:

Cuando no recordamos lo que nos pasa, nos puede suceder la misma cosa. Son esas mismas cosas que nos marginan, nos matan la memoria, nos queman las ideas, nos quitan las palabras . . . Si la historia la escriben los que ganan, eso quiere decir que hay otra historia: la verdadera historia, quien quiera oír que oiga. Nos queman las palabras, nos silencian, y la voz de la gente se oirá siempre. Inútil es matar, la muerte prueba que la vida existe.	When we don't remember what happens to us, the same things can happen to us again. They are those same things that marginalize us, they kill our memory, burn our ideas, Take away the words . . . oh . . . If history is written by the winners, that means that there is another story: the true story, Let anyone who wants to hear, listen. They burn our words, we are muted, but the voice of the people will always be heard. Useless is to kill, death proofs that life exists.

political, communicational and military power in the region, the culture of exclusion is alive and strong in the land of Palestine and beyond.

The account of the controversial establishment of the monarchy in Israel (1 Sam 8–13), which was the first attempt to build it as a State,[3] that is briefly consolidated only in the second period of the reign of David and during the time of Solomon, already shows traces of the justification and prejudice of the Jewish power, as well as the emerging resistances. The opposition appears from the beginning, since neither the Benjaminites nor the northern tribes recognize David, and are refractory from the beginning to this hegemony, which is only achieved after an intricate story of betrayals, murders and compromise policies (2 Sam 1–5). The so-called "rebellion of Absalom" (2 Sam 15–18) is a sign that there is ongoing disconformity of the various tribes, and the entire Davidic period, afterwards exalted as "exemplary," is a chain of uprisings and movements of resistance to the centralized power of the incipient State.

The story, in that regard, while acknowledging this concern, qualifies the State in negative terms. Those who confront the power of Jerusalem are designated as "conspirators" (qshr; 2 Sam 15:12), "useless or perverse" (bly'l; 2 Sam 20:1, note that this becomes a designation of the Satanic—Belial), among other similar adjectives. The story ends legitimating David on the throne, and therefore, with implied condemnation of all those who questioned his power, especially from the northern tribes, already designated several times as "Israel." David, according to this official history, being Judean, is the King of all Israel. Thus, the story begins to establish who really are the appointed and elected.

Nor Solomon's reign begins without incidents. In this case those who are opposed (legitimately, according to the laws of inheritance) are considered perverse and then murdered, after which Solomon is considered as an example of wisdom. However, the story (barely) hides the level of exploitation to which Solomon submits the people. When one considers the amount of taxes and gifts the King and his nobles received (1 Kgs 4–5) and what it would cost to keep its stables and army, one has to admit that this could only be achieved with the exploitation of thousands of peasants and slaves, product of the cams decreed by the King (1 Kgs 5:13). The statement clearly contradicts what the deuteronomic laws establish as the rule for monarchy (Deut 17:14–20). It is important

---

3. See Míguez, "El surgimiento del estado monárquico en el Israel Antiguo."

to emphasize this because it raises the question of the Samaritans not only as an ethnic issue, but also a matter of economic and social class.

The level of exploitation is evident at the death of Solomon. The people claim precisely because of the royal servitude (1 Kgs 12:4), but Rehoboam's response anticipates a greater burden and exploitation. The delegitimization of the protest and the subsequent division appears with the disqualification of the new King of Israel, Jeroboam, as a foreigner. It should be noted, however, that Jeroboam is announced as the future King of Israel (at least of ten tribes) by a prophecy (Ahijah the Shilonite, 1 Kgs 11:29–31), although he did not have the right to inherit the throne. But the same happened with David, when he was anointed by Samuel without being kin of Saul (1 Sam 16). The story then goes on to acknowledge the lordship of David, but condemns that of Jeroboam.

The stories of rebellion, conspiracies, murders and idolatries continue in both kingdoms, in details that we can not elaborate here. A series of prophecies are given about their wrongs and also the eventual ruin of both kingdoms. This culminates with the rejection of God and his annulment of the election of Israel, although the promise of the remnant (sh'r) is repeatedly reminded. Also, in this case we must attend the discursive strategy about the remnant. Initially it seems that remnant is from all Israel (2 Chron 34:9, 21), but then, and especially as we will see in Ezra and Nehemiah, it only recognizes the remnant of Judah, and this is applied almost exclusively to the returning elite.

The history of the destruction of the kingdoms begins to trigger from 2 Kgs 17 (fall of Samaria) and 2 Kgs 24 (fall of Jerusalem). However, the account of the fall of Samaria puts its emphasis on the occupation of the territory by displaced people from other nations (2 Kgs 17:24), and the consequent idolatry, as well as the anger of Yhwh. It is worth noting, because it relates to our theme, that the suffering is caused by the displaced peoples introduced in the land of Israel. These, which are presumably slaves or captives of other peoples and brought forcedly to the occupied territory, are both victims and the cause of their own distress. *We cannot escape this in consideration of the discursive strategy, since it is part of imperial discourses, and especially all the speech of the postmodern neoliberal Empire, that the victims are to blame for their own misfortune.* It is not the fault of the King who displaced them, but their own idolatry that attracts the anger of God and the punishment through the invasion of lions.

But this will also prove the impurity of the "people of the land" ('am ha'eretz), which will then mark all the religious and cultural construction of the Samaritans in the times of the "Second Temple." This becomes evident when we enter into the analysis of the texts of Ezra and Nehemiah.

In the so-called deuteronomistic history (Samuel and Kings) there is some tension and ambiguity, as well as in some references in Isaiah and some occasional passages elsewhere. Chronicles, on the other hand, shows bias in favor of Judah. Historicizing the kings of Judah, and only mentioning the Kingdom of Israel in a pejorative mood when it comes in contact with the Southern kings, it advances the project to declare Judaism as "all Israel." It at the same time rewrites history avoiding the negative incidents in the lives of David and of Solomon, which appear in the other narrative as derogatory of their Kingdom, and the division and fall of their kingdom. On the other hand, it makes a careful defense of some patriarchal lines and the priesthood, which will be significant when it comes to rebuild the legitimization of the returning elite of Babylon, and, complementarily, disqualify those whose political projects and/or class position, differ.

The purpose of reconstruction of the returnees, in its alliance with the Persian power and its elitist project, needs to hold their election and the "des-election" of the rest of Israel, installing a hegemonic ideology based on the concept of purity. The extensive genealogies and thorough list of the returnees, their census enumeration, is more than an administrative detail: their function is to reinforce the concept of purity. It is necessary for this discursive strategy to discern the "true Israelite" (Jewish or Benjaminite, and a sector of the Levites), from all others that might claim their Israelite right. The function of these casts is clear from the outset: already at the end of the first enumeration, the book of Ezra establishes that "there were others who also went to Jerusalem . . . though they could not prove their families or their descent, whether they belonged to Israel" (Ezra 2:59). These were excluded and "the governor forbade them to eat things sacred" (Ezra 2:61–63).

The replacement of "all Israel" by the proven descendants of Judah and Benjamin is made clear at the beginning of Ezra 4 where it is specified that "when the enemies (sr) of the descendants of Judah and Benjamin had learned that those who had returned of the captivity were rebuilding the Temple of the God of Israel" were to lend their collaboration, they are rejected. I emphasize this story and its use, because therein lies the discursive strategy. Those who come to offer their collaboration insist that they worship the same God and offer their sacrifices, even during the time of its submission to the King of Assyria. But there is a detail at the end of v. 2: "ever since the days of King Esar-haddon of Assyria who brought us here." This puts in the speaker's own mouth that they are displaced foreigners. The response progresses in its construction of the discourse of replacement, because those who respond do so in name, not of their respective tribes, but as "descendants of Israel" (v. 3a). Those of the tribes of Judah and Benjamin, who can prove their genealogy, and which are the returning elite held in captivity, become the only authentic descendants of the whole Israel. Therefore, they have to build the temple by themselves (*yhd*). To make the temple pure, ethnically pure, it should be built only by them.

The class effect is perceived in the following verse: "the people of the earth" is the opposite of the "people of Judah." The peasants, who stayed in the country and who suffered the Babylonian and Persian servitude, are opposed to the elite who marched into captivity, that was hard at times, but on the other hand it permitted them to hold in "purity" and allowed some privileges. Those that cannot show their lineage and ancestry are rejected even from worshiping God. Princes, nobles, and priests are now "All Israel," the only elected of the Lord.

After this first current led by Zerubbabel and Joshua, there is a second line led by Ezra (Ezr 7). Again, the discursive strategy advances in pointing out the ethnic identity of the new occupiers of Jerusalem, tracing the genealogy of Ezra to Aaron himself. Again, the favor of the Persian monarchy is a sign of legitimacy. Again, it submits any Israeli who wants to move to Judea and Jerusalem to the power and discretion of the new favorite of the King. And once again the genealogies and self appointing lists appear. Once more the entire story, in turn, legitimates the wealth of the returnees over against the situation of poverty which affects the population in general, as we will see later in the case of Nehemiah. The poor usually do not have the resources to justify ancestry, and at most are referred to as servants.

Again, taking women from the neighboring nations (then occupying the same territory) is considered sinful. The prayer of Ezra is an allegation of self-centered vindication. Among all the laws he could quote, Ezra chose those which target racial purity. But this episode adds an edict of reunion that may only include the tribes of Judah and Benjamin, including the confiscation of property of others (Ezra 10:7–9).

Finally, the book of Nehemiah, which is presented mainly as the autobiography of a pristine man, will crown this effort of exclusion, allied to the imperial power. Here again it begins to tell the story as if everything began again. The schema repeats the narrative structure of the episode of Zerubbabel and Ezra. Each story appears as a claim of prominence that seeks to subordinate others. They seem made in purpose to show what Jesus will denounce as the prayer of the self-indulgent Pharisee (Luke 18:11–12). Of the three, Nehemiah is with greater determination to establish the strategy of exclusion and in its search for legitimacy gives us more clearly the sample of this discursive maneuver.

It is not the case here to repeat what we have already pointed out in other accounts, with small variations and the addition of other names. But here is a revealing episode that clearly exposes also the class struggle that underlies the entire story. Chapter 5 presents the protest by poor people (or better, exploited people) over against their "Jewish brothers" (*'hjhm hjvdm*). Thus, the opposition of people-versus-Jews is established. The people are not Jewish brothers and Jewish brothers are not the people. These are exploited by the returnees—who returned with their riches and land claims. This exploitation produces hunger and it is caused by usury. We should note that the story highlights "women" to have a significant stake in this uprising. A few chapters later, when we consider again the topic of the expulsion of non-Jewish women, we should not forget this: they encouraged the people's claim, they held it with their presence, and they made their voice heard.

Later on the people's claim seeks to match the common people with the returnees, to show that the human condition does not tolerate these differences: "our bodies are like yours and our children as your children"; but at the same time exposes the extreme situation of selling their children to survive (and that they may survive).[4] The same text shows how the returnees took possession of the lands of the people that remained in Judea (vv. 11–12). Nehemiah's later boasting about his generosity demonstrates where the difference rests: in the favor of the imperial government and the wealth that it provides them. The economic exploitation is covered with the ethnic issue, which reduces the purity and legitimacy to the returning elite, and will then be a ruse of the pursuit of hegemony, of a small group that assumes to represent a totality incomparable to it,

---

4. The sale of children as servants should not be, as we might see it today, as a selfish act of the parents to ensure their own survival. In many cases it was the only way of ensuring the survival of the son or daughter, as servants would be dressed and fed by their employers, which the humble family could not assure. Always the hope remains, as the same text highlights, that with a change in the situation, they could rescue them through buyback.

as we have seen in the definition of Laclau and Mouffe, to which we will return in the final section.

The final episode of the book of Nehemiah, the expulsion of non-Jewish women and their children, which repeats a schema that we have already seen, is again significant. To the class and ethnic prejudice, we must add gender discrimination. The women are the stain of impurity that hinder the true elected. Nehemiah used torture against his own countrymen to succeed in having them expel their wife and children (Neh 13:25).

Example of the tension between this speech and other possible readings of Israel's relationship with other peoples is worth noting, through comparison with the episode in which Miriam and Aaron confronted Moses because "he took for himself a Cushite woman" (Num 12). There, Yhwh defends Moses and reproaches Aaron and punishes Miriam. Moses is the elected one and has the right to elect. Moses, who already was married with a Midianite and has a son with her, again takes a foreign woman. According to Nehemiah, Moses should be tortured, and his women and children expelled from Israel!

So the Judaism of the second temple creates its marks of exclusive identity: circumcision, the extreme enforcement of law, especially the ritual law and the sacrality of the Saturday, the concept of ethnic purity, and hidden in this legal tangle, gender discrimination and a situation of class where the urban elite despise the poor peasantry. The symbol of this exclusion is, precisely, the Samaritans, as it will be apparent in the period that follows, with the aggression, occupation of territories, exclusion of their priests and destruction of their temple. In all this, the new imperial forces will play their part: the Hellenic conquest, the games of power between the Ptolemies and Seleucids and pacts that the Jewish ruling class comply with them, and finally the presence of Roman power.[5]

Deconstruction of an Exclusion

With the exception of Mark, the other Gospels (also the book of Acts) refer to Samaria and its inhabitants. Elsewhere in the New Testament there are no references to the Samaritans, but the openness to gentile participation in

5. We don't have here the space to delve into the time of the Second Temple, and how the literature of the time reinforces that exclusion, as the dominant powers play in the times of the Maccabees. But what was said so far allows us to see how the anti-Samaritan speech was constructed in times of the second temple, which is basically the ideological situation that Jesus will face.

the community, one of the centers of Pauline theology, speaks indirectly of their inclusion. It is worth remembering that Paul does not present himself as a Jew, but as a Hebrew and Benjaminite (Phil 3:5; Rom 11:1). To identify himself he always uses Israelite or Hebrew, but never Jew. In Rom 9:1–5 he talks about his kin as Israelites, not Jews. Even in a strange sentence he writes: "To the Jews I became as a Jew, in order to win Jews" (1 Cor 9:20), implying that somehow his Jewish identity was assumed on the basis of the Gospel but that it had not conditioned his faith. Consider also that in his references to Jews, with only one exception (Gal 2:15), Paul speaks from a position of exteriority.

Matthew occasionally mentions the Samaritans (10:15) when Jesus sends his disciples in mission, telling them to not go to their land. This is part of the theology of this Gospel, which signals the opening to other peoples, beyond the Galilean frontier, only to the risen Jesus.

On the other hand, Luke indicates an opposite sense. Jesus sends his messengers to prepare his road through Samaria (9:52). When these are rejected, the disciples want to punish the Samaritans, but Jesus refuses to do so. Later, Jesus returns to take the route of Samaria (17:11 et seq.). This story tells the cure of ten lepers. The story highlights (v. 16) the attitude of the only one who returns to thank Jesus with a gesture of adoration and gratitude (prostrates on the ground): he is a Samaritan. That highlights the attitude of the Samaritan as recognizing Jesus, while the Jews are ungrateful and ignore him. This "stranger" (*allogenês*, literally, "one of other people") is then placed as a sign of faith: you are saved by your faith (v. 19).

Even stronger is the mention of a Samaritan in the well-known parable of Luke 10:30–37. The weight of this story is such that the word "Samaritan" becomes synonymous with compassionate. A dictionary of the English language defines it as (meaning 3): "one who is compassionate and helpful to a person in distress."[6] The choice of a Samaritan as an example of charity is not by chance, or only to indicate the figure of a foreigner: the Samaritan is also a figure for the excluded, the hated, the impure who enters history. And he enters in substitution of the most revered and pure, fulfilling the role of love that others refuse to perform. It is the one taking over the responsibility for the suffering other.

It is the deconstruction of the image formed over centuries of elitist politics, but it portrays the harsh reality: representatives of the elite (priest

6. http://www.dictionary.com/browse/samaritan.

and Levite) ignore the suffering, leave him at the side of the road. They become shills in the harm produced by the thieves. On the contrary, the excluded stands in solidarity with the excluded other, takes upon himself to restore the victim, reinserts him in the space of life (the Inn), gives continuity to his responsibility ("when I return"), undoes the work of thieves and is the agent of life over against the agents and accomplices of death.

In the continuity of the work of Luke, in Acts, Samaria is again given a significant place. The witness to the Christ in Samaria is already included in the mandate of the risen Jesus in Acts 1:8. In chapter 8, in response to the persecution in Jerusalem, Samaria served as a place of refuge. And not only that, but the people of Samaria received the Gospel, especially through the preaching of Philip, what then is corroborated by the presence of the Apostles Peter and John, and the realization of what we might call a "Samaritan Pentecost" (vv. 14–17). The presence of the Apostles and their recognition of the Samaritan believers is also a gesture of inclusion, according to this narrative: they constitute the first believers who do not come from Judaism. Peter and John, even before the vision of Peter in Joppa, accept and recognize the Samaritans as part of God's people, and confirm the presence of the Spirit among them. Even the episode with Simon Magus is inclusive: rather than expelling and punishing Simon, he is invited to reintegrate into the community through repentance and forgiveness, which he accepts. The recapitulation of 9:31 explicitly mentions the churches of Samaria together with Judea and Galilee, before the expansion to the gentile world. Then, once again, Samaria is included in 15:3, where the churches of Samaria rejoice for the conversion of gentiles: speech which excluded Samaria of the Israelite heritage has been left behind.

Certainly, one could see in Luke that this trend to set aside anti-Samaritan prejudice is linked with his Gentile origin. Different is the case of John, which is the Gospel that more explicitly includes the Samaritans among the followers of Jesus. So much so that several scholars of the New Testament and particularly in the studies of the Gospel of John discern from these mentions the fundamental characteristic of the community that gives origin to this Gospel as well as the formation of the text in its different times or stages.

There are two mentions of Samaritans, a more extended one in chapter 4, and another, almost casual, but not without importance, in chapter 8. In the story of John 4 Jesus does not avoid contact with the Samaritans but walks across the region. There the encounter with the woman at the well of Jacob becomes a theological construction around a plurality of issues: the water of life, the condition of God and its worshippers, the Messianic function, among others. We cannot on this site deal with all these significant issues, on which there are many and varied studies, but signal how it challenges the language of exclusion.

While the woman states the ethnic, gender and class difference as an obstacle, Jesus himself ignores them. On the other hand, the woman affirms the Samaritan claim to the Israelite heritage in the no way innocent phrase of "Jacob our father." Jesus does not question it. And while the dialogue at first seems to be a monologue between deaf, then it moves on when Jesus makes contact with the reality of the woman. Although there is a symbolic interpretation of the situation of Samaria, mixed with five nations, according to 2 Kgs 17, and an allusion to their dependence on Rome ("the one you have now is not your husband"—John 4:18), that same phrase is what reopens the dialogue.

Without going into a detailed exegesis of the chapter, it should be noted that Jesus remains in Samaritan territory another two days, and the whole village ends up recognizing him as Messiah; in the Samaritan tradition of the Messiah, this means master of wisdom. The statement that closes this passage (John 4:42) is a declaration: the first to recognize Jesus as Savior are the Samaritans!

Jesus' answer to Pharisaic aggravation in John 8:48—"Are we not right in saying that you are a Samaritan and have a demon?"—is very indicative: "I have no demon." Thus, in responding to the second accusation without defending himself from the first, he grants that calling someone a Samaritan is not offensive. He accepts the mock of being Samaritan, which was insulting for the accusers. Somehow Jesus "becomes Samaritan" when he accepts this qualification, and thus vindicates within his own messianic condition to be the excluded impure.

Discourse of Exclusion and Imperial Politics

The economic, military and political domain necessarily has to be accompanied by a cultural dimension that justifies and strengths it. So, the elite must impose a discursive fiction pretending the representation of a whole, as we have seen in the assertion of Laclau and Mouffe quoted in the opening of the text. That fiction presents domination as suitable, necessary, justified or, at least, inevitable. It is what Paul calls "all ungodliness and wickedness of those who by their injustice suppress the truth" (Rom 1:18), and which today we describe as the function of hegemony.

This political game is complicated in the projects of imperial building. Empires take the speech of the local ruling elite and make it play to its own domain. Thus, it performs a dual purpose: they attract the elite in its own favor and reinforces the sense of exclusion, coming eventually to bring into play the excluded themselves as justification of its actions, being divisive of the people. The course that we have examined in the case of the Samaritans exemplifies this, with an aggravating factor: the exclusion appears as a divine mandate, as cult. In consecrating the "canonicity" of the writings of exclusion, *exclusion becomes dogma*. It is repeated and affirmed as unquestionable truth: the hegemonic function is thus completed as religious speech. Meanwhile, the truth has been concealed in injustice.

The Gospel, in this case, shows an attempt to deconstruct this discourse by a different path: it takes the excluded as an expression of truth. The mercy that saves lives and the gratitude in the episodes narrated by Luke, the reception and empowerment by the power of the Spirit (Acts 8), the search for the truth and the confession of faith (in the case of the woman and the village of Sychar in John 4), and the inclusion of the Messiah himself in the whole of the despised, are set forth as the attributes of the excluded. Jesus challenges the divisions and posits justice against purity: that is its counter-hegemonic force.

The dominant discourse will always mark the submitted other as inferior, impure, dangerous. See the insulting expressions on Latinos, and especially on Mexicans that the former President of the United States Donald Trump launched during his campaign. Or the disparagement on refugees and economic migrants, which in some cases deny them their minimum rights of humanity. The history of the Samaritans serves to illustrate other stories that have accompanied imperial discourses on ethnic, class, or gender basis. And the evangelical inclusion encourages us to the deconstruction of these discourses, not from a similar opposition force, but from the potency of the excluded themselves.

Bibliography

Biglieri, Paula and Gustavo Guille. "The Deconstructivist Laclau." *The Undecidable Unconscious: A Journal of Deconstruction and Psychoanalysis* 4 (2017) 1–26. https://muse.jhu.edu/article/689767.

Laclau, Ernesto, and Chantal Mouffe. *Hegemonía y estrategia socialista. Hacia una radicalización de la democracia.* 2nd ed. Buenos Aires: Fondo de Cultura económica, 2004.

Míguez, Néstor O. "El surgimiento del estado monárquico en el Israel Antiguo. Aproximación desde la antropología política." *Cuadernos de Teología* 26 (2007).

Nebbia, Lito. "Quien quiera oír que oiga." https://www.youtube.com/watch?v=3mkhn 6oiqCM.

7

The Fluidity of Sacred Margins

The Letter to the Hebrews

MOTHY VARKEY

"When the world tightens its fist, be water"

TSHOMBE SEKOU

FOR MODERN READERS, THE book of Hebrews appears "alien" and "incomprehensible." This may be because, traditionally, scholars incline to limit their discussions pertaining to the author's wide-ranging use of various Jewish theological traditions, particularly the Melchizedek tradition, and focus on quotations and exegesis from the Hebrew Bible with christological motifs. Furthermore, the theology of the sacrifice of Christ in Hebrews seems to be locked in the presuppositions of the past. This perhaps best explains the "marginal" status of the epistle both in the canonical and in the broader context of the (re)search for "subversive hermeneutics" from which it was almost excluded.

But, being a (somewhat) diaspora text, Hebrews has more to offer to the new liberative quest for alternative hermeneutics that would not only (re)move the "margins," but also interrogate the so-called margins themselves, especially in the context of our renewed understanding of the liminality of human existence in the globalizing village. This chapter, therefore, investigates the use of Melchizedek tradition in the Letter to the Hebrews from the vantage point of postcolonial biblical interpretation. The merit of a postcolonial reading of Hebrews includes its ability to find liberating strands in the texts, while showing up the text's or its reception history's complicity in imperialist endeavors.

(Re)Mapping the Audience of Hebrews

Hermeneutical activity is always perspectival—whether consciously or unconsciously. This fittingly accounts for a detailed investigation of the "politics of the centripetal force" of the interpretation of Hebrews: the historical and theological situatedness of the audience of Hebrews. Instead of focusing on "the politics of identity," where very often identity is understood as essence,[1] this essay focuses on "the politics of location" because everyone belongs to and participates in a socio-political location and a member of a "distinct and identifiable social configuration" irrespective of the hybridity and heterogeneity of human subjectivity.[2] In Tolbert's view, the subversively close connection between "the politics of identity" and "the politics of location," while challenging the essentialization of human subjectivity, calls for a sliding, "fluid, shifting, and generally context-dependent" identity.[3] And the emerging nature of human subjectivity depends, to a great extent on "'*facts of blood*' (social, personal and familial alignments) and '*facts of bread*' (national, economic and political matters)."[4]

One cannot understand Hebrews outside of the socio-ethnic composition of its recipients. Firm evidence for the date at which Hebrews was written is almost entirely lacking; a judgment on this question depends on a "balance of probabilities" which suggests a date before the fall of Jerusalem. It is difficult to be more precise, and the discussion must remain inconclusive due to the lack of internal evidence. Notwithstanding, I find Hebrews to read more naturally in a pre-70 CE setting.

1. Tolbert, "Afterwords," 305–16.

2. Jasper, "Communicating the Word of God," 29–44.

3. Tolbert, "Afterwords," 305–16.

4. They are often at (violent) odds with one another. See Punt, "The Letter to the Hebrews," 342.

The next assumption concerns the ethnic identity of the audience, which is likely a mixed community of Jewish Christians and Gentile Christians,[5] but predominantly Jewish Christians.[6] Some scholars have argued that the recipients of Hebrews must have been unconverted[7] or converted[8] Essenes on the basis of the use of Melchizedek by the two communities. The resemblances between the two communities are only superficial; 11QMelchizedek appears to represent Melchizedek as a supernatural figure, with function similar to that of angel Michael. Both communities vehemently criticize Levitical priesthood and the Jerusalem cultus, but whereas the alternative for Qumran is that of a closed community governed by stringent religious and social rules, the alternative for Hebrews is a community inclusive of non-Jews. Whereas Qumran criticizes Jerusalem priesthood, Hebrews seeks to expose inadequacy of Levitical priesthood.

One can easily make out the presence of Jewish Christians from the extensive use of the Old Testament cultic regulations (Heb 9:1–10), tabernacle motif, and the Jewish exegetical rules which characterize rabbinic Judaism in the epistle.[9] Hebrews envisions one people of God; no break in salvation history;[10] Jews are not marginalized.[11] It is necessary to address the question of supersessionism in Hebrews because it is closely related to the Jewish background of the recipients; there is no issue if Christ "supersedes" Judaism or church "supersedes" Israel.[12] What we find in Hebrews is not Jewish messianic covenantalism, or attack on Judaism or its leaders.[13] Hebrews does not suggest that Jewish people have been replaced by Gentiles, instead new covenant as sustaining but transforming Israel's categories in the light of Christ event.[14] The title "to the Hebrews"

---

5. DeSilva, *Perseverance in Gratitude*, 2–3, 6–7.

6. Ellingworth, *The Epistle to the Hebrews*, 27.

7. Kosmala, *Hebräer, Essener, Christen*.

8. For detailed discussion see Bruce, "'To the Hebrews'? or To the Essenes'?"; Yadin, "A Note on Melchizedek and Qumran."

9. Cockerill, *The Epistle to the Hebrews*, 19–23.

10. Cockerill, *The Epistle to the Hebrews*, 21.

11. Cockerill, *The Epistle to the Hebrews*, 23.

12. Cockerill, *The Epistle to the Hebrews*, 22. See also Witherington III, *Letters and Homilies*, 25.

13. Hays, "Here We have No lasting city," 151–73.

14. Hays, "Here We have No lasting city," 151–73.

(Πρὸς Ἑβραίους) however cannot be taken as conclusive evidence to establish the identity of the audience because the label is not traditional.[15]

But it does not require the recipients to be Jewish because Gentile Christians would also be familiar with the Old Testament (literary knowledge, not first-hand acquaintance with the procedure in the Jerusalem temple) and manifested a lively interest in the Mosaic tabernacle and Levitical offerings.[16] Hebrews 11 denationalizes the heroes of the Jewish heritage in order to make them heritage of Gentile Christians: "Hebrews [. . .] opened the way for Gentile Christians to read Israelite history as if it were their own."[17] The mentioning of Timothy (13:23) strongly suggests that the audience must have formed as part of Paul's mission, which had its explicit goal of ministering to the Gentiles.[18]

In the light of the above considerations, it is best to assume that the recipients of Hebrews were predominantly but not exclusively Jewish Christian. Hebrews does not employ any ethnic categories to define its first readers;[19] "Jewish Christians" are "followers of Christ who have been acculturated into and continue to be attracted by Jewish religious practices regardless of their ethnicity."[20] Such acculturation may have happened to the Gentiles too primarily because many of their fellow believers were Jews. More importantly, Gentiles identified themselves with the synagogues as God-fearers. On the one hand, the audience of Hebrews were loyal to Christ, and on the other hand they were very particular about having continuous association with Jewish practices.[21] This explains why there is no direct polemic in the first 12 chapters of the epistle rejecting Judaism,[22] but rather a completionist argument;[23] there is no comparison or supersessionism of

15. Hagner, *Hebrews*, 2. But Witherington is of the view that "to the Jews" should not be considered as a mere conjecture; for him, "to the Jews" means "to the Jewish Christians" (see *Letters and Homilies*, 24).

16. Whitlark, *Resisting Empire*, 14–15; Hays, *The Conversion of the Imagination*, viii; DeSilva, *Perseverance in Gratitude*, 6–7.

17. Eisenbaum, *The Jewish Heroes of Christian History*, 220 (see 187–88, 218–25 for details).

18. DeSilva, *The Letter to the Hebrews*, 35.

19. Cockerill, *The Epistle to the Hebrews*, 20.

20. Cockerill, *The Epistle to the Hebrews*, 20.

21. Cockerill, *The Epistle to the Hebrews*, 20

22. Cockerill, *The Epistle to the Hebrews*, 20–21; the sustained *synkrisis* (comparison) with the Levitical cultus serves the ideological need of the Gentile readers, not the mixed community.

23. Witherington III, *Letters and Homilies*, 26; Ellingworth, *Hebrews*, 24.

contemporary Judaism but with the Old Testament institutions and Levitical priesthood. Therefore, the terms "Jewish Christians" and "Gentile Christians" may be used in a religious sense, not in an ethnic sense.[24] It shows the sensitivity of the author towards the ethnic texture of the audience. Had there been only either one of them, the epistle would not have displayed such exemplary and characteristic ethnic sensitivity.

The primary piece of external evidence points to the presence of Hebrews in Rome comes from 1 Clement. First Clement 36:1–5, which calls Jesus "high priest" (cf. 3:1), is taken from Heb 1:3–14.[25] The "shared terminology and contextual issues between Hebrews and other documents of Roman provenance" also connect Hebrews to Rome.[26] Timothy, mentioned in Heb 13:23, was also known to the Roman Church (cf. Rom 16:21).[27] Like the first recipients of Hebrews, the Roman church also suffered persecution (6:10–13; 10:32–34) and was known for generosity.[28] Eusebius reports the history of Rome's rejection of Pauline authorship of Paul (*Hist. eccl.* 3.3.4–5; 6.20.3).[29] Jerome also hints concerning the reservation of the "Latins" to accept canonicity of Hebrews partly because of the uncertainty concerning its authorship (*Epist.* 129.3).[30] All of these data have been considered collectively, and together they point to Rome as the destination of Hebrews; this is the fundamental assumption for this study.

It is evident from the above discussions that the nature and character of the followers of Christ in Hebrews is diasporic. They are "flesh-and-blood believers struggling to overcome the stranglehold of past traditions and adjust to the fresh movements of God in their fast-changing world."[31]

---

24. Cockerill, *The Epistle to the Hebrews*, 20

25. The use of Hebrews in *1 Clement* is not a conclusive proof of the Roman destination, given the mobility first-century Christ followers. See DeSilva, *Perseverance in Gratitude*, 22.

26. The word for "leaders" (ἡγουμένοις—Heb 13:7, 17, 24) was very frequently employed at Rome (*1 Clem* 1:3; 21:6; Herm. *Vis.* 2.2.6; 3.9.7); the generosity described in Heb 6:10–11 echoes the characteristic generosity of the early Christians in Rome (Lane, *Hebrews*, lviii); the issue of apostasy discussed in Heb 6:4–6; 12:16–17 recalls the issue concerning the possibility of repentance from apostasy or post-baptismal sin debated by Christ followers in Rome (Her. *Vis.* 5.7; cf. *Sim.* 9.20.1–21.3). See for details Whitlark, *Resisting Empire*, 7–8.

27. Hagner, *Hebrews*, 5.

28. Hagner *Hebrews*, 5.

29. Whitlark, *Resisting Empire*, 8.

30. Whitlark, *Resisting Empire*, 8.

31. Stedman, *Hebrews*, 9; Stibbs, *So Great Salvation*, 9–12.

As a diaspora community in Rome, the first recipients of Hebrews would have engaged the Roman imperial forces. Religiously and politically speaking, the audience of Hebrews were outside the "margins" of mainline Judaism and of the Roman imperial system. They did not belong to anywhere because both the Jews and the Romans viewed them as "undesirables" and "misfit"; they could not call either the Jewish world or the Roman political world their home. The reality of such a way of life creates a situation where diasporic people exist as "permanent strangers" in the Romans world and as "permanent aliens" in the Jewish world.[32]

Both the Jewish leaders and the Roman imperialist powers "pushed" the readers of Hebrews to the so-called "margins" through ideological and political discourses. This "epistemic behavior" achieves its effectivity through the practice of exclusion. Consequently, the dominant discourses of the Romans and the Jews "fix" the boundaries/margins of the first readers as a result of their loyalty to Christ (10:32–34; 11:1–40; 12:1–11).[33] The fixation of boundaries is sinful as it "fixes" people in "zones" of dependency and "peripherally." Ellingworth categorizes the dangers facing the recipients of the epistle as *passive* (lassitude, neglect, and immaturity), *active* (apostasy), and *external* (the pressure of ostracism and persecution).[34] The persecution included public harassment, imprisonment, confiscation of property, but had fallen short of martyrdom (12:4). Heb 12:4 contains a growing hostility against the believers and impending martyrdom.[35]

The anxiety at the traumatic "subjectification" may have been exacerbated by the delay of Christ's return (1:14; 10:36–39), rejection of the gospel (2:1–4; 5:11–6:8; 10:26–31; 12:14–17), and apostasy from Christ (6:1–18; 10:26–31). Some people have not fully grasped the full significance of what Christ had done and the continuing efficacy of his saving activity (5:11–6:8; 12:13) and abstained from worship (10:24–25).[36] Apostasy was a live option for the audience (2:3; 3:12; 6:4–6; 10:29). Therefore, people would have decided to renounce Christian faith and go back to

---

32. Segovia, "Toward a Hermeneutics of the Diaspora," 61–65.

33. Punt, "The Letter to the Hebrews," 361.

34. Ellingworth, *Hebrews*, 78–79. The present exposition assumes that their challenges were not separate but closely related.

35. DeSilva, *Perseverance in Gratitude*, 17; Graham Hughes, *Hebrews and Hermeneutics*, 28; Witherington III, *Letters and Homilies*, 27, 28, 29–30, 32; Brown, *The Message of Hebrews*, 13, 17.

36. DeSilva, *The Letter to the Hebrews*, 50.

Judaism.[37] It is natural to get attracted to privileges of the synagogues that would be theirs by compromising their faith and identifying with the imperial forces (12:14–17). They are like Esau who sold his birthright for a meal (12:16–17). Many, if not all, seem to have been frightened by the disparagement and marginalization that they suffered as a result of their Christian faith (11:1–41). They had "drifted away" from the message they had received (2:1–4).[38]

The author, however, exhorts his audience not to succumb to "othering" but to "resist evil" (12:4). As with any other diasporic community, "ethnocentric politics of identity" is one possibility and practice insular existence. But ethnocentric practice, which might be inevitable, would not only seal off all the possibilities of crossing borders/boundaries but they can also lead (though unintentionally) to "xenophobic rhetorics," "ethnic self-aggrandizement" and destructive essentialism. Return to universalization could very likely result in the universalization of dominant cultures and associated hierarchical values. More importantly, any attempt to evade interethnic critiques and moving the margins would invite the danger of being seduced by "celebratory romance of the past" or by an attempt at "homogenizing the history of the present."[39]

What then is the alternative to "ethnocentric insularity" or "enclosed community"? Is it the so-called universalization? This alternative could very likely result in the universalization of dominant cultures and the associated hierarchical values. But there is a crucial question here. Is the divide between Jewish Christians and Jews or between Jewish Christians and Rome visible? According to Bhabha—commenting on Franz Fanon's *Black Skin, White Masks*—diaspora existence is hybrid in nature because the space between the diaspora land and home land is not clear-cut.[40] Such a hybrid space ("dissembling image of being in at least two places at the same time")[41] is subversive because it challenges forced-assimilations, cultural mimicry, internalized self-rejection, and displacement. This hybrid space is otherwise known as "hyphens" where people live.

37. According DeSilva, it is "pedestrian inability" to live within the lower status, not persecution and attraction to Judaism that motivated apostasy (see *Perseverance in Gratitude*, 19).

38. Cockerill, *The Epistle to the Hebrews*, 16–17; DeSilva, *Perseverance in Gratitude*, 16; DeSilva, *The Letter to the Hebrews*, 50.

39. Bhabha, *The Location of Culture*, 9.

40. Bhabha, "Remembering Fanon," 117.

41. Bhabha, "Remembering Fanon," 117.

The author of Hebrews proposes the "Melchizedek tradition" in the Old Testament, where Abraham crosses the border and gives tithes to a Canaanite king-priest of Salem, as a political tool to re-invent the "margins" to where people are being pushed and a strategy to (re)read the Scriptures, thus reconceptualizes the "centres" that create "margins" and embrace "otherness" as a rhetorical site of liberation and resistance. The basic premise of such a strategy is contextualization which, for Segovia, implies two characteristics—otherness and engagement.[42] In so doing, the author's interpretation of the Melchizedek tradition in the epistle might have some kind of ethnocentric allusions or remarks, wittingly or unwittingly.

Melchizedek Tradition and Jesus's High Priesthood: Re-imagining Christology

There are two immediate reasons why the audience of Hebrews re-imagines a new Christology:

1. The Levitical priesthood is exclusive as it is territorial and centralized (7:11–14).

2. They believe that Christ fulfilled the Torah and all that it envisages for the salvation of humanity. Therefore, as followers of Christ, the audience of Hebrews stands in historical and soteriological continuity with Jewish heritage but Jewish leaders located them "outside" the orbit of Judaism(s).

Hebrews identifies a new de-territorialized priesthood in Jesus which defines margins as "rhetorical space" that transcends place and territory. This the author achieves by linking Jesus's priesthood with his divine sonship to the priesthood of Melchizedek. But it poses important questions. Why does the author present Jesus as the high priest over against the Levitical priesthood, not a king or an emperor over the Roman emperors? Is it simply a matter of exchanging the superiority of the Levitical priesthood for that of Jesus? How does it foster the geopolitical liberation of the audience of the letter? Answering these questions would tell us how the re-imagination of Christology in Hebrews becomes the political praxis of the hyphenated audience.

---

42. Segovia, "Toward a Hermeneutics of the Diaspora," 58–59.

The re-imagination of Christology engages the diaspora audience of the epistle in various ways. First, Jesus's high priesthood according to the order of Melchizedek destabilizes the so-called centrality of the "sacred center" (altar) that creates "sacred boundaries" by separating "holy land" from the "waste land"; instead it envisages multiplicity of altars. Diaspora people cannot relate to the territoriality of Levitical priesthood and that of God's promises. They need a new priesthood that is not territory based and altar centered. It is in Jesus that the author and the readers find a new de-territorialized and de-genealogical priest.

To validate such a priesthood of Jesus, the author extensively uses Melchizedek tradition. Abraham, the father of the nations, tithes to a Canaanite priest and received blessings from him. If Abraham, the forbearer Levi, accepts the priesthood of Melchizedek, who is not even a Jew, Jesus can also be accepted as a priest. More importantly, Jesus is the Son of God. But, while accepting the priesthood of Melchizedek, Abraham proposes a new understanding of God. For Abraham, the God of Melchizedek, "God of Most High" (*El Elyon*), is characteristically linked to places and natural phenomenon, which means they are static (see also *El-Roi*—Gen 16:13 and *El Elyon*—Gen 14:18). In contrast, for Abraham, his God is a de-territorialized and "detranscendentalized" God who cannot be knotted to any territory but to people and communities. The understanding of a journeying God is further evident in the sojourner or pilgrim motif (4:11; 13:1–7). To reinforce the concept of a journeying God further, Hebrews employs the term "tabernacle" instead of "temple." The same tradition can be found further in the Exodus tradition: Moses pitched a tabernacle outside the tent when he speaks face to face with God (Exod 33:7–11). It reflects the paradox of sovereignty; sovereignty is inside and outside at the same time.

In Hebrews, Jesus's priesthood is interpreted in view of the Yom Kippur instead of the Passover festivals as in the gospels. Sacrificial animals are killed outside the sacred boundaries, but only blood is brought inside the tent (Lev 16:12, 15; 17:3). "Outside the tent" is a place where one finds those who are ritually impure (Lev 24: 14, 23; Num 15:36), especially lepers (Num 5:2; 12:14); the defiled wait outside the tent for purification (Num 12:14–15; 31:19–20); law breakers are executed outside the tent (Num 15:32–36); "outside" is associated with death (Deut 2:4), especially by stoning (Lev 24:14, 23; Num 15:36). The author draws parallel between Jesus' death outside the city gate of the "holy city," Jerusalem (13:11), and the disposal of the "impure" bodies of the Yom Kippur sacrificial victims and the ritually impure. The letter also associates this boundary crossing imagery with the believers' eschatological city (13:14). This "permeable boundaries" define the new ontology of the diaspora community which positions itself in relation to a God, who in Jesus became a victim by himself, is with the victims on the hyphens.

Second, Hebrews' provocative re-imagination of Christology is a geopolitical praxis in many respects. Melchizedek (Gen 14:18–24) may be linked with Zadok, the later priest of David (2 Sam 8:17; 1 Kgs 1:8–12), if "Salem" (Gen 14:18) is an early reference to Jerusalem. In this regard, David must have used the Melchizedek tradition to validate his political agenda of centralizing religious power and political power in Jerusalem. This explains the formation of Ps 110:4. But the author of Hebrews uses the same Melchizedek tradition to expose how liturgical systems were ab/ used to territorialize Jewish cultic practices during the Davidic monarchy.

Furthermore, Herod replaced the Hasmoneans with foreign Jewish priestly families from Babylon (that of Hananel) and Egypt (beginning with Jesus son of Phiabi, then Simon son of Boethus) and Jerusalem (Matthias son of Theophilus) (cf. Josephus, *Ant.* 15:18–22, 40–41, 51–56, 319–322; 17:78, 161–167). The consequence was a weakened priesthood, now appointed by the imperial political authority. Because these new priestly families lacked legitimacy, they collaborated with Herodian dynasty and Roman imperial regimes. But the letter to the Hebrews outrightly disavows the empire nominated/appointed priests by re-imagining Jesus as their eternal high priest. So they rejected not only the authority of the Roman empire to appoint priests in Jerusalem but the empire itself.

Third, the superior cult of Jesus contests not only the claims of Levitical priesthood appointed by the empire but also that of the Capitoline city itself built with the money extracted from the Jerusalem temple tax (*fiscus Judiacus*) to the Capitoline treasury. Unlike the Capitoline (*imperium*), the new community (*basiliea*; 12:28) constituted outside the "sacred boundaries" is not a city (13:11–14). Such a position on the precariousness of the city is an explicit criticism of the Roman city culture. To reinforce the volatility of the imperial city claims, Hebrews proposes the term "sojourner" to re-constitute the identity of the members of the new community with porous boundaries as opposed to the term "citizen." The new *basiliea* on the margins, of the marginalized and by the marginalized is unshaken because it has no margins or center. Fixity of both the center and the margins is an illusion. Such a socio-political proposition perfectly fits into the diasporic/marginal experience of the audience.

Fourth, the transaction between Abraham and Melchizedek opens up the possibility of a new way of engaging the borders and negotiating the power relations built on differences. Both Abraham and Melchizedek were not suffering from xenophobia; instead they were hyphenating each other by positioning themselves in a radical relation to each other. For Abraham and Melchizedek, the so-called geographical boundaries are not lines of division that neatly divide one from the other, but a site of liminality and elusive zones of negotiation.

Such spatial practices envisage a non-territorial spatiality (nomadic spatiality). Though Abraham and Melchizedek had geographical and political boundaries/territories, their understanding of territory was different from the "sedentary territory" which views land as a fixed plane. For Abraham and Melchizedek, "nomadic spatiality" does not parcel out a space to people; nomads are localized but delimited. Therefore, one cannot find any conflict between "homeland" and "borderland" in the transactions of Abraham and Melchizedek because they re-imagined space in such a way that it transcends place and boundaries.

Conclusions

By going outside the tent, Jesus the high priest according to the order of Melchizedek engages in a new nomadic spatial practice, which calls for a new politics of location. The author of Hebrews invites his readers for such a praxeological re-imagination of Christology and spatiality so as to challenge the marginality of the margin and the centrality of the center and thereby politically transforms hyphenality as privileged fields of encounter and as dialogical and deconstructive space. Such a transfigured experiencing of spatiality will ensure that the audience of the epistle will experience their time in diaspora as the "time of the end" (messianic time), where one is invited to experience *eschaton* in history, in relation to "the end of time" (apocalyptic time).

Bibliography

Bhabha, Homi. "Remembering Fanon: Self, Psyche and the Colonial Condition." In *Colonial Discourse and Postcolonial Theory: A Reader*, edited by Patrick Williams and Laura Chrisman, 112–23. New York: Columbia University Press, 1994.
———. *The Location of Culture*. London: Routledge, 1994.
Brown, Raymond E. *The Message of Hebrews*. The Bible Speaks Today. Downers Grove, IL: InterVarsity, 1982.

Bruce, F. F. "'To the Hebrews? or To the Essenes'?" *New Testament Studies* 9 (1962–63) 217–32.

Cockerill, Gareth Lee. *The Epistle to the Hebrews*. New International Commentary on the New Testament. Grand Rapids: Eerdmans, 2012.

DeSilva, David A. *The Letter to the Hebrews in Social Scientific Perspective*. Eugene, OR: Cascade Books, 2012.

————. *Perseverance in Gratitude: A Socio-Rhetorical Commentary on the Epistle "to the Hebrews."* Grand Rapids: Eerdmans, 2000.

Eisenbaum, Pamela M. *The Jewish Heroes of Christian History: Hebrews 11 in Literary Context*. SBL Dissertation Series 156. Atlanta: Scholars, 1997.

Ellingworth, Paul. *The Epistle to the Hebrews: A Commentary on the Greek Text*. New International Greek Testament Commentary. Grand Rapids: Eerdmans, 1993.

Hagner, Donald A. *Hebrews*. New International Biblical Commentary 14. Grand Rapids: Baker, 1983.

Hays, Richard B. "'Here We Have No Lasting City': New Covenantalism in Hebrews." In *The Epistle to the Hebrews and Christian Theology*, edited by Richard Bauckham et al., 151–73. Grand Rapids: Eerdmans, 2009.

————. *The Conversion of the Imagination: Paul as Interpreter of Israel's Scripture*. Grand Rapids: Eerdmans, 2006.

Hughes, Graham. *Hebrews and Hermeneutics: The Epistle to the Hebrews as a New Testament Example of Biblical Interpretation*. Society for New Testament Studies Monograph Series 36. Cambridge: Cambridge University Press, 1978.

Jasper, Allison "Communicating the Word of God." *Journal for the Study of the New Testament* 67 (1998) 29–44.

Kosmala, H. *Hebräer, Essener, Christen: Studien zur Vorgeschichte der frühchristlichen Verkündigung*. Studia Post-Biblica 1. Leiden: Brill, 1959.

Lash, Nicholas. *Theology on the Way to Emmaus*. 1986. Reprint, Eugene, OR: Wipf & Stock, 2005.

Punt, Jeremy H. "The Letter to the Hebrews." In *A Postcolonial Commentary on the New Testament Writings*, edited by Fernando F. Segovia and R. S. Sugirtharajah, 338–68. London: T. & T. Clark, 2009.

Segovia, Fernando F. "Toward a Hermeneutics of the Diaspora: A Hermeneutics of otherness and Engagement." In *Reading from This Place*. Vol. 1, *Social Location and Biblical Interpretation in the United States*, edited by Fernando F. Segovia and Mary Ann Tolbert, 57–73. Minneapolis: Fortress, 1995.

Stedman, Ray C. *Hebrews*. Downers Grove, IL: InterVarsity, 1992.

Stibbs, Alan M. *So Great Salvation: The Meaning and Message of the Letter to the Hebrews*. Exeter, UK: Paternoster, 1970.

Tolbert, Mary Ann. "Afterwords: Christianity, Imperialism, and the Decentering of Privilege." In *Reading from this Place*: Vol. 1, *Social Location and Biblical Interpretation in the United States*, edited by Fernando F. Segovia and Mary Ann Tolbert, 305–16. Minneapolis: Fortress, 1995.

Whitlark, Jason A. *Resisting Empire: Rethinking the Purpose of the Letter to "the Hebrews."* Library of New Testament Studies 484. London: Bloomsbury, 2014.

Witherington, Ben, III. *Letters and Homilies for Jewish Christians: A Socio-Rhetorical Commentary on Hebrews, James, and Jude*. Downers Grove, IL: InterVarsity, 2007.

Yadin, Y. "A Note on Melchizedek and Qumran." *Israel Exploration Journal* 15 (1965) 152–154.

8

Dispersion of *Minjung* in Mark and Asian Diasporas in the Americas

JIN YOUNG CHOI

THE TERM "DIASPORA" COMBINES the Greek words *dia* (through) and *speirein* (to sow or disperse) and connotes the idea that the subject(s) has been dispersed, scattered or sown into new locations. As "diaspora" implies "dispersion from," it presupposes "a notion of a center, a locus, a 'home' from where the dispersion occurs."[1] The idea of separation is thus intrinsic to the concept of diaspora. Moreover, the experiences of diaspora comprise crossing or going through (*dia*) a border that separates physical spaces. The border crossing results in dislocation (from the old) and

1. Brah, *Cartographies of Diaspora*, 178. While in the ancient Greek diaspora was referred to "as migration and colonization," historically it signifies the Jewish people's collective trauma in the exile to Babylon (Smith, "Migrancy, Hybridity, and Postcolonial Literary Studies," 254). However, Cohen argues, "Jewish migratory experiences were much more diverse and more complex than the catastrophic tradition allows" (Cohen, *Global Diasporas*, 22–23). Moreover, scholars in diaspora studies apply this term broadly because the idea that the identity of a dispersed people "can only be secured in relation to some sacred homeland to which they must at all costs return," expelling other residents, is itself an imperialist one. Rather, according to Hall, "diaspora identities are those which are constantly producing and reproducing themselves anew, through transformation and difference" (Hall, "Cultural Identity and Diaspora," 235).

relocation (to the new). Diasporic journeys are often accompanied with "traumas of separation and dislocation" and, at the same time, the finding of new homes.[2] Fernando F. Segovia describes the diasporic experience in this way:

> On the one hand, we live in two worlds at one and the same time, operating relatively at ease within each world and able to go in and out of each in an endless exercise of human and social translation; on the other hand, we live in neither one of these worlds, regarded askance by their respective populations and unable to call either world home.[3]

Being in the diaspora generates the sense of otherness even after finding a new home. Since the sixteenth century, Asians have made diasporic journeys to the Americas and found homes in the New World. Their traumas were not only derived from separation and dislocation but were also caused by forced labor migration and slavery. Their otherness was multiplied when the master narrative of American histories erased not only the presence of Asians in the Americas but also the vestiges of European colonialism in Asia.[4] While cultural hybridization is often celebrated in the increasingly globalized world,[5] diaspora as a concept should be historicized rather than being essentialized or idealized. What makes Asian multiple journeys "configure into one journey [to the Americas] via a confluence of narratives as it is lived and re-lived, produced, reproduced and transformed through individual as well as collective memory and re-memory"?[6] What are the socio-cultural, political, and economic conditions that mark the trajectories of Asian diasporas to the Americas?

I situate the earlier period of Asian diasporic experience in the Americas in the context of European and American colonialisms and the ensuing forced migrations in the forms of slavery and indentured labor. Addressing the confluence of historical narratives is beyond my

---

2. Brah, *Cartographies of Diaspora*, 190.

3. Segovia, "Toward a Hermeneutics of the Diaspora," 61–62.

4. Hu-DeHart and López, "Asian Diasporas," 10.

5. Asian diaspora is not unique in this phenomenon. For example, "Mexicans enjoy their pan chino with coffee for breakfast, Peruvians swear on their uniquely named chifa restaurants that they have the best Chinese food in the world, and Cubans love the lottery game they call la charada china" (Hu-DeHart and López, "Asian Diasporas," 11).

6. Brah, *Cartographies of Diaspora*, 180.

expertise and the scope of this chapter. Rather, the argument that I make here is that rereading the Gospel of Mark around the themes of home, dispersion, and border can inform the historicizing of the Asian diasporic formation in the Americas, and vice versa. I find the concept of minjung (the "masses"), which was developed in the 1970s by several Korean theologians, particularly Ahn Byung-Mu, is a heuristic device. The concept of minjung helps not only focus on the migration and exclusion of people both in the social and narrative contexts of the Gospel and in the Asian diaspora, but also leads us to see realities of today's minjung.

Diasporas in the Americas

The Asian migrations to, and presence in, the Americas are traced back to the mid-sixteenth century, but this history has been obscured in American history. Especially, the history of Asian slavery is relatively unknown due to the overwhelmingly painful history of African slavery. European and American empires employed different forms of exploitation and oppression of different peoples to maintain their colonial systems. Thus, Asian diasporic experiences in the Americas need to be historicized in their own right. I aim to develop my argument as follows. First, Asian migrations to the Americas were closely related to European and American colonialisms and the systems of slavery and indentured labor. Second, the U.S. controlled Asians' immigration and citizenship through restrictive laws and policies, and this systemic exclusion influenced Asian's exclusion in Latin America. Last, historicizing the Asian diaspora helps us see today's diasporic minjung, who migrate and cross borders under the regulations of imperial-colonial and racist regimes.

Forced Colonial Migrations

For two hundred and fifty years, the Spaniards developed the worldwide trade system through the Manila Gallon Trade between Acapulco in Mexico and Manila in the Philippines, both of which constituted New Spain (1565–1815).[7] Western America, particularly Mexico, functioned as the post from which colonial empires stretched to Asia and finally all over the world "in the name of commerce and Christianity."[8] From the late

7. Hu-DeHart and López, "Asian Diasporas," 9.
8. Hsu, *Asian American History*, 1–2.

sixteenth to seventeenth centuries, a vast group of people from the Indian subcontinent and Southeast Asia migrated to Mexico and other parts of Latin America through the passage of the transpacific slave trade. These Asian slaves were, without distinction, assigned the identity of "chinos."[9]

Catarina de San Juan (original name, Mirra) was one of the chino slaves who migrated to the Americas under force and endured enslavement in the Spanish colonies.[10] Catarina was abducted from her home on the west coast of India by Portuguese slavers around 1610. She was sold at Spain's slave-trading station in Manila and arrived in the Mexican city of Puebla as a "china slave."[11] She was freed and called *la china poblana*, meaning "the Chinese woman from Puebla." After her death in 1688 she was revered as a popular saint.[12] The construction of the Pueblan Chinese woman as "a national gendered icon," which signifies "cultural unity among Mexicans," both obscures the history of Asian slaves and demonstrates the subjectivity that made their integration into the Spanish colonies possible.[13]

Postslavery World Trade and Restrictive Immigration Law

As the British Empire officially abolished the African slave trade in 1807, massive migrations of people from India, China, and Japan transpired due to the demand for new sources of labor. About 225,000 Chinese contract laborers (*culíes*) arrived in Cuba and Peru between 1847 and 1874.[14] The coolie trade replaced slaves as the New World's work force, constructing infrastructures such as the transcontinental railroad and working in the gold mines.[15] A thousand Japanese disembarked in Hawaii as three-year contract laborers at sugar plantations and more immigrants came in at

9. Seijas, *Asian Slaves in Colonial Mexico*, 1–3.

10. Seijas, *Asian Slaves in Colonial Mexico*, 8–31; Sánchez, "Deconstructing the Rhetoric of Mestizaje," 215–40.

11. Seijas, *Asian Slaves in Colonial Mexico*, 2. Chinos were preferred as domestic slaves because they looked accommodating and submissive.

12. Hsu, *Asian American History*, 3–4; Hu-DeHart and López, "Asian Diasporas," 10–11.

13. Sánchez, "Deconstructing the Rhetoric of Mestizaje," 216, 228. The small group of Japanese who arrived in Mexico in 1614 also succeeded in integration into the local society.

14. Hu-DeHart and López, "Asian Diasporas," 10, 14.

15. Hu-DeHart and López, "Asian Diasporas," 14.

other destinations such as Guatemala, Mexico, and Peru before the end of the nineteenth century.[16] However, colonialists and plantation owners feared rebellions of these indentured workers, so they began to limit the numbers of people from any one nation.[17]

When the U.S. recruited Chinese contract workers, who provided docile and cheap labor, it had already passed a naturalization law in 1790 that limited citizenship only to "free, white immigrants."[18] The Chinese workers' contributions to and sacrifice in building the nation were paid back by the 1882 Chinese Exclusion Act, which banned Chinese immigration for ten years but actually remained in effect until 1943. The US restrictive immigration policies were a factor increasing Asian migration to Latin America. Responding to the US demand for minerals and other economic resources, Northern Mexico's economy grew rapidly and this, in turn, demanded labor of many Chinese migrants on the border between northwestern Mexico and the western U.S.[19] The US Exclusion Acts not only reinforced the protection and expansion of the border but also influenced the Mexican state to follow the U.S. exclusive immigration policies restricting the admission of Chinese women and Chinese-Mexican marriages. During the late nineteenth century and the early twentieth, Chinese became the target of exclusion, discrimination, and violence both in the U.S. and Mexico and many fled to their borders. Thus, Chinese people's forced migration is first related to Spanish colonialism and then to the expansion and colonialism of the U.S.[20]

I have briefly discussed Chinese coolies in the borderlands, but other Asian peoples' situations in the Americas were not really different. From 1850 to World War II, immigration legislation continued to replace immigrant workers: Chinese were replaced by Japanese and Koreans, and then by Filipinos, and finally by action restricting all Asian immigrations.[21] The downturn of slavery and the colonial expansion of

16. Hu-DeHart and López, "Asian Diasporas," 13.

17. Hsu, *Asian American History*, 10–11.

18. Lowe states: "Up until 1870, American citizenship was granted exclusively to white male persons; in 1870, men of African descent could become naturalized, but the bar to citizenship remained for Asian men until the repeal acts of 1943–1952" (Lowe, *Immigrant Acts*, 11). An American who married an "alien ineligible to citizenship" lost her own citizenship (Hu-DeHart and López, "Asian Diasporas," 14).

19. Sánchez, "Deconstructing the Rhetoric of Mestizaje," 231.

20. Sánchez, "Deconstructing the Rhetoric of Mestizaje," 230–34.

21. The Immigration Act of 1924 set a national origins quota, excluded all

world markets brought indentured laborers from Asian countries, and then those Asian workers and migrants became the victims of the restrictive immigration policies in the Americas.

Asian American Diasporas in the Era of Globalization

It is estimated that there are currently more than four million people of Asian origins in Latin America, constituting 1% of its population. However, Asian immigrants or people of Asian descent in Latin America are no longer viewed as providers of cheap labor. Instead, extensive capital from China, Japan, Korea, and other global economic powers has been invested to take advantage of Mexico's natural resources, the "cheap labor and the low tariffs that result from the North American Free Trade Agreement (NAFTA)."[22] Along the US-Mexican border are factory plants called Maquiladoras where multinational corporations manufacture imported components into lower priced-goods for export to the U.S. While the Maquiladora industry may contribute to employment and development of Mexico's economy, issues of environmental pollution and human rights of women and children have been raised.

On the other hand, Asian Americans' educational and economic success in the U.S. granted them the model minority position, which is actually the product of the policies of limiting and screening Asian immigration.[23] The model minority myth not only resulted from differential colonizations and racializations; it also obliterates the history of institutionalized exclusions of Asian Americans. Lisa Lowe examines the agency of Asian immigrants and Asian Americans, which she calls "immigrant acts." Although Asian diasporas in the Americas have been "subject to" imperial-colonial exploitation and racist exclusion, they have also been "subjects" who venture on voyages to the new world, find new homes and adopt new ideas, religions and lifestyles. Moreover, Asian immigrants have been "agents of political change, cultural expression, and social transformation."[24]

---

immigrants from Asia, and limited the number of immigrants by country. During World War II, Japanese *issei* (the first generation of immigrants to North America) and even their American-born children were forced into concentration camps. Hu-DeHart and López, "Asian Diasporas," 13.

22. Flores, "Misery in the Maquiladoras."

23. Hsu, *Asian American History*, xix.

24. Lowe, *Immigrant Acts*, 9.

Such agency is actualized not necessarily based on Asian Americans' model minority status but through "the acts of labor, resistance, memory, and survival, as well as the politicized cultural work that emerges from dislocation and disidentification."[25] The agency of Asian Americans that brings about social change is based on their experience of dispersion and exclusion. It is for this point that I revisit and reimage the minjung, rereading the Gospel of Mark in this ever-changing context of globalization and thus turning our eyes to the others who are dislocated and disenfranchised today.

Ochlos in the Gospel of Mark

Ahn Byung-Mu and Ochlos-Minjung

Ahn Byung-Mu, a Korean New Testament scholar trained in German historical criticism, was a primary contributor to the development of minjung theology and hermeneutics. Ahn argued that it was the crowd (*ochlos*) in the Gospel of Mark who transmitted the Jesus tradition, not the institutionalized church that the disciples represent.[26] According to Ahn, the *ochlos* was not merely the background of Jesus's ministry, but Jesus loved and sided with the *ochlos*. And more importantly, the *ochlos* is found among the contemporary minjung in Korea.

Ahn explores the sociopolitical makeup of the *ochlos* based on the Jesus tradition as preserved in part by Mark. The *ochlos* surrounded and followed Jesus in Galilee—the people of the land (*'am ha'aretz*) who were socially despised and alienated, including the sick, sinners, and tax collectors. They were separated by the purity laws and rejected by the ruling powers. Ahn's reading of the *ochlos* in Mark leads him to search for the minjung in the Korean society. He describes the minjung as:

> weary and burdened, the lost sheep, the uninvited, the poor, the disabled, the blind, the crippled, the mistreated prodigals wandering the streets and alleys of towns; they are the unemployed roaming the streets, the oppressed, the imprisoned, the hungry, the naked, the moaning and the persecuted.[27]

25. Lowe, *Immigrant Acts*, 9.
26. Ahn, "Jesus and Minjung," 49.
27. Ahn, "*Minjok, Minjung,* and Church," 95.

Suffering defines the reality of minjung. It should be noted, however, that the *ochlos*-minjung is neither a monolithic group nor a fixed entity. The minjung are not necessarily religious like Latin America's Christian base communities. They are "not the proletariat as [in] the Marxist fueled liberation theology."[28] Unlike black liberation theology, the minjung does not constitute a certain racial group. They cannot be defined in nationalistic, racial/ethnic, and economic terms.[29] They are divergent and even "ambivalent toward powers when pressed by the empire."[30]

In this fluid concept of minjung, there is the possibility that minjung hermeneutics continues to have relevance to any society where people suffer and struggle against oppression and injustices. This hermeneutics asks the question: who are the minjung today? While the minjung were originally designated the suffering people or nation of Korea, the concept has been expanded to or reappropriated for Asian minjung (Yong-Bok Kim), transnational minjung (Jin Young Choi), black masses (Mitzi Smith), as well as women in US military camptowns (Keun-Joo Christine Pae) and sexual minorities (Min-Ah Cho) in South Korea.[31]

I am joining in the collective, politicized cultural work by finding today's minjung through interpreting the Gospel of Mark around the themes of exclusion and migration. Following Ahn Byung-mu's reading of *ochlos* as the focal character in the Gospel, I shall examine the portrayal of *ochlos* as presented by Mark not only in Galilee but also across geographical and ethnic boundaries.

Galilee and Ochlos

In Ahn's interpretation, Galilee is the context of both Jesus and the *ochlos* and has a "minjung-like character."[32] Politically, Galilee had suffered from foreign invasions throughout its history, so that it was treated as "the

28. Sugirtharajah, *Jesus in Asia*, 200–201.

29. Ahn, "Jesus and Minjung," 56.

30. Kim and Kim, *Reading Minjung Theology*, 9. Sánchez argues that Galilean *ochlos* are transformed into Jerusalem *ochlos*, who negotiate colonial power in the "imperial epicenter." The *ochlos* are "'border-straddlers' between ethnic Galilee and colonial Jerusalem" (Sánchez, "Ambivalence, Mimicry, and the *Ochlos*," 136.

31. Kim and Kim, *Reading Minjung Theology*, 101–19, 164–83, 184–99; Yong-Bok Kim, "Jesus Christ among Asian Minjung"; Choi, *Postcolonial Discipleship of Embodiment*, 97–107.

32. Ahn, "Minjung Theology," 73.

land of Gentiles" (Isa. 9:2; Matt. 4:15–16). As a part of the ancient tribal alliance of Zebulun-Naphtali, Galilee was differentiated from Judea, which was the successor of David's kingdom.[33] Galilee was conquered by Assyria in 733 BCE (2 King 15:29) and it continued to come under the rule of foreign nations such as Babylon and Persia. It is recorded that Simon Maccabeus rescued a minority group of the Galilean Jews during the Maccabean War (1 Macc. 5), yet cities in Galilee eventually became colonies of the Greek Empires, Ptolemy and Seleucid. Finally, about sixty years before Jesus was born, the Romans conquered Galilee, Judea, and other districts of Palestine. As noted by Richard Horsley, people in Galilee as well as in Judea suffered from repeated wars of conquest, the extraction of tribute, and its shifting arrangements of client rulers.[34]

Politically oppressed by foreign nations, Galilee was the object of contempt by its own people of Israel (cf. John 1:46). Although "an all-too-simple dichotomy between Galilee and Judea" would be in need of further nuance, scholars argue that Galileans were viewed from the first century Judean perspective "as having a politically suspect background, a lack of education, the temperament of a farmer, and a deficiency in orthodoxy."[35] As a socially and culturally alienated region, Galilee was "the center of an anti-Roman movement and the center of political and military resistance" and thus became "the target of Roman and Herodian purges."[36]

It is important to note that Jesus starts his kingdom preaching in this dangerous place, Galilee (Mark 1:14b–15), and at an especially dangerous time—when John the Baptist was imprisoned by Herod Antipas. According to Josephus, "John was executed as a Roman political prisoner; he was a false prophet who had the power to deceive the minjung like a demon (*daimonion*)."[37] When Jesus is accused of having Beelzebul (Mark 3:22; cf. Matt. 11:18, "He has a demon"), it connotes that "he

---

33. Ahn, "Minjung Theology," 76.

34. Horsley, *Covenant Economics*, 82.

35. Scholars often take the example of Yohanan ben Zakkai's famous dictum, "O Galilee, Galilee, you hate the Torah! Your end will be by 'oppressors'!" in *y. Shabbat* 16.8/3 (15d). Deines, "Galilee and the Historical Jesus," 18; cited from Vermes, *Jesus the Jew*, 48–57.

36. Ahn, "Minjung Theology," 73, 77.

37. Ahn, "Minjung Theology," 71–72. As Jesus was executed by Roman authorities, Ahn argues, political persecution by the ruling authorities of Judah and Rome was inevitable for the eyewitnesses of Jesus (Ahn "The Transmitter of Jesus-Event Tradition," 37).

instigated the minjung."[38] While in Matthew, Jesus's home is Bethlehem and Jesus flees to Galilee, Mark presents Jesus going back home to Galilee.[39] Nevertheless, what Mark highlights is the fluid concepts of home and of mobile subjects who cross boundaries throughout the Gospel. In Mark, Jesus was a migrant, and so were the *ochlos*.

Exclusion Laws

Galilee is home to Jesus. Yet, he does not have the conventional concept of family. When people say to Jesus, "Your mother and your brothers and sisters are outside (*exō*), asking for you" (Mark 3:32; cf. 4:11), he responds, "Who are my mother and my brothers? . . . Here are my mother and my brothers!" (3:33–34). He was referring to the *ochlos* sitting around him.[40] By embracing the *ochlos* as family, Jesus reconstitutes the existing kinship system.

While he will challenge the social systems or institutions such as marriage and divorce, wealth, political power, the temple-state and its economy, Roman taxation, the Law, and the scribal group later in the Gospel (Mark 10–12), Jesus's earlier ministry in Galilee focuses on subverting his own tradition—the Jewish symbolic order represented by the purity laws.[41] As a way of preserving social order and national identity, these laws not only required people to keep ritual purity from any defilement (*koinoō/koinos* in Mark 7:2, 15, 18, 20, 23), but also labeled those who could not follow or who trespassed the laws as "sinners." This meant that "those in lowly professions, the poor, and the sick" suffered further social marginalization and were systematically criminalized.[42] These are the *ochlos* in Galilee whom Jesus accepted as family.

Dispersion and Border Crossings

I argue that while Ahn stresses only the *ochlos* in Galilee, actually the *ochlos* appear to be heterogeneous people in terms of race/ethnicity, who

38. Ahn, "Minjung Theology," 72.

39. Ahn, "Minjung Theology," 72.

40. Ahn observes that in Matthew's parallel passage (12:49), Jesus indicates that the disciples are his family (Ahn, "Jesus and Minjung," 52).

41. Clevenot, *Materialist Approaches*, 78.

42. Ahn, "Jesus and Minjung," 55.

cross borders even in the earlier time of Jesus's ministry. The *ochlos* as mobile subjects are found not only within the periphery of Galilee but also between peripheries and centers. It is striking that Mark depicts "people from the whole Judean countryside and all the people of Jerusalem" as coming to be baptized by John the Baptist (1:5). Why do the Judeans and Jerusalemites come to confess their sins and to be forgiven in this marginal place? Some scholars note that Mark describes that this ritual of cleansing sins happens in the periphery, not in the center, the temple in Jerusalem.[43] Soon afterwards (from 2:4), Mark begins to call these people the *ochlos*.

Furthermore, Mark 3:7–8 illustrates that a great multitude followed him from Galilee but that they also came "from Judea, Jerusalem, Idumea, beyond the Jordan, and the region around Tyre and Sidon."[44] Later the *ochlos* in "the regions (*horia*) of Judea and beyond (*peran*) the Jordan" gathered around Jesus, and he taught them according to his custom (10:1). As in this particular passage, Jesus is often depicted as crossing borders, particularly traveling beyond the Jordan River or opposite sides of the Galilean Sea (3:8; 4:35; 5:1, 21; 6:45; 8:13; 10:1). Moreover, Jesus's movement reaches to other regions (*horia*) such as Gerasenes (5:17)[45] and Tyre and Sidon (7:24, 31). More significantly, Jesus's movements, alongside the *ochlos*, start in Galilee where his home is, and Mark's Gospel ends with the promise that he will return home.

> 1:14 Now after John was arrested, Jesus came to Galilee, proclaiming the good news of God.
> 16:7 . . . he is going ahead of you to Galilee.

Jesus's return home to Galilee would give hope to the *ochlos* dispersed elsewhere; wherever Jesus is, there is their home (3:33–35). Ahn argues, "During Mark's time, the Jews, including Jewish Christians, were exiled from their homeland, and were wandering like sheep without a

---

43. Bruce Worthington argues that considering the status of the temple as the economic, political and social hub of ancient Palestine, as well as "the visceral presence of God in the world," Jesus's strategy focused on villages is conspicuous. The *ochlos* "leaves Jerusalem in order to follow Jesus in Galilee" (Worthington, "Jesus the Pervert," 179).

44. Although the "multitude" in this passage is *plēthos* not *ochlos* in Greek, those who followed Jesus are not only the disciples but also the *ochlos* (5:24).

45. Many interpreters observe the imperial military presence in this scene, but it should be noted that there is a possibility that the imperial-colonial force was involved in controlling the local economy in Gerasenes, which caused conflicting interests between the colonized people and the border-crosser, Jesus, who challenges the imperial power.

shepherd."[46] Immediately after the violent execution of John the Baptist at Antipas's royal banquet (6:14–29), the *ochlos* are described as "coming and going" (6:31) in order to be healed or liberated from their "sins" by Jesus. They hurried "there on foot from all the towns and arrived ahead of" Jesus and his disciples (6:33). How dramatic it is to imagine that far more than the five thousand *ochlos* finally encountered him! Jesus saw the countless *ochlos* and his gut moved toward them because "they were like sheep without a shepherd" (6:34).

Jesus's compassion was not limited to the *ochlos* in Galilee but included those across other borders around the region of the Decapolis (7:31; 8:2; cf. 1:41; 9:22). In these two feeding stories, the motivation for Jesus's acts was the condition of the *ochlos*—not only that they were without food, but also their migrant situation.

> I have compassion for the crowd, because they have been with me now for three days and have nothing to eat. If I send them away hungry to their homes, they will faint on the way—and some of them have come from a great distance. (8:2–3)

The *ochlos* are those who might be fainting on the way home because they came far away from home. The *ochlos* with whom Jesus was concerned are migrants who might have their home but cannot reach home because of poverty, hunger, and the incompetency and violence of the ruling authorities. Or they have homes but do feel unhomeliness because they are socially and culturally alienated.[47]

Just as the numbers of five or four thousand in Mark's descriptions are not actual but symbolic, the three days of the migrancy condition is symbolic of distance and barriers. Galilee is a symbolic place where Jesus reconstitutes home for the *ochlos* in Jesus's time and today. Yet, we still see displaced people in Jesus's home, Palestine. We hear news of the Palestinians in Gaza who cannot cross the border set by the modern state of Israel; their attempt to move toward home, which is only a few miles away, has been frustrated. Many of them have fainted and been killed in the few minutes it took them to attempt to get home, and this singular event has occurred, literally, for seventy years. And, poignantly, they are the *ochlos* whom Jesus saw two thousand years ago in that land.

---

46. Ahn, "Jesus and Minjung," 50.

47. Choi, *Postcolonial Discipleship of Embodiment*, 80, 167.

Concluding Remarks

Images of exclusion and migration are prevalent in the Gospel of Mark. The system of purity laws separates people, places, and culture, and it creates the Other—the *ochlos*. The *ochlos* are not limited to Galileans but are the displaced who cross borders within the larger Roman Empire. Notwithstanding, they are relocated, alongside Jesus. As Mark describes the *ochlos* as dispersed migrants across ethnic, national, and geographical boundaries, I use the lens of minjung as a heuristic tool to remember the trace of Asian diasporas in the Americas. Asian diasporas were the *ochlos*-minjung—slaves, indentured workers, and (im)migrants, whose admissions and settlements were continuously rejected and manipulated.

However, not all of Asian immigrants and diasporas today are socially and culturally excluded. Avtar Brah states, "the concept of diaspora places the discourse of 'home' and 'dispersion' in creative tension, *inscribing a homing desire while simultaneously critiquing discourses of fixed origins*" [italics in original].[48] As the *ochlos* in the Gospel are ambivalent in mimicking colonial powers, a reflection on Asian diaspora in the Americas—past, present and future—also leads to the critical question: who is then the *ochlos*-minjung? What is the configuration of neoimperialism-colonialism and racist regimes today, and who are the most suffering people under those powers?

As the sinners in Jesus's time were not able to carry out the requirements of the law and thus criminalized, certain border-crossers are publicly proclaimed to be criminals today. Among them are illegal immigrants, war victims, refugees, and other minority peoples. As I am writing on diaspora, migration, and the *ochlos*-minjung, thousands of a so-called caravan of people are fleeing from poverty and violence and crossing thousands of miles on foot from Central America through Mexico and ultimately to the southern U.S. borders. Today critics are called to revisit the histories of the displacements of slavery, colonization, and conquest and listen to the stories of these displaced people, including Asian diasporas in the Americas and beyond.

48. Brah, *Cartographies of Diaspora*, 189.

Bibliography

Ahn, Byung-Mu. "The Transmitter of Jesus-Event Tradition." In *Reading Minjung Theology in the Twenty-First Century*, edited by Yung Suk Kim and Jin-Ho Kim, 27–48. Eugene, OR: Pickwick Publications, 2013.

———. "Jesus and Minjung in the Gospel of Mark." In *Reading Minjung Theology in the Twenty-First Century*, edited by Yung Suk Kim and Jin-Ho Kim, 49–64. Eugene, OR: Pickwick Publications, 2013.

———. "Minjung Theology from the Perspective of the Gospel of Mark." In *Reading Minjung Theology in the Twenty-First Century*, edited by Yung Suk Kim and Jin-ho Kim, 65–90. Eugene, OR: Pickwick Publications, 2013.

———. "Minjok, Minjung, and Church." In *Reading Minjung Theology in the Twenty-First Century*, edited by Yung Suk Kim and Jin-Ho Kim, 91–97. Eugene, OR: Pickwick Publications, 2013.

Brah, Avtar. *Cartographies of Diaspora: Contesting Identities*. Gender, Racism, Ethnicity. London: Routledge, 1996.

Choi, Jin Young. *Postcolonial Discipleship of Embodiment: An Asian and Asian American Feminist Reading of the Gospel of Mark*. Postcolonialism and Religions. New York: Palgrave Macmillan, 2015.

Clevenot, Michel. *Materialist Approaches to the Bible*. Translated by William J. Nottingham. Maryknoll, NY: Orbis, 1985.

Cohen, Robin. *Global Diasporas: An Introduction*. 2nd ed. New York: Routledge, 2009.

Deines, Roland. "Galilee and the Historical Jesus in Recent Research." In *Galilee in the Late Second Temple and Mishnaic Periods*. Vol. 1: *Life, Culture, and Society*, edited by David A. Fiensy and James Riley Strange. Minneapolis: Fortress, 2014.

Flores, Esteban. "Misery in the Maquiladoras." *Harvard International Review, Special Supplement* 38 (Winter 2017) 10–12.

Hall, Stuart. "Cultural Identity and Diaspora." In *Colonial Discourse and Post-colonial Theory: A Reader*, edited by Patrick Williams and Laura Chrisman, 227–37. London: Harvester Wheatsheaf, 1994.

Horsley, Richard A. *Covenant Economics: A Biblical Vision of Justice for All*. Louisville: Westminster John Knox, 2009.

Hsu, Madeline Y. *Asian American History: A Very Short Introduction*. Oxford: Oxford University Press, 2017.

Hu-DeHart, Evelyn, and Kathleen López. "Asian Diasporas in Latin America and the Caribbean: A Historical Overview." *Afro-Hispanic Review* 27.1 (2008) 9–21.

Kim, Yong-Bok. "Jesus Christ among Asian Minjung: A Christological Reflection." *Religion Online*. https://www.religion-online.org/article/jesus-christ-among-asian -minjung-a-christological-reflection/.

Kim, Yung Suk, and Jin-Ho Kim. *Reading Minjung Theology in the Twenty-First Century*. Eugene, OR: Pickwick Publications, 2013.

Lowe, Lisa. *Immigrant Acts: On Asian American Cultural Politics*. Durham: Duke University Press, 1996.

Sánchez, David Arthur. "Ambivalence, Mimicry, and the *Ochlos* in the Gospel of Mark." In *Reading Minjung Theology*, edited by Yung Suk Kim and Jin-Ho Kim, 134–47. Eugene, OR: Pickwick Publications, 2013.

Sánchez, Martha Chew. "Deconstructing the Rhetoric of Mestizaje through the Chinese Presence in Mexico." In *Strange Affinities: The Gender and Sexual Politics of Comparative Racialization*, edited by Grace Kyungwon Hong and Roderick A. Ferguson, 215–40. Durham: Duke University Press, 2011.

Segovia, Fernando F. "Toward a Hermeneutics of the Diaspora: A Hermeneutics of Otherness and Engagement." In *Reading from This Place*. Vol. 1, *Social Location and Biblical Interpretation in the United States*, edited by Fernando F. Segovia and Mary Ann Tolbert, 57–73. Minneapolis: Fortress, 1995.

Seijas, Tatiana. *Asian Slaves in Colonial Mexico: From Chinos to Indians*. Cambridge Latin American Studies 100. New York: Cambridge University Press, 2014.

Smith, Andrew. "Migrancy, Hybridity, and Postcolonial Literary Studies." In *The Cambridge Companion to Postcolonial Literary Studies*, edited by Neil Lazarus, 241–61. Cambridge Companions to Literature. New York: Cambridge University Press, 2004.

Sugirtharajah, R. S. *Jesus in Asia*. Cambridge: Harvard University Press, 2018.

Worthington, Bruce. "Jesus the Pervert: A Žižekian Response to Mark 11.15–17." *Biblical Interpretation* 22 (2014) 168–87.

Part 2

Politics of Othering

9

Women and Masculinity

Hindu India and Second Temple Judah

MONICA JYOTSNA MELANCHTHON

NOTIONS OF ALTERITY, OTHERNESS and difference are controversial. The Other is often disparaged, demonized and seen as inferior, unacceptable or dangerous. The process of othering is sustained by the dominant community to enforce its superiority and hegemony. The marginalization of the Other (read: women) defines the center (read: masculinity). Diversity is not celebrated for the richness it brings. Instead, it has created untold challenges for the harmony and well-being of the society.

India, in the climate created by the current BJP (Bharatiya Janata Party) regime, is experiencing heightened tensions and violence between religious, caste and ethnic groups. Social analysts and scholars attribute the conflicts to assertions of identity, which is "the most contested today often rallying around issues of power relations, socio-cultural locations, resources, political support and other external interventions."[1] Conflicts occur when dominant groups manipulate social, political, economic, and ideological factors to construct nationalist identities.

When identity is threatened, the bodies of men and women (and societal ideas around masculinity and femininity) become metaphors for expressing community, nation, religion. The human body becomes

1. Tripati and Singh, "Prologue," xiii.

123

a mode of consciousness, a starting point in the creation of a view of the world. As Merleau-Ponty notes, "the body is the place where appropriations of space, objects and instruments occurs," a primary receptacle of ideological scripts.[2] The human body is used to inscribe and project differences amongst human communities.

> The body is a political site, insofar as it marks points of difference and sameness among individuals and allows for correlative regulations of these categories. In the generic understanding of a political process as one that emerges out of structures of power, and works towards the subsequent reinforcement of such structures, the body develops an architecture of signs and markers of difference, "accounted for the distribution of material, spatial, temporal resources" and a necessary . . . classification of population.[3]

The tensions between Hindus and Muslims created by the struggle for Indian independence in the early 1900s saw renewed efforts by varied movements to define the nation. While male bodies were inscribed with who or what type of behavior was good for the nation, women's bodies became embattled sites, actively engaged in the construction of a new nation and new models of womanhood. Indian and feminist scholar Charu Gupta calls attention to the fact that within the Hindu movements of this time, gender was an important means used to define and sharpen differences between the Hindu and Muslim communities.[4] Through these movements, attempts were made to construct a "full bodied masculine Hindu male" who would strengthen community identity while also participating in the nationalist struggle. For the promotion of this "aggressive chauvinism," the Hindu woman was invited to participate in the communal conflict by taking on the male persona to defend the community's honor.[5] Sikata Banerjee also calls attention to the cultural expressions and masculinized vision of nation and its implications for women who are coopted into this masculine environment with ascribed roles.[6] This chapter draws upon the work of these two Indian women scholars and apply their insights to understanding similar issues of gender (male and

2. Merleau-Ponty, *Phenomenology of Perception*, 154.

3. Jackson III, *Scripting the Black Masculine Body*, 15.

4. Gupta, *Sexuality, Obscenity, Community*, 222; see also, Gupta, "Articulating Hindu Masculinity and Femininity."

5. Gupta, *Sexuality, Obscenity, Community*, 222.

6. Banerjee, "Armed Masculinity;" see also Banerjee, *Make me a man!*

female), the project of nation building and identity formation in Second Temple Judah.

The question that drives this essay relates to Hindu and Judean constructions of masculinity and femininity at a time of crisis, when differences between groups were heightened and in tension. The aim here is to register the process of othering in the literature that arose during such periods and attend to how men and women were used to define the insider against the Other (foreigner, Samaritan, visionary, non-elect, anti-elect). Even though women are the Other in these two cultures, and their place in society was rigidly controlled, they were also the "insider others," the essential, and their bodies were monitored and regulated to differentiate insiders from outsiders.[7] Of particular interest is how powerful ideologies and institutions regulate and control women's bodies and how women (as embodied beings) cope, negotiate, and resist these forces.

India, Identity, and Nation (1900s)

The early 1900s saw colonized India intensify its efforts to oust the British in a bid for freedom, independence, and self-government. Mohandas K. Gandhi's organized resistance to the 1919 law that gave British authorities free rein to imprison suspected insurgents without trial resulted in the Jallianwala Bagh massacre of hundreds of innocent civilians in Amritsar by the British in April of 1919.[8] Gandhi launched the Non-cooperation Movement[9] in September 1920 but his sudden cancellation of the civil disobedience campaign at the height of public enthusiasm in February 1922[10] and the resultant decline of the Non-cooperation Movement resulted in the deterioration of Hindu-Muslim relations. Unity between these two communities was a mere memory and the politics between the two communities was bitter. The Muslims felt that fighting for freedom was not worth their time unless their place within an Independent India was recognized as being equal to the Hindus both in terms of political power and resourcefulness.

7. Walsh, "Women on the Edge," 122.

8. "Jallianwala Bagh Massacre." https://www.britannica.com/event/Jallianwala-Bagh -Massacre.

9. "Noncooperation Movement." https://www.britannica.com/event/noncooperation -movement.

10. Gandhi claimed that the cancellation of the campaign was necessary to end the violent outbreaks associated with it.

The Hindu leadership was threatened by what they saw as a growing and dangerous awakening among Muslim masses through the co-
alescence of the non-cooperation movements and the Khilafat,[11] while
Muslim leadership questioned whether they too quickly followed the
lead of the Hindu dominated Indian National Congress in fighting for
a political order in which their own interests were not given sufficient
attention.[12] The atmosphere was one of mutual suspicion and fear, with
every incident at that time analysed with mistrust and scepticism and
every move by one community created tensions between the two.

The late 1800s and early 1900s also saw a dramatic rise in conversions to egalitarian faiths, namely Christianity, Islam, and Buddhism,
popularly known as the era of "mass movements" in Christian mission
histories.[13] Entire villages and sub-castes converted collectively, which
did not seem to be a major issue at the local level but increased fears elsewhere. These conversions contributed to the notion of Hindu decline and
was contrasted with the growth and strength of other faiths, particularly
of Islam. Conversion to Islam and Christianity became a major grievance
and was identified as a central issue and cause for Hindu decline.

> In 1923, Veer Damodar Sarvakar's ideological pamphlet *Es-
> sentials of Hindutva*,[14] in which he endorsed the idea of India
> as a *Hindu Rashtra* (Hindu Nation),[15] fired strong Hindu senti-
> ments and set the terms of the debate for a significant segment
> of India's population, especially the aggressive and socially
> conservative Hindu-nationalist ideological-political bloc. To
> achieve "political consolidation" of the Hindu people Sarvakar
> advocated a definition of "Hindu" that combine the concepts
> of motherland (*matrubhumi*), ancestors (*pitrubhumi*) and holy
> land (*punyabhumi*). "Thus a Hindu is someone born of Hindu
> parents, who regards India—'this land of Bharatvarsha, from

11. "Khilafat Movement: Indian Muslim Movement." https://www.britannica.
com/event/Khilafat-movement.

12. Cf. Nanda, *Road to Pakistan*, 94.

13. Sarkar, *Beyond Nationalist Frames*, 232.

14. Republished as *Hindutva: Who Is a Hindu?* (1928).

15. India is the land of the Hindus since their ethnicity is Indian and the Hindu
faith originated in India. "Savarkar also argued that a Muslim or a Christian, even if
born in India, could not claim allegiance to the three essentials of Hindutva: 'a common nation (*rashtra*), a common race (*jati*) and a common civilization (*sanskriti*), as
represented in a common history, common heroes, a common literature, a common
art, a common law and a common jurisprudence, common fairs and festivals, rites and
rituals, ceremonies and sacraments'" (Tharoor, "Veer Savarkar").

the Indus to the Seas'—as his motherland as well as his holy land, 'that is the cradle-land of his religion.'"[16]

Appropriation of nationalism based on Hindu majoritarianism, identity, and the indigenous origin of Hinduism, resulted in Islam and Christianity being labeled "alien religions" and "unpatriotic by definition."[17] Hindus were a "nation," while Muslims were a "community."[18] Sarvakar's distinction between "nation" and "community" and the formation of the Rashtriya Sevak Sangh (RSS) in 1925, reinforced and made explicit the unequal status between the two communities.

> In the British Indian political system . . . separate electorates encapsulated the minority status of Muslims . . . Instead of negotiating the terms of accommodating cultural differences within the Indian nation, those excluded from the definition of a "Hindu" had to either seek incorporation by adopting a territorially based religious identity or go in the opposite direction through a self-generated process of separation.[19]

Both communities engaged in aggressive revivalist ardor to organize their communities. "Save the dying race" became the slogan of the Hindus who asserted their religious community identity through two reformist movements, namely the *Shuddhi* and *Sangathan*, which sought to "purify" and "reconvert" marginal groups and castes that had converted to other faiths which they believed was mainly forced. Sarkar writes, "Social upliftment efforts, which in strict logic could have been directed towards all subordinated lower castes and untouchables, became in practice exercises in policing and modifying the borders between religious communities."[20]

The period saw the rise of significant movements on both sides of the religious divide. *Shuddhi* (purify) Movement was started by the *Arya Samaj* (society of nobles) to bring back the people who converted to Islam, Christianity and Sikhism. The goal of the *Arya Samaj* was not to "reconvert" individuals to Hinduism. The *Sangathan* movement that accompanied the *Shuddhi* sought to organize, build, and consolidate the

16. Tharoor, "Veer Savarkar."

17. Sarkar, *Beyond Nationalist Frames*, 235.

18. Sarvakar, *Essentials of Hindutva*, 4, as cited by Iqbal, *The Life and Times of Mohamed Ali*, 312.

19. Jalal, *Self and Sovereignty*, 258.

20. Sarkar, *Beyond Nationalist Frames*, 94.

Hindu community. Both movements were fueled and flared by strong anti-Muslim sentiments. In response, the Muslims in North India started the
communal and revivalist movements *Tabligh* (propagation)[21] and *Tanzim*
(organization)[22] to strengthen the Muslim identity and presence in Indian
politics. The former was a militant proselyting effort to counteract the
Shuddhi movements, while the latter fostered Muslim identity. The Hindu
effort was exerted to gain an edge in the numbers game, while the Muslims sought to protect and advance their provincial dominance against the
Hindu leadership which was an economically powerful minority and part
of an all-India majority. These movements, both Hindu and Muslim, were
important contributing factors[23] to the deterioration of Hindu-Muslim
relations, with unity being the main fatality.[24]

Postexilic Judah—Conflict and Identity

The exile and postexile periods are known for conflict, chaos and threat.
The nature of the conflict and the identity of the conflicted parties differ
between accounts.[25] The protagonists include Judahites and Samaritans,[26]
returning exiles and those left behind in Palestine,[27] Zadokites (pro-tem-
ple) and Visionaries (anti-temple, disenfranchised Levites and those left
in the land),[28] the elect versus the non-elect and anti-elect.[29] The issues
of conflict included temple construction, worship, priesthood, social and

21. Started by Maulana Muhammad Ilyas in 1923. Its primary goal was to convey
shariat based guidance to followers of Islam. Using a vernacular translation of the
Quran it encouraged observance of the Islamic law, and practice, prayer, fasting, dress-
ing, modest marriage celebrations. Arabic *Madrassas* and *Maktabs* were established
and mosques were built to impart religious education and to equip every student with
skill to become an effective transmitter of Islam. "Chapter 3," 83.

22. Started by S. D. Kitchlew in 1923, to encourage the organization of political
groups to play a more active role in the affairs of the country. Directed both against the
government and the Hindus, it promoted Muslim identity. "Chapter 3," 88.

23. "Chapter 3," 89.

24. Jalal, *Self and Sovereignty*, 258.

25. Cf. Bedford, *Temple Restoration in Early Achaemenid Judah*, 11.

26. Rowley, "The Samaritan Schism in Legend and History," 215; compare Hensel
who suggests a different paradigm in "On the Relationship of Judah and Samaria in
Post-exilic Times."

27. Smith, *Religion of the Landless*, 179–200; Rom-Shiloni, *Exclusive Inclusivity*.

28. Hanson, *The Dawn of the Apocalyptic*.

29. Kaminsky, "Israel's Election and the Other," 18.

religious degeneration of those who remained in Palestine, and other social and economic issues (eunuchs, famine, foreigners). The period also saw some of the clearest articulations of Israelite and non-Israelite relations and the threat that the presence of non-Israelite influences had on the cohesion of the Israelite community, depicted in the prohibitions against mixed marriages in Ezra and Nehemiah. These postexilic texts reflect various self-conceptions and examples of belonging and attest to the discourse involved in the constitution of a postexilic community.[30] Identity was a contested issue, and the period was one in which "imagining the Other was a continual process deeply involved in and crucially facilitating ongoing negotiation of and re-negotiating of identity."[31]

In summary, it was a period that saw the strengthening of identity against the backdrop of exile, and differentiation between those taken into exile and those left in the land. Identity was constructed along lines that benefit a certain group of stakeholders, namely the decisive community comprised of returnees, the *golah* for whom the exile was a fundamental and self- defining experience.[32] Drawn from among those who were wealthy and influential, and from among the priestly classes, they were in many ways an extension of the Persian empire but indigenous/ with ancestry to/in the land of Judah. They were returned to the land to pursue and to further the colonial project of the Persians by enforcing a colonial strategy that would be beneficial to them. They took advantage of the instability in internal boundaries; by employing concepts such as "holy seed," "purity," "separation" and "ritual" (Sabbath, sacrifice, reading of the Torah), among others, which were "linguistic guise[s] for the non-linguistic realities of reclaiming land rights, ethnic and religious discrimination, as well as social exclusion."[33] Hence a Judahite during the Persian period was a returnee seen as remnant, holy, pure (not married to a foreign woman),[34] righteous, loyal to the nation and who expressed

30. Häusl, *"Denkt nicht mehr an das Frühere!"*

31. Edelman, "Introduction," iii.

32. Cf. Camp's interesting discussion on the significance of space in the construction of identity in "Home of the Mother, Exile of the Father."

33. Vaka'uta, *Reading Ezra 9–10 Tu'a wise*, 139. See also Hoglund, "Achaemenid Imperial Administration," 380–453 (cited in Eskenazi, "Out from the Shadows," 35).

34. The question regarding the identity of the "women of the land/foreign wives" has been the subject of scholarly debates. Compare the NRSV translation of Ezra 9:1–2 with the JPS version. The JPS rendering states that the people of Israel had not separated themselves, "from the peoples of the land whose abhorrent practices *are like* those of the Canaanites, the Hittites. . ." Such a rendering leaves the actual ethnic

this loyalty through participation in the reconstruction of the temple, of the city, of reinstating worship and observance of ritual.

Other than the expression of disdain against foreign women, these texts say very little about the Israelite woman and her identity and to what extent her experience was considered in the construction of nationalism. Women's experience is rarely if ever regarded as the starting point for such constructions or even for understanding the experience of colonization and the resistance to it. The construction of nation has always been a heteromale project, a community of fraternal relationships based on "masculinized memory, masculinized humiliation and masculinized hope."[35] It has always been about the emasculation and subjugation of men within an imperial context. While women are the bearers of the nation, they are denied any agency in the construction of identity or nation. The very elided presence of women signified their very absence. The common theme of the nation as female, which implies the gendering of the citizen as male, sets limits on the forms of belonging available to women. Can one assume that holiness, maintenance of purity, observance of ritual was also imposed on Judahite women? It is not clear what contributions women might have made to the reconstruction of temple and nation. It is more likely that a woman's political relation to the nation was engulfed by her social relation to a man through marriage. Hence, we have texts such as Prov 31:10–31 that allude to the fact that the woman's contribution to nation building was confined to the domestic sphere, the administration and maintenance of home and the wellbeing of husband and children.

Masculinities in Colonial India and Post-exilic Judah

Masculinity is socially, politically, and religiously constructed and hence one can discern competing forms of masculinity at any given time; but there is a form of masculinity that is dominant and hegemonic. Colonialism is a highly "gendered process" and "driven by a gendered process of subordination."[36] Colonization therefore impacts the masculinity of both the colonizer and the natives. The British Public School system instilled in their men what has been termed "muscular Christianity," and "moral 'manliness,'" through which colonialism came to be identified as divine

---

background of the women unspecified.

35. Enloe, *Bananas, Beaches and Bases*, 44.

36. Dasgupta and Gokulsingh, "Introduction," 8.

calling as a rite of passage for 'real' men."[37] The masculinization of the British male resulted in the feminization of the natives which attributed feminine attributes to Indian Hindu male and thus lower further the feminine gender identity and overwrite "indigenous contexts where gender identities continued to be ambiguously inflected."[38]

The response of the Indian nationalist was to provide a counter image to refute this image and rejuvenate Indian masculinity. Hindu intelligentsia sought insight on manliness in traditional Indian texts while modern thinkers accepted the association between science and masculinity. The *shuddhi* and *sangathan* movements provided images of Hindu manliness that both bolster community identity and carry out a militant nationalist struggle. This was in opposition to the British construction of the Indian male as well as the principle of *Ahimsa* advocated by Gandhi,[39] which they believed emasculated the Hindu nation. They wanted a society organized into a force that would "give blow for blow with equal mercilessness."[40] Physical prowess was the remedy against the colonial influences which was bolstered by fear of and anger against the growing strength of the Muslims. Conversion to Islam or Christianity was said to lead to loss of power, weakness and misery which could be reversed, and manliness restored through *shuddhi*. This emphasis on physique promoted the martial spirit amongst them. Military schools, gymnasiums, training in boxing flourished with *sangathan* strengthening the emphasis on body building, wrestling and lathi-wielding.[41]

The idea of the Hindu warrior was an ideological commonality across movements fighting against colonization. The image was rooted as Banerjee suggests in "a notion of hegemonic masculinity defined by attributes of decisiveness, aggression, muscular strength and a willingness to engage in battle . . . opposed to a notion of femininity that is defined by traits such as weakness, non-violence, compassion and a willingness to compromise."[42]

37. Srivastava, "Sane Sex," 32.

38. Srivastava, "Sane Sex," 33–34.

39. Gandhi's attempt to reverse notions of femininity and masculinity by his emphasis upon "feminine" strengths was rejected by militant Hindu organizations. Virtues of docility, tolerance, and peace were dropped in favor of the self-reliant militant hero. Cf. Gupta, *Sexuality, Obscenity, Community,* 233.

40. Gupta, *Sexuality, Obscenity, Community,* 233.

41. Gupta, *Sexuality, Obscenity, Community,* 234.

42. Banerjee, "Armed Masculinity," 65.

The long experience of imperialism and colonization by succes-
sive foreign powers influenced and configured ideas of masculinities in
Judah. As colonized subject it had to define itself against a supposedly
"effeminate colonial other" and, on the other hand, create a masculine
cultural space where it could resist this feminization. Given that it was in
loggerheads with terms set by the varied colonial powers, its nationalist
response while incorporating the ideals of hegemonic masculinities was
also varied. Israel did not always replicate colonial ideas but was itself
an imaginative configuration of nationalist myths and icons based on
conventional cultural ideas aimed at confronting foreign colonial rule.

Hegemonic masculinity[43] (masculinity entwined with power) was
complex in ancient Israel. Biblical hegemonic masculinity is a "consistent phenomenon" that requires analysis.[44] Following the lead of David
Clines,[45] scholars have provided an inventory of traits[46] that might help
us construct biblical masculinity (which is a volatile and shifting negotiation of several factors).[47]

Notions of masculinity in the literature from postexilic Judah did
not emerge in a vacuum. They unfolded against a context of political and
economic anxiety that may have heightened the prominence of particular types of masculinity. They yielded images of the Hebrew male as a
combination of both a fighter (valorizing physical strength) and spiri-
tual/religious person incorporating ideas of spiritual/religious strength
and moral courage. The type of masculinity that seems to dominate
postexilic literature is advocated by the returnees from exile and the male
body became the site on which they negotiated their religious and cultural concerns. I also suggest that the early post-exile period (under the
Persian regime) was a period of emerging religious nationalism which

43. Carrigan, Connell and Lee, "Toward a New Sociology of Masculinity."

44. Oakland, "Requiring Explanation," 482.

45. Clines in "David the Man" identifies the following traits in David: active warrior,
verbal prowess, persuasiveness, great beauty, bonding with other men and music lover.

46. Haddox identifies honor (to protect and provide for family and those beyond,
hospitality, honesty, and forthright speech), potency (skill in warfare, in leadership,
and in the sexual realm, physical wholeness and autonomy), and wisdom (good judgment and appropriate action) as possible springboards to understand constructions of
masculinity in the Hebrew Bible. She concludes that all these need to be accompanied
by submission to God. Hence "biblical masculinity can be seen as countercultural,
resisting the drive to complete power." Haddox, "Is There a 'Biblical Masculinity'?," 13.
See also Haddox, "Masculinity Studies of the Hebrew Bible."

47. Oakland, "Requiring Explanation," 482.

saw an emphasis on a form of militancy that was spiritual and moral, expressed with terms such as—holy, pure, strict observance of the sabbath, submission to YHWH, the Torah, the Temple, which in the latter period (Greek), was combined with the "warrior" and the emphasis on raw power and physical strength (Maccabees). As extensions of the Persian empire, early returnees saw no benefit or did not have the power to organize themselves in military fashion for the "Persian kings were brutal in their treatment of nations that were disloyal."[48] Adopting the strategy they did, they were able to regain and consolidate power within the land, while profiting from the handouts of the Persian government for being loyal subjects. Effeminized as colonized subjects in the public sphere, and still very much under the imperial gaze, they could only respond by asserting their masculinity in the inner world of Judah (domestic space). Manliness was therefore understood as creation of the loyal subject— devoted to structures of religion and thereby faithful to the collective nation. The nation would be served in their role as loyal, pure, and holy individuals submissive to God and the Temple. Although the image of masculinity focused on male bodies, it is plausible that some exceptional women could also embody these traits of the masculine Israelite (Esther, Judith, Susannah). But the foreign woman deserved special mention.

Foreign Woman: The Converted

The abductions of Hindu women came to be viewed as a characteristic Muslim activity. Hindu publicists used the figure of the pure, victimized and the abducted Hindu woman to promote an identity agenda, emphasizing fear of a common enemy, and stories were written to buttress this idea and to describe the difficulties experienced by the abducted woman.[49] Gupta suggests that writing novels and stories about abductions of Hindu women, sensationalizing cases of abduction by Muslims and metamorphizing the abducted Hindu woman into a sacred and violated symbol of the Hindu community was an orchestrated campaign by Hindu communalists.[50]

48. Perdue, Carter, and Baker, *Israel and Empire*, 110.

49. For example, *Pinjar*—a 1950 Punjabi *novel* by noted poet and novelist Amrita Pritam. It is the *story* of a Hindu girl, Puro, abducted by a Muslim man, Rashid; Puro's parents refuse to accept the defiled girl when she manages to escape from Rashid's home.

50. Gupta, *Sexuality, Obscenity, Community*, 243–66. The partition of India and Pakistan in 1947 saw thousands of women from both sides of the religious divide and many

These stories of abduction were set against the heroic Hindu male who courted the Muslim woman with romance, not abduction.[51] These stories of love and romance between a Hindu male and a Muslim woman provided entertainment, titillation, and a sense of jubilation.[52] The conversion of Muslim women to Hinduism was encouraged though there were few instances of Muslim women converting, but the point being made was that Hindu males were "recovering" Muslim women for something better.[53] The issue was how to enlarge the Hindu fold—and this can be done through the seduction and conversion of the Muslim woman. This rhetoric about absorption of the Muslim woman into the Hindu fold was complemented by an aggressiveness towards and humiliation of the woman of the "other." The conversion of the Muslim woman was encouraged and so the instruction was to abduct Muslim women not for adultery, but *shuddhi*.

Abduction of women during conflict and engaging in a form of genocidal rape is a well-known fact in the Hebrew Bible (Deut 21: 10–14; Numb 31).[54] Women seen as war booty were abducted for sexual pleasure, but also for keeping the line of the tribe alive (Judges 21). Most of these instances were violent abductions and in large numbers—32,000 (Num 31: 35), 400 (Judges 21: 12). The ethnicity or religious belonging of these women did not matter since they were booty and would enable an increase in the numbers of the tribe.

But the foreign woman who is not part of war booty is a contentious character within the Hebrew Bible, especially the one (Jezebel) who resisted attachment to the God of Israel. The one welcomed into the fold was

Sikh women abducted and forced into conversion with women also being complicit in these abductions. Cf. Menon and Bhasin, "Recovery, Rupture, Resistance," WS2-WS11.

51. Cf. Pandey Bechan Sharma, also known by his pen name "Ugra" who wrote several novels uplifting social causes and championing the cause of nationalism. His 1926 social romance novel, titled *Cand hasīnoṁ ke khutūt* (Letters of Some Beautiful People),is an example of a Muslim woman who marries a Hindu male and campaigns against the Islamic culture.

52. Gupta, *Sexuality, Obscenity, Community*, 241.

53. It is significant that Muslim women were asked to give up certain Islamic customs such as the burial of the dead, *nikah*, visiting dargahs and circumcision, rather than the imparting of Hindu religious knowledge to new converts. The movement was motivated much less by the desire to promote spirituality and religious values than by strong anti-Muslim passion. Gupta, "Articulating Hindu Masculinity and Femininity," 729.

54. Rey, "Reexamination of the Foreign Female Captive"; Niditch, "War, Women, and Defilement in Numbers 31."

the foreign woman who was willing to attach herself (Ruth, Rahab) both to the people and to the God of Israel. The short story of Ruth tells the story of a Moabite widow who follows her widowed mother-in-law back to Judah and is subsequently married to Boaz and becomes the ancestor of King David. It has been argued that the book was composed as a polemic in post-exilic times to counter Ezra and Nehemiah's condemnation[55] and prohibition[56] of exogamy with non-Israelites.[57] That view maintains that Ruth's status as David's grandmother legitimates marriage to foreign women.

Is this the only motive for such a story in the Hebrew Bible? Can we ascribe another agenda in the light of the Indian use of such stories? Could the book of Ruth have been written to showcase another way in which foreign woman could be co-opted into the Israelite fold especially when there was resistance to conversion by foreign women? The story is carefully crafted to stress the camaraderie between the two women, and the lack of resistance on Ruth's part to any suggestion made by Naomi with 1:16–17 understood as love, and loyalty of Ruth for Naomi. A story such as Ruth endorses images of heroism, kindness, romance all without treachery, cowardice, force or abduction and complicit in all this, is Naomi. It signifies control, conquest, subjugation and victory over foreign women—made particularly persuasive because it did not involve coercion and suppression, a strategy for absorbing the foreign woman into the fold and into the faith.

Conceiving the Other—
Foreign Woman as Evil and a Seductress

The rhetoric of assimilation of the foreign woman into the Israelite fold was complemented by an aggressiveness towards and humiliation of this woman of the Other, especially if she resisted absorption. Communal

55. "Then Ezra the priest stood up and said to them, "You have trespassed and married foreign women, and so increased the guilt of Israel" (Ezra 10:10).

56. "In those days also, I saw Jews who had married women of Ashdod, Ammon, and Moab; and half of their children spoke the language of Ashdod, and they could not speak the language of Judah, but spoke the language of various peoples. And I contended with them and cursed them and beat some of them and pulled out their hair; and I made them take an oath in the name of God, saying, "You shall not give your daughters to their sons, or take their daughters for your sons or for yourselves" (Neh 13:23–25).

57. Farmer, "Ruth," 383; Jones, *Reading Ruth in the Restoration Period*, 9.

identity has to be built in opposition to the Other and the image of the seductress, prostituting foreign woman was also evoked aggressively in colonial India. The picture of the violent, prostituting woman gained significance, strengthened shared prejudices and justified *Shuddhi* and *Sangathan*. Gupta calls attention to pamphlets that portrayed Islam as using prostitutes for the purpose of proselytizing.[58] Muslim women leaders, begums and queens became easy targets in the press. The most notable among them were the Begums of Bhopal, a dynasty of four powerful women (1819–1926) and inspirational figures who fought against patriarchal norms to create their own destiny. They had to counter and negotiate both the British and the men in their communities to acknowledge women's right to political power and to accept them as rulers. They asserted themselves in public life, trained in the martial arts and engaged in battle when needed, encouraged the arts, and led in projects (education) for the wellbeing and welfare of their subjects.[59] Identified as the "daughters of reform" within the Islamic world, they contributed to the reformist discourse and built "on traditional norms in order to introduce incremental change" for the betterment of Muslim women.[60] Yet, these women, especially the last Begum of Bhopal, Nawab Sultan Jahan Begum (1858–1930, reigned 1901–1926), were demonized and demeaned as dangerous and branded as prostitutes. In and through the attack on them, the Hindu community imagined the defilement of the enemy community.

This treatment of the Muslim woman and female leader is reminiscent of Jezebel the "bad girl" (1 Kgs 17–19) by Hebrew writers. There is no woman with a poorer reputation than Jezebel, the ancient Phoenician queen who is said to have corrupted a nation. As one who met one of the ghastliest fates in the Bible, her name alone has come to represent sexual promiscuity and depravity. Even so, a lot has been written about her. She was framed by two factors—her identity as a foreigner and her worship of Baal—besides the common discriminatory attitudes against all women.

Like the pamphlets written against Muslim women, Hebrew authors malign Jezebel's Phoenician origins and made her suspect as one who uses sexual prowess for her own benefit. She was considered dangerous because she breaches the borders of the native society as a sexual associate/partner and as counselor of a man who held near absolute power. Jezebel

58. Gupta, *Sexuality, Obscenity, Community*, 242.
59. Shaikh, "The Begums of Bhopal."
60. Hurley, *Contesting Seclusion*.

was strong, independent and courageous, and as wife of Ahab and queen she was a danger to the stability of the state. She had to be maligned so she did not wreak influence on other women; and men had to be warned of the dangers of foreign women of which Jezebel was the prototype.

Scholars have maintained through textual analysis that she was framed by the Deuteronomic Historian to be consistent with the demands and expectations of the priestly and scribal elite's stress on religious fidelity to Yahweh, expressed through ethnic exclusivity called "purity." Jezebel never converted to Yahwism, and hence was singled out as the ultimate Baal worshipper to be avoided. Alexander Fore has convincingly shown from his analysis of 1 Kgs 21 that the verses pertaining to Jezebel were inserted later, most possibly in the fifth century BCE.[61] Yet centuries of interpretation and tradition have buried this woman under mounds of spite, hatred, ridicule, and suspicion.

Representing femininity that turns its wiles against YHWH and luring Ahab to his doom, Jezebel encapsulated the worst scenario the reformers could envision.[62] "Misogyny rooted in the primordial otherness of female sexuality, kept dancing at the edge of the author's consciousness, tempting them to blame this woman for the wickedness of the realm."[63] These are obvious dynamics in the Jezebel stories. More subtle are the plays on fertility religion and the indications that femininity is opposed to the true God.

Invoking images of the evil regime of a Muslim woman/Phoenician princess who did not conform to norms of Hindu/Judahite patriarchy helped supply a subtext to the idea that women rulers were calamitous, more so if they were Muslim/foreign. "Political power if conceded to women, could create havoc, it was much better to keep men in charge and women under their control."[64]

Militarizing Women— Woman as Chaste, Pure, and Sister in Arms

Religion, caste, and class mediate gender through women becoming agents of violence against Muslims/non-Israelites. Reimagining the

61. Fore, "The Vineyard of Naboth."
62. Pippin, *Apocalyptic Bodies*, 32–42.
63. Carmody, *Biblical Woman*, 52.
64. Gupta, *Sexuality, Obscenity, Community*, 242.

Hindu within the community was intended to make women active and consenting constituents of a communalised community.

The story of Judith in the Apocrypha presents a model for gender boundary crossing in the world of Hellenised Judaism. It is a very Jewish story giving hope in the post-Maccabean period. She reinvented Israelite identity around the issue of gender at a time when the Jewish community was confronted by the overpowering influence of Hellenism and their nation threatened by Greek invaders.[65] Judith is an excellent example of the weak overthrowing the strong, of females usurping male power, and she also represents the powerless since she is a widow.[66] She is the masculinized warrior defining women's participation in the ideological work on masculine Judaism. Her participation is tamed by the erasure of visible markers of her sexuality—she is a widow, who dresses as a widow until she sets off on this mission. She uses her sexuality, chastely I might add, to behead Holofernes and thereby questions his masculinity. But she returns to her pure, uncorrupted and widowed life when the mission is completed. She embodies two models of woman in the nation—the heroic woman and the masculinized celibate, chaste woman warrior, loyal to her husband even though he is no longer alive, and to the nation. She is an ideal model of faithful Israel by virtue of being named "Jew," faithful to Torah, and uses erotic power chastely. Her act is powerful given her marginal status as woman and as widow; her act of courage is celebrated.

Judith's story is akin to legends and myths of brave Rajput and Aryan woman disseminated by Hindu movements.[67] These stories were invoked to emphasize both *pativrata* (loyalty to husband) and heroism.[68] To defend their honor and chastity, they were encouraged to take arms against Muslims. As fighters, these women freed from traditional restrictions, project warrior strength onto the nation. Through stories such as of Judith and the Indian warrior women, women are invited to channel their power, embrace their feminine traits (not as limiting but as empowering), while emulating their warrior mentality. They are submerged in images of masculinity and empowered as agents of violence. They are

---

65. Esler, "Ludic History in the Book of Judith," 139.

66. Wilson, "Pugnacious Precursors and the Bearer of Peace," 455.

67. Jhansi Rani Laxmibai, a leader in the rebellion of 1857 against the British in what is now known as India's first battle for independence, is one such figure.

68. Gupta, *Sexuality, Obscenity, Community*, 237.

sisters in arms! As sisters, the women warriors are de-sexed and help the idea of an activist masculinity.[69]

Judith is eventually domesticated and colonized since she resists neither patriarchy nor racism (against Gentiles), nor class within her own community. Once peace is restored, Judith "withdraws from the public sphere to the silence and privacy of her home."[70] She works within the framework of patriarchy and continues to be controlled and monitored by societal structures. The Hindu woman was invited to be a part of the *Sangathan* on the premise that her chastity and her honor need protection. So, while she was an agent for the movement, she was also a victim that needed protection. By co-opting her into the movement, both these roles came under the observation and scrutiny of the movement.

In Conclusion

Both postexilic Judah and Hindu nationalists constructed strict and strictly enforced definitions of masculinity and femininity in response to the other—foreigner/Muslim. Gender was used to sharpen differences and define the identity of the community. Women were therefore both "active and passive markers of communal difference"; they were not simply by-products of history; they acted and were acted.[71] The identity of the community though described in male terms was construed and inscribed in relation to women whether Israelite or non-Israelite, Hindu, or Muslim. Gendered discourses constrain the role of women in the national imaginary to be supporters, nurturers and sisters of an androcentric notion of "nation," rather than themselves constituting the nation. When identity, especially that of the male is construed on the basis of religious ideals, women are limited, and gendered power imbalances become pronounced and women from both within and outside the community pay with their bodies.

69. Gupta, *Sexuality, Obscenity, Community*, 233.
70. Dube, "Rahab says Hello to Judith," 67.
71. Gupta, *Sexuality, Obscenity, Community*, 266.

Bibliography

Banerjee, Sikata. "Armed Masculinity, Hindu Nationalism and Female Political Partici pation in India: Heroic Mothers, Chaste Wives and Celibate Warriors." *International Feminist Journal of Politics* 8 (2006) 62–83.

Banerjee, Sikata. *Make Me a Man! Masculinity, Hinduism, and Nationalism in India.* SUNY Series in Religious Studies. Albany: State University of New York, 2005.

Bedford, Peter Ross. *Temple Restoration in Early Achaemenid Judah.* Journal for the Study of Judaism Supplements 65. Leiden: Brill, 2001.

Camp, Claudia V. "Home of the Mother, Exile of the Father: Gender and Space in the Construction of Biblical Identity." In *Contesting Religious Identities: Transformations, Disseminations, and Mediations*, edited by Bob Becking et al., 18–38. Studies in the History of Religions 156. Leiden: Brill, 2017.

Carmody, Denise Lardner. *Biblical Woman: Contemporary Reflections on Scriptural Texts.* New York: Crossroad, 1992.

Carrigan, Tim, R. W. Connell, and J. Lee. "Toward a New Sociology of Masculinity." In *The Making of Masculinities: The New Men's Studies*, edited by Harry Brod, 63–100. Boston: Allen & Unwin, 1987.

"Chapter 3: Emergence of Muslim Communal Organizations." https://shodhganga. inflibnet.ac.in/bitstream/10603/113141/5/05_chapter%203.pdf.

Clines, David J. A. "David the Man: The Construction of Masculinity in the Hebrew Bible." In *Interested Parties: The Ideology of Writers and Readers of the Hebrew Bible*, 212–43. Journal for the Study of the Old Testament Supplement Series 205. Sheffield: Sheffield Academic, 1995.

Dasgupta, Rohit K., and K. Moti Gokulsingh. "Introduction: Perceptions of Masculinity and Challenges to the Indian Male." In *Masculinity and Its Challenges in India: Essays on Changing Perceptions*, 5–26. Jefferson, NC: McFarland, 2014.

Dube, Musa W. "Rahab Says Hello to Judith: A Decolonizing Feminist Reading." In *Toward a New Heaven and Earth: Festschrift for Elisabeth Schüssler Fiorenza*, edited by Fernando F. Segovia, 54–72. Maryknoll, NY: Orbis, 2004.

Edelman, Diana V. "Introduction." In *Imagining the Other and Constructing Israelite Identity in the Early Second Temple Period*, edited by Ehud Ben Zvi and Diana V. Edelman, xiii–xx. Library of Hebrew Bible/Old Testament Studies 456. London: Bloomsbury, 2014.

Enloe, Cynthia. *Bananas, Beaches and Bases: Making Feminist Sense of International Politics.* Updated edition with a new Preface. Berkeley: University of California Press, 1990.

Eskenazi, Tamara C. "Out from the Shadows: Biblical Women in the Postexilic Era." *Journal for the Study of the Old Testament* 54 (1992) 25–43.

Esler, Philip F. "Ludic History in the Book of Judith: The Reinvention of Israelite Identity." *Biblical Interpretation* 10 (2002) 107–43.

Farmer, Kathleen. "Ruth." In *The New Interpreters Study Bible*, edited by Walter J. Harrelson, 383–84. Nashville: Abingdon, 2003.

Fore, Alexander. "The Vineyard of Naboth: The Origin and Message of the Story." *Vetus Testamentum* 38 (1988) 89–104.

Gupta, Charu. "Articulating Hindu Masculinity and Femininity: 'Shuddhi' and 'Sangathan' Movements in United Provinces in the 1920s." *Economic and Political Weekly* 33/13 (Mar 26–Apr 3, 1998) 727–35.

Gupta, Charu. *Sexuality, Obscenity, Community: Women, Muslims, and the Hindu Public in Colonial India*. Delhi: Permanent Black, 2001.

Haddox, Susan E. "Is There a 'Biblical Masculinity'? Masculinities in the Hebrew Bible." *Word & World* 36 (2016) 5–14.

———. "Masculinity Studies of the Hebrew Bible: The First Two Decades." *Currents in Biblical Research* 14 (2016) 176–206.

Hanson, Paul D. *The Dawn of the Apocalyptic: The Historical and Sociological Roots of Jewish Apocalyptic Eschatology*. Philadelphia: Fortress, 1979.

Häusl, Maria, ed. *"Denkt nicht mehr an das Frühere!" Begründungsressourcen in Esra/ Nehemia und Jes 40–66 im Vergleich*. Bonner biblische Beitäge 184. Göttingen: Vandenhoek & Ruprecht, 2018.

Hensel, Benedikt. "On the Relationship of Judah and Samaria in Post-Exilic Times: Farewell to the Conflict Paradigm." *Journal for the Study of the Old Testament* 44 (2019) 19–42.

Hoglund, Kenneth G. "Achaemenid Imperial Administration in Syria–Palestine and the Missions of Ezra and Nehemiah." PhD diss., Duke University, 1989.

Hurley, Siobhan Lambert. "Contesting Seclusion: The Political Emergence of Muslim Women in Bhopal, 1901–1930." PhD diss., University of London, 1998.

Iqbal, Afzal. *The Life and Times of Mohamed Ali: An Analysis of the Hopes, Fears, and Aspirations of Muslim India from 1878–1931*. 2nd ed. Lahore: Institute of Islamic Culture, 1979.

Jackson, Ronald L., III. *Scripting the Black Masculine Body: Identity, Discourse, and Racial Politics in Popular Media*. SUNY Series, The Negotiation of Identity. New York: New York University Press, 2006.

Jalal, Ayesha. *Self and Sovereignty: Individual and Community in South Asian Islam since 1850*. London: Routledge, 2000.

Jones, Edward Allen, III. *Reading Ruth in the Restoration Period: A Call for Inclusion*. Library of Hebrew Bible/Old Testament Studies 604. London: Bloombury, 2016.

Kaminsky, Joel S. "Israel's Election and the Other in Biblical, Second Temple, and Rabbinic Thought." In *The "Other" in Second Temple Judaism: Essays in Honor of John J. Collins*, edited by Daniel C. Harlow et.al., 17–30. Grand Rapids: Eerdmans, 2011.

Menon, Ritu, and Kamala Bhasin. "Recovery, Rupture, Resistance: Indian State and Abduction of Women during Partition." *Economic and Political Weekly* 28.17 (1993) WS2-WS11.

Merleau-Ponty, Maurice. *Phenomenology of Perception*. Translated by Colin Smith. London: Routledge, 1962.

Nanda, B. R. *Road to Pakistan: The Life and Times of Mohammed Al Jinnah*. London: Routledge, 2010.

Niditch, Susan. "War, Women, and Defilement in Numbers 31." In *Women, War, and Metaphor: Language and Society in the Study of the Hebrew Bible*, edited by Claudia V. Camp and Carole R. Fontaine, 39–57. Semeia 61. Atlanta: Scholars, 1993.

Oakland, Jorunn. "Requiring Explanation: Hegemonic Masculinities in the Hebrew Bible and Second Temple Traditions." *Biblical Interpretation* 23 (2015) 479–88.

Perdue, Leo G., and Warren Carter. *Israel and Empire: A Postcolonial History of Israel and Early Judaism*. Edited by Coleman A. Baker. London: Bloomsbury, 2015.

Pippin, Tina, *Apocalyptic Bodies: The Biblical End of the World in Text and Image*. London: Routledge, 1999.

Rey, M. I. "Reexamination of the Foreign Female Captive: Deut 21:10–14 as a Case of Genocidal Rape." *Journal of Feminist Studies in Religion* 32 (2016) 37–53.

Rom-Shiloni, Dalit. *Exclusive Inclusivity: Identity Conflicts between the Exiles and the People Who Remained (6th–5th centuries BCE).* Library of Hebrew Bible/Old Testament Studies 543. New York: Bloomsbury, 2013.

Rowley, H. H. "The Samaritan Schism in Legend and History." In *Israel's Prophetic Heritage: Studies in Honor of James Muilenburg,* edited by Bernhard W. Anderson and Walter Harrelson. New York: Harper, 1962.

Sarkar, Sumit. *Beyond Nationalist Frames: Postmodernism, Hindu Fundamentalism, History.* Bloomington: Indiana University Press, 2002.

Sarvakar, Veer Damodar. *Essentials of Hindutva.* Bombay: Veer Savarkar Prakashan, 1923.

Shaikh, Hiba. "The Begums of Bhopal: A Dynasty of Powerful Women." Feminism in India (May 25, 2018). https://feminisminindia.com/2018/05/25/begums-of-bhopal-female-dynasty/.

Smith, Daniel L. *Religion of the Landless: The Social Context of the Babylonian Exile.* Bloomington, IN: Meyer-Stone, 1989.

Srivastava, Sanjay. "'Sane Sex', the Five-Year Plan Hero and Men on Footpaths and Gated Communities: On the Cultures of Twentieth-Century Masculinity." In *Masculinity and Its Challenges in India: Essays on Changing Perceptions,* edited by Rohit K Dasgupta and K Moti Gokulsingh, 27–53. Jefferson, NC: McFarland, 2014.

Tharoor, Shashi. "Veer Savarkar: The Man Credited with Creating Hindutva Didn't Want It Restricted to Hindus." *The Print* (26 February 2018) https://theprint.in/pageturner/excerpt/veer-savarkar-hindutva-india/38073/.

Tripati, R. C., and Purnima Singh, "Prologue." In *Perspectives on Violence and Othering in India,* edited by R. C. Tripati and Purnima Singh. Delhi: Springer, 2016.

Vaka'uta, Nāsili. *Reading Ezra 9–10 Tu'a Wise: Rethinking Biblical Interpretation in Oceania.* International Voices in Biblical Studies 3. Atlanta: Society of Biblical Literature, 2011.

Walsh, Carey. "Women on the Edge." In *Imagining the Other and Constructing Israelite Identity in the Early Second Temple Period,* edited by Ehud Ben Zvi and Diana V. Edelman, 122–43. Library of Hebrew Bible/Old Testament Studies 456. London: Bloomsbury, 2014.

Wilson, Brittany E. "Pugnacious Precursors and the Bearer of Peace: Jael, Judith, and Mary in Luke 1:42." *Catholic Biblical Quarterly* 68 (2006) 436–56.

10

Reading Her Story in His Narration

Zuleika and Her Otherness in Genesis 39

SWEETY HELEN CHUKKA

It is not sexuality which haunts society,

but society which haunts the body's sexuality.

—M. GODELIER[1]

NARRATIVES THAT CONCERN WOMEN in the book of Genesis unsettle the male world with their wisdom ways, subversive strategies, and transgressive ideologies. Most of these women's voices are buried under the narrator's voice; their voices are unearthed and sacralized either because they participate in God's promise to the patriarchs or for giving birth to male children who play a crucial role in a genealogy.

Feminist biblical scholars applaud female subjectivity and challenge prejudices in the narration and its reception. However, a woman like Potiphar's wife (hereafter called Zuleika[2]), due to her foreignness

1. Godelier, "The Origins of Male Domination," 17 (cited in Levinson, "An-Other Woman").

2. Jewish and Islamic traditions named Potiphar's (Aziz in Qur'an) wife Zuleika/

and "outrageous" behavior is treated by scholars as feisty,[3] villainy,[4] willy,[5] sexually intense. Reflections on Gen 39 have traditionally focused on the virtues of Joseph. While Zuleika is portrayed as a seductress ("negative" temptress),[6] Joseph was elevated to a wise interpreter of dreams. According to the narrator, Joseph found favor in God's sight (Gen 39:2,3), in Potiphar's sight (39:4), in Zuleika's sight (39:7), and in the chief jailer's sight (39:21).[7]

The Qur'an allocates an entire Sura discussing the events between Joseph and Zuleika. The details in Sura 12:23–32, 50–53 essentially depict the "craftiness" of Zuleika, yet it also records her remorse for such activity.[8] A Midrash suggests Zuleika's persistence to "seduce" Joseph was because "the court astrologers told her that she would be the mother of Joseph's descendants."[9] However, the highest negativity ascribed to Zuleika is found in the biblical text.[10] This negativity could be due to her foreignness, her sexual desire and her "deception." This essay is vigilant to the narration of Zuleika's story in Gen 39. This vigilant reading unmasks the dynamics of power prevalent in the text (that subdues the voice of Zuleika in order to elevate the status of Joseph) and deconstructs the narrator's understanding of the foreign woman's sexuality.[11]

Zuleikha/Zelicah meaning "lovely and brilliant" (as well as Rāʿīl). See Goldman, *The Wiles of Women/the Wiles of Men*, 85; "The Book of Jasher."

3. McKay, "Confronting Redundancy as Middle Manager and Wife."

4. Frymer-Kensky, *Reading the Women of the Bible*, 74–77.

5. Goldman, *The Wiles of Women/the Wiles of Men*, 31–56.

6. Athalya Brenner-Idan, *The Israelite Woman*, 112.

7. Joseph's beauty is central to many in the rabbinic literature and the Qur'an. They give extensive details about the "assembly of ladies" scene. This scene legitimizes the actions of Zuleika (see Kugel, *In Potiphar's House*). In the following reading, my questions are embodied, and my perspectives are prejudiced towards Zuleika. Discussing the hyperfeminization of Joseph, Rachel E. Adelman juxtaposes Joseph with Esther. She discusses their Jewishness, their foreignness, their diaspora experience and focusses on how they "rise to power in foreign court" (Adelman, *The Female Ruse*, 198–230).

8. Sura 12:51 read "The king asked the women, 'What happened when you tried to seduce Joseph?' They said, 'God forbid! We know nothing bad of him!' and the governor's wife said, 'Now the truth is out: it was I who tried to seduce him—he is an honest man.'"

9. See Goldman, *The Wiles of Women/the Wiles of Men*, 38.

10. See Kugel, *In Potiphar's House*, 94.

11. Most scholars present Joseph as the central figure, Klaus-Peter Adam maintains that, the genre of Gen 39 is "a diaspora novella" that focusses on the individual who immigrates into Egypt—"If the main plot is the immigrant story, naturally the lead character gets the main attention. That is the simple rule of the genre" (private

Approaches to Genesis 39

The "seduction/attempted rape" of Joseph by Zuleika caught the attention of the early church fathers, who approached the text either morally, ideally or typologically.[12] Biblical scholars of the 20th and 21st centuries went beyond these three types.

For Alice Bach, "Getting at the suppressed story of the female in male-authored literature requires both filling the gaps in the narrative and reading the text for the patriarchal agenda that has shaped the telling of the story."[13] Scholars filled the gaps differently. Susan Tower Hollis studies the Potiphar's wife motif and "argues that it is also possible to view this 'negative' woman as effecting a positive change when the narrative includes a return or resurrection."[14] James L. Kugel engages in an ancient biblical interpretation by using "reverse engineering" as a strategy. For him, Biblical texts do not record everything and he fills the biblical narrative gaps using information available in extra biblical sources.[15] Alice Bach compares Gen 39 with the *Testament of Joseph* and states that "recollected, re-membered version in the *Testament of Joseph* . . . provides an opportunity to examine the literary effect of this new story created from the skeleton of the old."[16] Heather A. McKay employs management theory and social anthropology to build a "positive" reading of Rahpitop[17] (Zuleika) as a marginal, childless woman whose "primary goal was not power but pregnancy."[18] Robert C. Gregg engages the "early history of interpretation among Jews, Christians, and Muslims and opines that the questions arising from their interpretation sharpen the understanding of the biblical text."[19] Mindful of these works, I engage with the ambivalent spaces of the text and add another reading informed by my embodied Dalit experience.

---

e-mail). However, given the patriarchal context of the text that hardly records women's voices, I listen/excavate Her-story in HIStory.

12. Fee further Gregg, "Joseph with Potiphar's Wife."

13. Bach, "Breaking Free of the Biblical Frame-Up," 318.

14. Hollis, "The Woman in Ancient Examples of the Potiphar's Wife," 29.

15. Kugel, *In Potiphar's House*, 251.

16. Bach, "Breaking Free of the Biblical Frame-Up," 319.

17. McKay reverses 'Potiphar's' name and calls Potiphar's wife "Rahpitop" which in Egyptian means "Ra (or sun)-on head." See McKay, "Confronting Redundancy as Middle Manager and wife," 216.

18. McKay, "Confronting Redundancy as Middle Manager and Wife," 215.

19. Gregg, "Joseph with Potiphar's Wife," 326.

My Presuppositions

Scholars employ positive and negative approaches in analyzing Gen 39.[20] Common to these approaches is the polarization of Zuleika as villain and Joseph as a pious man, with a few who are sympathetic to Zuleika while affirming Joseph's righteousness. My approach consciously disengages with the dichotomy of Zuleika and Joseph and thus detach from a moral, ideal and typological reading. I here declare three presuppositions with which I read the text.

First, Gen 39 is a male-authored text that favors Joseph. The intentionality of the narrator in valorizing Joseph is apparent in the entire tale of Joseph, hence Gen 39 should not be read in isolation from Gen 37–50. To fulfill this goal, the narrator introduces Zuleika as a literary tool to elevate Joseph's position. Joseph is exalted for his faithfulness, righteousness, self-control and Zuleika is condemned for her sexual misconduct and deception. The narrator's bias in favor of Joseph is also apparent in his repeated claim that God was with Joseph (Gen 39:2,3,5, 21, 23). Gen 39:1–6, which is exclusively the narrator's report or introduction to what follows, mentions Yhwh five times. "The reader discovers that Yhwh is with Joseph (v. 2), his master knows Yhwh is with him (v. 3), Yhwh is the cause of Joseph's success (v. 3) and Yhwh has blessed the Egyptian's house and possessions (v.5)."[21]

Second, Joseph is portrayed by many scholars as the victim of sexual assault and they thereby explore the power dynamics. Tikva Frymer-Kensky sees Joseph at the bottom of the social ladder. She maintains that Joseph is "after all, her husband's slave."[22] Samuel Logan Ratnaraj from India reads Joseph as a Dalit.[23] Joseph is a pseudo-Dalit, who forgets that he was a Dalit and exploits his fellow Dalits when elevated to power in Egypt. Logan Ratnaraj asserts Joseph's Dalitness but denies him that identity for not participating in the liberative activity of his people. He says, "when the privileged Dalits are elevated socially and economically, they look down on their own people hiding their identity and betray

---

20. While McKay and Bailey offer positive interpretations of Potiphar's wife, Alice Ogden Bellis, Athalya Brenner etc. viewed Potiphar's wife negatively. See Bellis, *Helpmates, Harlots, and Heroes*.

21. Kaltner, *Inquiring of Joseph*, 27.

22. Frymer-Kensky, *Reading the Women of the Bible*, 75.

23. Ratnaraj, "Reconstructing the Dreamer Narrative."

other Dalits."[24] To the contrary, I do not see Joseph as a Dalit.[25] Dalits are less privileged and are considered uncompromisingly polluting, their success is vehemently undermined, and beauty was never their thing. Joseph has the promise of God; he is part of the power structure and controls the household of Potiphar. If he was enslaved, his "enslavement" was not real.[26] Writing from a much later period, the narrator projects the later experience of slavery into Joseph's experience. If there was any slavery in this text as others would see, it is condemnable.[27] Joseph, in Gen 39 and in the full narrative, was neither considered as a slave[28] nor was he treated as one; he comes from privileged lineage with whose names God identifies Godself. Joseph was never a man without privilege—he was temporarily de-robed of his privilege when he became a "Hebrew servant" but even in his predicaments he can neither be a representative of the slaves nor of the slavery system. Early church fathers like Ambrose present Joseph as a "mirror of purity."[29] Read from a Dalit perspective, purity does not make one marginalized; pollution does. Joseph, by being touchable, does not bear the marks of a Dalit.

Third, Zuleika is not a villain. Zuleika is referred to as the wife of the Egyptian guard Potiphar. We are not sure if she is an Egyptian herself. If she is an Egyptian, then she is the Other for the Jewish narrator.

24. Ratnaraj, "Reconstructing the Dreamer Narrative," 124.

25. I do not apologize for reading Her story. I read Gen 39 from a Dalit perspective. I consider Joseph as a non-Dalit because of his promise, power and privilege (denied to Dalits). This is not to undermine the experience of my African American colleagues who would like to read Joseph as a slave. I am simply reading from an Indian context.

26. I maintain that Joseph was not enslaved. That is not his embodied experience. I translate Hebrew root *qnh* as "ransomed" (traditionally "bought"). I argue that Potiphar ransomed Joseph from the Ishmaelites (cf. Gen 37:25ff).

27. In the book of Genesis, עֶבֶד is used more than 80 times. While NRSV interchanges "slave" and "servant" based on the context, JPS uses "servant" in all instances. In most of the occurrences, "servant" is implied when there is a reference to "subordinate/helper/assistant," who can be elevated to a higher rank. On the other hand, "slave" is implied to identify a person who is a possession (e.g., Gen 30:43). Slavery was widespread in the ANE.

28. Sepher HaYashar notes Joseph's presence in Egypt. In a conversation between Medanim and Potiphar regarding Joseph, Potiphar questions the "slave" status of Joseph and asks Medanim for proof that Joseph was a slave. Joseph's appearance doesn't convince Potiphar about his "slave" status (see "The Book of Jasher," chapter 44).

29 Gregg, "Joseph with Potiphar's Wife," 339.

If she is not an Egyptian, then she was probably treated as a slave within her own household.[30]

I imagine her as a female outsider who was not part of the promise and neither had the power[31] nor the privilege as Joseph did. I, therefore, do not assign any specific ethnicity to her. The male narrator undermines Zuleika as the villain and sets her against Joseph, the righteous one. In order to present and carry forward this "pure" image of Joseph, the narrator introduces a character who can be scapegoated. The minimal information available about Zuleika makes her a marginal character. She has no name, no ethnicity and perhaps no children. The narrator has not only marginalized her by not disclosing her information, but also allowed her to be demonized beyond repair.[32]

SthreeChesed Reading

For a close reading of Gen 39, I disengage in a legal, moral, ideal, and typological reading explored by biblical scholars. I, as a Dalit woman, claim Zuleika as an Other—eventually a Dalit, intend to seek justice and stand in solidarity with her in her shame and in her moment of vulnerability by expressing "loving kindness."[33] I employ *SthreeChesed* as a hermeneutical key to unlock the text.

The first part of *SthreeChesed*, is the Sanskrit word "Sthree"[34] which means "woman." It is commonly used in our vernacular bibles and

30. In Gen 41:45, Asenath is named as Joseph's wife. Pharaoh's daughter Asenath is named but Potiphar's wife is not.

31. McKay argues that Potiphar's wife has "much of his authority," (see McKay, "Confronting Redundancy as Middle Manager and Wife," 221).

32. I condemn sexual assault on any gender. Seeking sexual favor by force is unacceptable. In this essay, I argue that this story is not historical and has been fabricated to elevate Joseph and establish his "purity."

33. "When the *hesed* shown Esther is ascribed to her having pleased Hegai (Est 2:9) and to the king's loving her more than the other women (2:17), what is described is not an act but a situation that is not established by Esther's own actions" (Zobel, "Hesed," 49). As a Dalit, I presuppose that Zuleika is falsely charged by the narrator as having "deceived" her household and Potiphar by "fabricating" an incident. So, this loving kindness is an act of Dalit solidarity. Branding Dalit women as "witches" and "seductresses" is common in Indian context. In Oct 22, 2018, "a 70-year-old woman's tongue was chopped off after she was branded a witch in a Bihar village in Rohtas district" (https://www.firstpost.com/india/villagers-in-bihars-rohtas-brand-70-year-old-dalit-woman-a-witch-chop-her-tongue-off-police-probe-underway-5421591.html).

34. Anderson-Rajkumar coined "Sthreeology" as a term that combines feminist

despite its brahminical overtones, I use it as a tool. However, I disengage from the brahminical understanding of *Sthree* who is domesticated, who should be in *madi*, a pristine state, with limited sexual desires, with little interest in material things, devoting oneself to God and to husband. The expression *pathiye prathyaksha deivam* (God manifested in husband) is very common among brahmin women and I am inviting readers to disjoin from these brahminical overtones in understanding the character of a woman. The *Sthree* that I engage with is disengaged from any power, purity and privilege. Similar to Evangeline Rajkumar' assertion about the centrality of women's experiences to Sthreeology, Zuleika's experiences and silences play a crucial role in my reading. By affirming Zuleika as a *Sthree,* a word used only for "respectful" women, I acknowledge Zuleika as a "respectful" woman. Even though in a brahminical sense Zuleika is not in a pristine state (*madi*), and her non-compliance to the principle of *pathiye prathyaksha deivam* makes her less-*Sthree*, in my reading, she does not fall short of respect.

The second part of the *SthreeChesed, Chesed,* is the Hebrew word חסד translated as loving kindness or everlasting love. *Chesed* is employed as a call to move beyond the information offered by the text to engage in a creative imagination that gives the reader access to the unexplored ambiguous spaces in the text. Defying the narrator's interest in showing *chesed* to Joseph, I show *chesed to* Zuleika. I suggest that the narrator's phobia towards Zuleika was also projected onto Joseph. The combination of *Sthree* and *Chesed* is both an affirmation and a call. An affirmation of her respectfulness and a call to exhibit loving kindness amidst the harassment she receives from her interpreters. In this essay, I employ *Sthree-Chesed* as hermeneutical tool to show Zuleika loving kindness through my interpretive strategies.

Her Story in His Narration

Genesis 39 is positioned right after Judah's sexual encounter with Tamar in Gen 38. Wenham, Brayford, Niditch suggest that Gen 38 is an interpolation[35] and disjoin Gen 39 from the preceding chapters. Amos on the

---

and womanist perspectives to foreground the experiences of women. The primary source for Sthreeology are women's experiences. See Anderson-Rajkumar, "'God' in the light of Women's Experiences," 265.

35. See Wenham, *Genesis 16–50*, 377; Susan Brayford, *Genesis*, 402.

other hand sees Gen 39 intrinsically connected with Gen 37 and 38, with themes that are common to all three chapters. She maintains that "the three chapters have been introduced by the final example of the *toledoth* formula that describes the section as "the story of the family of Jacob."[36] The discussion on the relation of these chapters identify the intentionality of the narrator in positioning the text. Themes such as "deception, cultural otherness, woman's sexuality, garment"[37] converge in Gen 38 and 39 to underscore God's steadfast love to the patriarchs despite foreign women's interventions to thwart it. The narrator's agenda to valorize Joseph and his God in Gen 39 is a His (the narrator's, Joseph's and perhaps his God's too) story.

Genesis 39 is located in three different spaces—in an undisclosed space, in Potiphar's house, and in prison. Each space clarifies the events and reveals the biases of the narrator. Even though Joseph is an "outsider" to the space where the events take place, he is the prime focus and the story revolves around his beauty, his resistance to temptation, and God's guidance, in two sections.

Genesis 39:1–6

The narrator depicts Joseph as an attractive and upright young man. As the plot unfolds, Joseph is upgraded from being a foreigner to an overseer. Gen 39:1–6 introduces characters, personalities and events that unwind in Gen 39:7–23. It establishes Joseph's righteousness, his ruthless selling and divine providence.

Genesis 39 begins with a *toledoth* formula that is described as "the story of the family of Jacob."[38] The stories of Jacob's family exhibit literary unity and continuity. By depicting Judah and Joseph as vulnerable men in Gen 38 and 39, the narrator summons the readers to defend Jacob's descendants and reject foreign women. Sarna rightly notes the narrator's skillful elevation of Joseph's identity over against the Egyptian: "the national identity of Joseph's master is repeated three times for emphasis (vv. 1, 2, 5)."[39] Sarna believes that this emphasis is "probably because the sale of Joseph into Egyptian slavery sets the stage for the looming enslavement

36. Amos, "Genesis," 15.

37. Amos, "Genesis," 15.

38. Amos, "Genesis," 15.

39. Sarna, *Genesis*, 271.

and subsequent redemption of Israel."[40] For the narrator, Gen 39 is crucial in the tale of Joseph, for it complements the plot begun in Gen 37:8–10 where Joseph is elevated above his brothers and parents.

Genesis 39:1–6 records intricate details about Joseph and Potiphar. The narrator informs readers that Potiphar bought (קנה)[41] Joseph, neither Potiphar nor the narrator call Joseph a slave. Zuleika calls Joseph "the Hebrew servant" in Gen 39:17. He was designated successful (v.2), having God's presence (v.3), prospered (v. 3), found favor (v.4), was in charge (vv. 4, 6), overseer (vv. 4, 5), and blessed (v.5). These details describe Joseph's power and privilege dispute his being bought to be a slave. The Surah gives additional information:

> The Egyptian who bought him said to his wife, "Treat him well during his lodging. Perhaps he will be of benefit to us and we will take him as a son." Thus, did We establish Joseph in the land, and We taught him the interpretation of events. Allah controlled his affairs although most people do not know. When he reached maturity, We gave him wisdom and knowledge. Thus, do We reward those who are good. (Surah 12:21–22)

Joseph's success, favor from Yhwh/Allah and the favor he finds from Potiphar suggest that he was probably not bought as a slave but rather, that he was ransomed.

The narrator impresses upon the readers that Yhwh was with Joseph. In Gen 39:1–6, "the reader discovers that God is with Joseph (vv. 2, 3, 5)."[42] In ascribing all the credit to Yhwh, the narrator polarizes Israelites and Egyptians—Joseph prospered not because of the generosity of the master who ransomed him and gave him power but because Yhwh was with him. The narrator's bias towards Joseph is further disclosed in v. 6b. The events in 39:7–23 clarify the need for introducing Joseph's beauty in v. 6b.

---

40. Sarna, *Genesis,* 271.

41. The Qal form of קנה (bought) is used in several contexts in the Hebrew Bible. "The primary usage of the verb קנה is concrete and economic." The verb has been used in several occasions to refer to buying a slave (Gen 39:1; 47:19–20, 22–23; Exod 21:2 etc.). Though, the current text lays emphasis on Potiphar buying Joseph, the content of the text does not give any evidence to the "slave" status of Joseph. In the contemporary parlance, slavery meant all forms of exploitation, humiliation, confinement etc. Since the experience of Joseph does not correspond with his experience in the house of Potiphar, I do not consider him as a slave. As Dalit theologian Samuel Logon Ratnaraj proposes, Joseph is not a slave but the father of slavery. Cf. Kondasingu Jesurathnam et al., *Liberation Hermeneutics in the Indian Interpretation of the Bible,* 124–32.

42. Kaltner, *Inquiring of Joseph,* 27.

The second character introduced in Gen 39:1–6 is Potiphar. Except his association with Pharaoh, information about Potiphar is withheld. Two things are obvious about Potiphar: he is an officer/eunuch and captain of the guard. Sarna notes, "the full name and titles are here given to draw attention to the aristocratic nature of the household into which Joseph is sold."[43] If the narrator's intention was to introduce us to the household that Joseph entered, these details would have been elaborated as the narration progressed. The insignificance of his character in the tale is evident in the fewer details provided about him. One of the two details about Potiphar that are crucial for our reading is: he was an "eunuch" (given the Hebrew and Aramaic translation).[44] Brayford notes that Potiphar is already introduced in Gen 37:36 and translates the Septuagint τῷ σπάδοντι Φαραω, ἀρχιμαγείρῳ as "eunuch and chief butcher of Pharaoh." She adds, "the narrator again describes him as a eunuch and chief butcher but uses another Greek word ὁ εὐνοῦχος (eunuchos) to translate the Hebrew סָרִיס."[45] Carden identifies Joseph as queer and comments, "The city (Egypt) has long served as a place of refuge for queer people fleeing the confining homophobic environment of family and small town."[46] While Joseph's queerness is not obvious to me, Potiphar's is. The presence of eunuchs in the royal courts is not unique to Gen 39.[47]

In addition to the promise of God, Potiphar confers power, privilege and position on Joseph. The authority bestowed upon Joseph by Potiphar is noticeable in v. 6b, "he left everything that he had in the hand of Joseph. And he did not know anything but the food which he ate." Alter observes that the repetition of כל (everything), בית (house), יד (hand) connects the events.[48] ביד occurs in 39:1, 3–4, 6, 8, 12–13, 22–23 and denotes the authority given to Joseph by Potiphar and the chief jailer.[49]

---

43. Sarna, *Genesis*, 271.

44. Havea, "Sea-ing Ruth with Joseph's Mistress."

45. Brayford, *Genesis*, 402.

46. Carden, "Genesis."

47. The biblical texts records queer people holding positions of power in the royal courts—in Est 2:15 "keeper of women," or in Jer 52:25 "overseer of men"—but not the captain of the guard and the responsibility of the entire household as in Gen 39:1.

48. Huddlestun, "Divestiture, Deception, and Demotion," 59.

49. Huddlestun, "Divestiture, Deception, and Demotion," 59.

Genesis 39:7–23

Genesis 39:7–23 forms the crux of the Joseph and Zuleika narrative. The narrator now introduces Zuleika. She is introduced by her "actions" and by her relationship with Potiphar (as wife) and not by her name. Havea says, "The narrator does not care enough about a character to remember her or his actual name."[50] "Namelessness is lack of respect,"[51] hence Jewish and Islamic traditions name her Zuleika, a name that means "lovely and brilliant"; Zuleika is a suitable counterpart to Joseph who is "beautiful in form and fair in appearance."

While Joseph upgrades from pit(y) to power, Zuleika degrades from moral digression to deception. The intentionality of the narrator in inserting a tale which has equivalence in 13th century BCE Egyptian "Tale of Two Brothers"[52] dichotomizes masculinity and femininity. While Joseph is embraced, Zuleika is doubly Otherized—as a woman and a foreigner. This points to two dichotomies in the narrative: gender dichotomy (masculinity and femininity), and ethnic dichotomy (Jewish and foreign Other).

Dichotomy of Masculinity and Femininity

Joshua Levinson briefly summarizes the history of interpretation of the "seduction scene" and uncovers how "the rabbinic cultural formation (ca. 70–600 CE) utilized the seduction scene both to stage and challenge the ways 'society haunts the body's sexuality.'"[53] As I have noted earlier, the dominant reading of Gen 39 is that, while Joseph is the "mirror of purity,"[54] a "para-

---

50. Havea, "Sea-ing Ruth with Joseph's Mistress," 155.

51. Havea, "Sea-ing Ruth with Joseph's Mistress," 155.

52. In the Egyptian tale of the two brothers, Anubis the older one is married but Bata the younger is not. Bata is a handsome young man and his sister-in-law tries to seduce him. Bata's refusal enraged his sister-in-law who reported to Anubis that Bata attempted to seduce her and beat her up when refused. Anubis attempts to kill Bata and god Pre-Harakhty rescues him. Anubis learns the truth from his brother. Bata cuts his genitalia to prove his innocence and throws it into the water and a fish eats it. After several deaths at the hand of a divinely formed wife given to him by gods he is finally reborn from her as a crown prince and accedes to the throne. Cf. Day, *Gender and Difference in Ancient Israel*, 33–34.

53. Levinson, "An-Other Woman," 271.

54. Quoted Ambrose from Gregg, "Joseph with Potiphar's Wife," 339.

gon of virtue and self-control,"[55] who "embraces all the characteristics of a
hero,"[56] Zuleika is "often portrayed as driven by her passions to the point
of madness."[57] This dichotomy of masculinity and femininity is obvious in
the biblical text and with some reservations in Surah 12 as well. Levinson
writes, "many scholars have shown that a dominant code of self-fashioning
in the Greco-Roman world, where self-control, especially in its sexual form,
was a *sine qua non* of masculine gender identity, while women are constantly portrayed as "constitutionally unable to constrain themselves."[58] This
norm of the Greco-Roman world was imposed on readings by exegetes who
demonstrated immense grace and steadfast love to Joseph and none to Zuleika. Where the text is ambiguous, readers provide interpretations that (in
their estimation) uphold the agenda of the narrator. With rare exceptions
in biblical literature the narrator tends to be an omniscient, third-person
voice who is not a character in the story.[59] In his omnipresence, the narrator
decides whose (side of the) story needs to be heard; in Gen 39, we hear His
instead of Her's. In Gen 39:7, Zuleika is depicted as sexually perverse who
commands Joseph to lie with her. Judith Mckinlay notes the Qal imperative
"lie with me" (עמישכבה) and states that this was "not much an invitation as
a command."[60] Though the use of imperative indicates command, the status
of Zuleika in her household deprives her of the right to command. As Havea
notes, Zuleika "is not a subject in her own rights but a possession of her
husband."[61] Genesis 39:7–10 records the exchange of words between Joseph
and Zuleika; Zuleika is precise and direct; she has three words to say/ask,
"lie with me." Interestingly, Joseph does not say that he does not like her. His
response is in vv. 8–9.

> 8 But he refused and said to his master's wife, "Look, with me
> here, my master did not know what is in the house and every-
> thing he has, he put in my hand. 9 Nothing is greater in this
> house than me, he did not refrain from me anything except you,
> because you are his wife. How shall I do this great wickedness
> and sin against God?" (my translation)

55. Levinson, "An-Other Woman," 271.
56. Bach, "Breaking Free of the Biblical Frame-Up," 322.
57. Levinson, "An-Other Woman," 271–272.
58. Levinson, "An-Other Woman," 272.
59. Kaltner, *Inquiring of Joseph*, 25.
60. McKinlay, "Potiphar's Wife in Conversation," 72.
61. Havea, "Sea-ing Ruth with Joseph's mistress," 155.

For Alice Bach, "The biblical Joseph, who bragged of his superiority in Gen 37, has undergone no change in personality."[62] Joseph brags about himself (the narrator already gave this information in v. 6a) and flaunts the power and privilege bestowed on him. Like in Gen 37, where his dreams are correlated to the dreams to the patriarchs, here his "purity" is due to his loyalty to his master and God. According to the narrator, Joseph oversees everything that the master had which includes his wife too perhaps as some would argue.

For Havea, the narrator's comment on "except the food that he ate" could literally mean food or metaphorically, wife.[63] I contend that the narrator is talking about food and not euphemistically about wife. Genesis 43:32 informs the readers that Egyptians refused to eat food with the Hebrews. The special food practices of Egyptians are probably the reason Potiphar cared about what he eats and did not allow Joseph to neither decide nor have anything to do with Potiphar's food. McKinlay relates the elaborate response of Joseph to his vulnerability in this powerplay.[64] However, here Joseph is powerful, and Zuleika is not.

Monica Melanchthon's insight on Gen 38 is helpful here: "Tamar does not have Judah's power and therefore pleads to a greater justice by using the power of her sexuality, her body; she divests herself of all that is considered respectful—submission and reputation and she risks her life in order to have and give life."[65] Like Tamar, Zuleika also had no access to the power Joseph has. He is in control of the entire household. Zuleika does not even have the care of her husband, who "knows" nothing. Knowing that her husband is a eunuch, as Havea puts it, "She wanted Joseph, who is described as good looking."[66] There is ambiguity as to why the foreign woman Tamar is "more righteous than I," but the foreign woman Zuleika is "seeking to do wickedness." The narrator would probably point to the wrong that was done Tamar, but Zuleika also was wronged by being denied "the knowing" of her husband. In this sense, I would say *sthree* does not have to be in *madi* (pristine state) when circumstances and embodied experiences urge something else. The concept of *pathiye prathyakshya deivam* (God manifested in husband) needs to be transcended when betrayal

---

62. Bach, "Breaking Free of the Biblical Frame-Up," 331.

63. Havea, "Sea-ing Ruth with Joseph's mistress," 156.

64. McKinlay, "Potiphar's Wife in Conversation," 72.

65. Melanchthon, "Luther on Tamar," 16.

66. Havea, "Sea-ing Ruth with Joseph's mistress," 156.

and objectification become reality. Zuleika experiences detachment from her husband (being a eunuch; and we do not know at what point she came to know about this). Denied of any privilege in her household, she seeks the next powerful one in the household to "lie beside her." Her constant appeal day after day is contrasted with his constant refusal day after day. As Hagar, Zilpah, and Bilhah were accessible to their masters, so should Joseph have been accessible to Zuleika.

Joseph was however not accessible to Zuleika. She beseeches him with love and waits for him to respond. For many days, and maybe years.[67] In the verses that follow, Zuleika sees Joseph in the household when no man was there and proposes to him, but he flees. Zuleika is introduced into the tale to elevate Joseph. I suppose this tale is not even historical. The narrator strategically polarizes Zuleika and Joseph. The dichotomy between the male and the female in the narrative is obvious in Zuleika's appeal and Joseph's refusal; her brevity and his elaborateness; her evilness and his piety; her perversion and his righteousness. Zuleika is Otherized in the tale due to her femaleness and for asserting her sexuality.

Zuleika and Her Otherness

The namelessness of Potiphar's wife is understood by Havea as disrespect.[68] However he interprets the ambiguity in namelessness as "freeing."[69] Havea claims, "the nameless character cannot be pinned down to a particular label; she or he cannot be named or blamed. She or he might be the possession of another character to whom blame and praise could be directed, but as far as the nameless character is concerned, she or he is free of specificity or particularity."[70] It is because of this *freeness*, I chose to call her Zuleika as in the Jewish and Qur'anic traditions. Zuleika was not just nameless but also "identity" less. The narrator chose not to give her ethnic details leaving it to the interpreters to assume that she could be an Egyptian. Potiphar was clearly an Egyptian, but Zuleika's ethnicity is not revealed. I assume that Zuleika probably belonged to an "inferior" ethnic background compared to the Hebrews and Egyptians. In what follows,

67. Bach, "Breaking Free of the Biblical Frame-Up," 335.
68. Havea, "Sea-ing Ruth with Joseph's mistress," 155.
69. Havea, "Sea-ing Ruth with Joseph's mistress," 155.
70. Havea, "Sea-ing Ruth with Joseph's mistress," 155.

I propose two aspects of Zuleika's otherness. I argue that Zuleika is an Other even if she belongs to Egypt ethnically.

Scholars who argued for Zuleika's Egyptianness have not explored the dichotomies between the Hebrews and the Other. Greifenhagen explains that "the majority (83 percent) of the references to Egypt in Genesis appear in the Joseph narrative (37:1—50:26), a narrative that involves migration from Canaan into Egypt and then is largely set in Egypt."[71] While Greifenhagen draws attention to the positive and negative implications of Egypt, I briefly focus on Egypt's otherness and Zuleika's otherness. Greifenhagen articulates the dichotomy between Egyptian and Hebrew succinctly. He says, "although, Egypt is connected with ideas of success, it is also a place of deception and danger; this is the same ambiguity associated with Egypt in the earlier narratives of Genesis."[72] By focusing on the deception and danger put forward by Zuleika, interpreters make moral judgments against her character and her geographical location. Greifenhagen demonstrates that Egypt had negative overtones even in the Abraham story cycle. He points to three significant features that would clarify the Israelite relationship to Egypt.

1. To see Israel's origins as clearly non-Egyptian,

2. To see any connection between Israel and Egypt as temporary and fraught with danger,

3. To see any yearning on Israel's part for Egypt as disastrous.[73]

Reading Gen 39 against the background of the three points above allows us to understand the dynamics of Hebrew versus Egyptian, man versus woman, in Gen 39. The narrator opens Gen 39 by inviting readers to view Egypt as a negative counterpart of Israel. Joseph was bought by Potiphar and brought into his Egyptian household. We are not given any details regarding when Joseph came into power. By depicting Potiphar as buying a person, we learn that slavery already existed in Egypt; Egypt is an embodiment of economic exploitation of slaves and hence often referred to as the house of bondage. However, the following chapters in Joseph's cycle informs us that Joseph's exploitative practices gave rise to slavery. In this connection Logan Ratnaraj sees Joseph as the father of slavery. I propose an alternative image.

71. Greifenhagen, *Egypt on the Pentateuch's Ideological Map*, 24.

72. Greifenhagen, *Egypt on the Pentateuch's Ideological Map*, 35.

73. Greifenhagen, *Egypt on the Pentateuch's Ideological Map*, 30.

First, given that Joseph was entrusted with power and privilege in the household of Potiphar, I see Potiphar buying Joseph not in the same sense as the buying of a chattel slaves but buying to "ransom" (as in the book of Ruth). Potiphar generously ransoms Joseph from the hands of Ishmaelites and brings him to his household and appoints him overseer of everything and did not have a concern (know) for anything including his wife. Second, by ascribing Joseph's success to Yhwh (v. 5) and not to Potiphar, the narrator once again discloses his bias against Egypt. Third, Joseph becomes the "endangered ancestor"[74] and the danger lurks around in the form of the Egyptian mistress. I refuse to call her "his mistress" (as Havea suggests) because I do not believe that she has power over anything. Fourth, some interpreters wonder about the absence of men in the household when Zuleika "seduces" but they do not wonder why Joseph entered the household when no men were there. It is conceivable that Joseph as the overseer of the household was aware of the absence of the men. Despite knowing that, Joseph entered the household first and then the space of Zuleika. Joseph probably did have a love affair with Zuleika and then mocks at her, her sexuality and her Egyptianness. The narrator dichotomizes Zuleika and Joseph first and then her Egyptianness and his Hebrew-ness. This intentional polarization privileges and elevates one culture over the other and one gender over the other.

I suggest that Zuleika is a foreigner both to the Hebrew Joseph who "mocked" at her and to the Egyptian Potiphar who did not "know" (euphemism for sexual intercourse) her. I interpret Potiphar's lack of "knowing" as denying sexual intimacy with his wife, because he was a eunuch. Though the text does not give any clue regarding the foreignness of Zuleika, the book of Esther reveals that courts do have foreign women as wives. Esther becomes the wife of king Ahasuerus and she was a Jew. The king did not know about her Jewish identity, but he did not deny her the privilege when he knows it. We can assume that Zuleika also landed in Potiphar's house as a foreigner. Due to her foreignness, she was denied full respect and kindness. This respect and kindness are what readers ought to show her, as she embraces her new given identity and yearns for a partner, companion and friend. Levinson says that "Potiphar's wife functions not only as Joseph's sexual other but as his cultural other as

---

74. Greifenhagen, *Egypt on the Pentateuch's Ideological Map*, 35.

well"[75] and I opine that this cultural Otherness is not her Egyptianess but her unknown foreignness.

Conclusion

The presence of Zuleika in the tale of Joseph functions as a literary tool to elevate the status of Joseph. As the narrative progresses, Joseph is elevated from pit(y) to power, and Zuleika is deposed from inside to outside. The literary elimination of Zuleika beyond the confines of Gen 39 verifies her exploitation. The narrative bias against Zuleika the "foreign woman" and her sexuality makes her a marginal character. Literary sexual exploitation of Zuleika corresponds to the sexual exploitation of Dalit women in India. Just as Zuleika is Othered by the narrator and by interpreters, Dalit women are the targets of the dominant in India. In a context where Zuleika's and Dalits women's reputation are demoralized beyond repair, there is a need for *Swabhiman Yatra* (self-respect march) to reclaim the rights and dignity of women who have been de-robed. To that end, this essay attempted to show *chesed* to the *Sthree* Zuleika restoring to her dignity and respect.

Bibliography

Adelman, Rachel. *The Female Ruse: Women's Deception and Divine Sanction in the Hebrew Bible.* Hebrew Bible Monographs. Sheffield: Sheffield Phoenix, 2017.

Amos, Clare. "Genesis." In *Global Bible Commentary* edited by Daniel Patte et al., 1–16. Nashville: Abingdon, 2004.

Bellis, Alice Ogden. *Helpmates, Harlots and Heroes: Women's Stories in the Hebrew Bible.* Louisville: Westminster John Knox, 2007.

Botterweck, Zobel. "Hesed." In *Theological Dictionary of the Old Testament,* edited by G. Johannes Botterweck and Helmer Ringgren, 5:44–64. Translated by Geoffrey W. Bromiley. Grand Rapids: Eerdmans, 1986.

Brayford, Susan. *Genesis.* Septuagint Commentary. Boston: Brill Academic, 2007.

Brenner-Idan, Athalya, ed. *A Feminist Companion to Genesis.* Feminist Companion to the Bible 2. Sheffield: Sheffield Academic, 1993.

———. *The Israelite Woman: Social Role and Literary Type in Biblical Narrative.* 2nd ed. T. & T. Clark Cornerstones. London: Bloomsbury, 2014.

Carden, Michael. "Genesis/Bereshit." In *The Queer Bible Commentary*, edited by Guest Deryn, 21–60. London: SCM, 2006.

Day, Peggy L., ed. *Gender and Difference in Ancient Israel.* Minneapolis: Fortress, 1989.

75. Levinson, "An-Other Woman," 298.

Frymer-Kensky, Tikva. *Reading the Women of the Bible: A New Interpretation of Their Stories*. New York: Schocken, 2002.

Goldman, Shalom. *The Wiles of Women / The Wiles of Men: Joseph and Potiphar's Wife in Ancient Near Eastern, Jewish, and Islamic Folklore*. Albany: State University of New York Press, 1995.

Gregg, Robert C. "Joseph with Potiphar's Wife: Early Christian Commentary Seen against the Backdrop of Jewish and Muslim Interpretations." *Studia Patristica* 34 (2001) 326–46.

Greifenhagen, F. V. *Egypt on the Pentateuch's Ideological Map: Constructing Biblical Israel's Identity*. Journal for the Study of the Old Testament Supplements 361. London: Sheffield Academic, 2002.

Havea, Jione. "Sea-ing Ruth with Joseph's Mistress." In *Islands, Islanders, and the Bible: RumInations*, edited by Jione Havea et al., 141–61. Atlanta: Society of Biblical Literature, 2015.

Huddlestun, John R. "Divestiture, Deception, and Demotion: The Garment Motif in Genesis 37–39." *Journal for the Study of the Old Testament* 98 (2002) 47–62. https://doi.org/10.1177/030908920202600403.

Kaltner, John. *Inquiring of Joseph: Getting to Know a Biblical Character through the Qur' an*. Collegeville, MN: Liturgical, 2003.

Kugel, James L. *In Potiphar's House: The Interpretive Life of Biblical Texts*. Cambridge: Harvard University Press, 1994.

Levinson, Joshua. "An-Other Woman: Joseph and Potiphar's Wife. Staging the Body Politic." *Jewish Quarterly Review* 87 (1997) 269–301. https://doi.org/10.2307/1455187.

McKay, Heather A. "Confronting Redundancy as Middle Manager and Wife: The Feisty Woman of Genesis 39." *Semeia* 87 (1999) 215–31.

McKinlay, Judith. "Potiphar's Wife in Conversation." *Feminist Theology* 10 (1995) 69–80.

Melcher, Sarah J. et al., eds. *The Bible and Disability: A Commentary*. Studies in Religion, Theology, and Disability. Waco, TX: Baylor University Press, 2017.

Melanchthon, J. "Luther on Tamar: A Subaltern Response." *Consensus (Online)* 38/1 (November 2017) 1–16.

Niditch, Susan. "Genesis." In *Women's Bible Commentary*, edited by Carol A. Newsom, Sharon H. Ringe and Jacqueline E. Lapsley, 27–45. 3rd ed. Louisville: Westminster John Knox, 2012.

Rajkumar, Evangeline Anderson, "'God' in the Light of Women's Experiences: An Indian Perspective." DTh diss., Serampore University, 1998.

Ratnaraj, Samuel Logan. "Reconstructing the Dreamer Narrative: Joseph the Father of Slavery." In *Liberation Hermeneutics in the Indian Interpretation of the Bible*, by Kondasingu Jesurathnam et al., 124–32. Bangalore: SBSI, 2012.

Sarna, Nahum M. *Genesis*. JPS Torah Commentary. Philadelphia: Jewish Publication Society, 2001.

Wenham, Gordon J. *Genesis 16–50*. Word Biblical Commentary 2. Waco, TX: Word, 1994.

Wiles, Maurice, et al. "Joseph with Potiphar's Wife: Early Christian Commentary Seen against the Backdrop of Jewish and Muslim Interpretations." *Studia Patristica* (2001) 326–46.

11

"And No One Shall Rescue Her Out of My Hand"

Gomer and Hosea 2 in a World of Battered Women

Bethany Broadstock

In Australia, an online campaign keeps a running tally of every reported violent death of women. In 2015 these numbered almost eighty, and by the end of July 2016 they were already approaching sixty. Not only does this campaign keep count of their number, but it ensures that their experiences and identities are not left in a shadow.[1] Among them is a sixty-year-old woman stabbed to death alongside her four-year-old grandson; a pregnant woman in her mid-twentys and her seven-year-old son both killed by shooting; a twenty-two-year old woman found decomposed in the boot of a car; a woman murdered with an axe, despite a protection order against her ex-partner; a woman at forty-four, who jumped from a moving vehicle out of fear for her life and died from her injuries; a twenty-five-year-old woman found with her throat slashed; and the list goes on. For every identity and story there are at least five more which are similar, and many more not reported, and this campaign makes for painful but necessary reading. The stories of these women echo the story narrated in Hosea 2.

1. Cf. https://www.facebook.com/notes/destroy-the-joint/counting-dead-women-australia-2015-we-count-every-single-violent-death-of-women-/867514906629588.

Yahweh as Husband

A disturbing parallel may be drawn between the stories of contemporary domestic violence in Australia, with Hosea's metaphorical imaging of Yahweh as "husband" to biblical Israel. In general, the defining narrative of biblical prophetic texts is that Yahweh is a covenant partner which means that, in the heteronormative world of the Hebrew Bible, Yahweh is male. The problems with this imagery have been well documented. The community of Israel is presented not in social terms but personified in the figure of a sexually active woman—a wife—whose alleged infidelity is met with an unstable and violent diatribe which threatens her isolation, abuse, humiliation, and death. While the murders recorded by the "Counting Dead Women" project are not limited to domestic or family violence, these comprise the majority, because one woman (on average) is murdered by an intimate or former partner every week in Australia.[2] It is through the lens of this statistical and lived reality that I read Hosea's prophetic metaphor.

Although the metaphor crystallizes in Hos 2, it is located within a narrative arc that lays the groundwork earlier (1:1–9). The situation itself, and then the metaphor to follow, arises from "a word of the Lord" which commands Hosea "*take* for [himself] a wife of *whoredom*" (1:2, my italics). This wife is Gomer, of whose willingness to enter the marriage or engage in a sexual relationship we hear and know nothing, only that Hosea "went and took" her and she then conceived (1:3). The infidelity that Gomer represents is ambiguous; the text does not clarify whether it is sexual, social, cultic, or something else. But a generic allusion to her "unfaithfulness" within the context of marriage is sufficient to open the way for a prophetic address of Israel's own unfaithfulness to their obligations as a community living under Yahweh.

Double Entendre

The passage that follows is characterized by the double-communication of the metaphor, wherein the words spoken to and about Gomer are presented as direct address, but Israel is understood to be their true object (cf. 1:2,4,6–9). This discussion will not attempt historical reconstruction,

---

2. National Homicide Monitoring Program report, *Australian Institute of Criminology*, 2015.

partly because the text is resistant to this, but it takes the covenantal context for granted as a fundamental concern of the book and its content.[3]

That the escalating violent and threatening language employed by the text functions on these two levels raises two problems, one is theological and the second one extends into the contemporary social moment. The first relates to the implication entailed by the metaphor that violence and disproportionate anger hover as a threat over God's way with God's people, and may comprise the divine response God makes to a fractured relation in the context of the covenant.

Note that with the command to marry Gomer, the Lord "*first* spoke through Hosea" (1:2; my italics). If we assume that the author intends to mean that this speaking continues, then the words ascribed to Hosea's character are also, in some way, ascribed to the character of God. The words of God are the words of Hosea; the words of Hosea are the words of God. We proceed on the assumption that it is acceptable, if not necessary, to interrogate and evaluate the projections of God implied herein. The second problem is that if a reader in the present time understands this divine response to be justified, the text leaves itself vulnerable to exploitation by those who would seek to theologically legitimate certain forms of violence in the context of marriage or other intimate settings. In other words, the words of God may be taken by abusers as their words.

Yahweh as Male

It is worth examining the logic and application of the metaphor more closely to consider its implications, particularly in relation to gender contrasts and dynamics. In the very act of speaking "for" Yahweh, the text equates the male Hosea with God, and God with maleness.[4] This is compounded by the fact that in and through Hosea's own situation he is uniquely placed to identify with God's jilted position.

By contrast, the female Gomer is likened to the unfaithful community subject to judgement. She is doubly othered from God: in this representation, and then by her gender. Hosea, the text tells us, is loyal

3. There is disagreement as to whether Hosea's own marriage was itself a metaphor or a reality. This discussion does not consider it necessary to resolve this issue. The text is being read as text, as literature and theology; historical considerations are secondary. The text of Hosea is also poorly preserved, and very little is known about either Hosea or Gomer. These factors mean that the text resists historical reconstruction.

4. O'Brien, *Challenging Prophetic Metaphor*, 34.

and long-suffering while she cannot help but to "pursue her lovers" (2:7); he is consistent while she lacks in self-control; he is forgiving though her behavior warrants death, and her restoration can be credited only to his non-pursuit of the retaliation available to him.[5] He speaks freely while her voice is either silenced or manipulated, along with those of her children, and she cannot be reached by them or by anyone: "and no one shall rescue her out of my hand" (v.10).

The autonomous female sexuality Gomer represents stands in contrast to Hosea's "neutral male standard,"[6] and is considered inherently negative, to be condemned and suppressed. Towards this end she is threatened with public nakedness, humiliation and voyeurism (2:3,9,10), death by starvation and thirst (2:2,3,9), isolation and barricades (2:6,7,10), life without joy (2:11), and other punishments left undefined (2:13). She suffers sexually-loaded verbal abuse; the NRSV translation renders Hebrew references to illicit sexual activity as "whore" and "whoredom." Unfaithfulness is the cause for judgement, but because it is described in terms of unrestrained sexual freedom (the use of the Hebrew *zenut* implies she is neither subject to control nor subjugation[7]), female sexuality becomes that against which fidelity is defined.

More Than Metaphors

There are primarily two assumptions which underpin this discussion. The first is that the potential to harm entailed by a metaphor should not be discounted simply because it is "only" a metaphor.[8] Metaphors are careful, deliberate constructions employed for the purpose of illuminating and speaking of an object or subject so as to deepen understanding—which may raise no easy questions about Hosea's comprehension of God's character. The second is that the difficulty of the text lies in the reality that the violence entailed by the relationship between "husband" and "wife" is not in fact metaphorical. In the Australian context, women are three times more likely than men to experience violence from an intimate

5. O'Brien, *Challenging Prophetic Metaphor*, 32.

6. T Setel, "Prophets and Pornography," 87.

7. Setel, "Prophets and Pornography," 91.

8. Graetz, "God Is to Israel as Husband Is to Wife," 135.

partner,[9] five times more likely to require subsequent hospitalization, and five times more likely to report fearing for their lives.[10]

Further, the events implied are no less dangerous because they are only threatened within the text. Threats "which are likely and able to be carried out" have been included in definitions of violence, including one used by the Australian Bureau of Statistics in a 2012 assessment of personal safety.[11] In addition to those deaths which have been a matter of the public record, there are countless lesser-known stories of women who do not lose their lives but suffer in other ways and/or live in fear of the potential escalation of their situation. The text cannot but echo with the lived experience of abused, dominated and threatened women for whom its images will not be easily reconciled with the sacred status they are ascribed. It would perhaps not be an overstatement to suggest women would be within their right to fear for their lives were they to fall into the hands of the God imaged by Hosea ("a terrifying thing" [Heb 10:31]), but also, crucially, those whose violence the text has the potential to perpetuate and justify. This is not to suggest that rejection is the only option available; there is also contextual reinterpretation.

Family Matters

Of the women who experience intimate violence in Australia, half have children in their care.[12] While many interpreters have labelled Hosea's metaphor a marital one, Gomer has given birth to three children (1:2–9), and it is thus familial. The chapter begins with Hosea's plea to his children (2:1–2), from which we may infer that they remain first-hand hearers of all that follows. In the text, as in reality, children are disempowered witnesses to and frequently the collateral damage of violence within the home. They are even some of its most tragic victims, as in the well-known

9. In 2012, 17% of all women and 5% of men had experienced violence by a partner since the age of 15. Australian Bureau of Statistics (2013), *Personal Safety*, Australia, 2012, Cat. No. 4906; http://www.abs.gov.au/ausstats/abs@.nsf/mf/4906.0).

10. Mouzos, *Femicide*.

11. The 2012–2013 report is available online: https://www.ausstats.abs.gov.au/aus stats/subscriber.nsf/0/B19374AFCCC38354CA257C150019CF65/$File/abs_annual_rep_2013_web.pdf.

12. National Crime Prevention, *Young people and domestic violence: National research on attitudes and experiences of domestic violence* (Crime Prevention Branch, Commonwealth Attorney-General's Department, Canberra, 2001).

Australian case of 11-year old Luke Batty who was murdered at a public cricket training session by his father (estranged from his mother) despite a violence order against him.

Echoes of these dynamics can be heard in the text, which implicates Hosea's children in the judgement to which their mother is subject, and whose "very names stand as symbols for rejection": *Lo-ruhamah* ("not pitied") and *Lo-ammi* ("not my people").[13] The third, Jezreel, is an overtly political toponym. The three are placed clearly in view but are given no opportunity to answer Hosea, like their mother, who is the "key defining factor in [the text's] structure and message but remains in the shadows."[14] Hosea's words negate her choice and personal agency: "you *shall* respond . . . you *will* call me . . . she *shall* say" (v.7, my italics). One does not know what she might say if she spoke for herself. Arguments can only be made from silence, because these voices go unheard independent of the meaning construed for them.

It is crucial to highlight that this is due largely to the text's construction from the male perspective. Readers of the text are not always conscious of this, but feminist interpretation is aware, because to read from the female perspective is to run immediately into problems. The text is under Hosea's control, in addition to the controlling behavior it describes. Thus, the reader must subconsciously adopt the male perspective in order to relate to the text and "evaluate positively the image of God it represents."[15] It is from and because of this perspective that, despite its methods, the text is still able to elicit reader-sympathy for the prophet, and has continued to elicit condemnation for Gomer in the history of interpretation.

It is a recurring cultural refrain that women who behave in particular ways deserve, invite or expose themselves to, the extreme responses and critiques which follow. Almost every mainstream attempt to read Gomer has rested on the assumption that her reputation needs improvement,[16] while simultaneously accepting uncritically the ideology which needs to portray her in the way it does.

Hosea's second chapter is almost a microcosm of other prophetic texts, and many of the psalms, in that a period of severe disruption or

13. Kelle, *Hosea 2*, 7.

14. Fontaine, "A Response to 'Hosea,'" 67.

15. O'Brien, *Challenging Prophetic Metaphor*, 67.

16. Yvonne Sherwood undertakes a highly interesting survey of the dominant ways in which interprets have attempted to "deal, with Gomer (see Sherwood, "Boxing Gomer," 106–17).

disorder abruptly finds some kind of theological resolution. At v. 14, the tone and nature of the pericope shifts from violent and abusive to more tender, restorative language, marked by a jarring move from the phrase "will punish" (v.13) to "will allure" in the following line (v.14). Dominant readings have privileged this second half; it is also the only extract provided by the Revised Common Lectionary for use in public worship. This perhaps encourages communities of faith to identify the positive theological message lying beneath preceding imagery, which is related to the fidelity of God despite the flaws and failures of God's people.

Violence and Love

The chapter is marked in three places by the word "therefore" as a link between unfaithfulness and its consequences (vv. 6, 9, 14). At the third "therefore" (v. 14), one expects to meet the climax of God's judgement, but finds instead a relational renewal when what had come before seemed to rule this out as a viable possibility warranting genuine hope. Where there should be a final "doing away" with the community, a resignation to the more flawed and frail edges of human existence is reclaimed again to find its identity in belonging to Yahweh and recalibrate its life accordingly. The ultimate theological word of the text is a summary of arguably the key affirmation of the Hebrew scriptures and broader biblical witness, that God is inexhaustible in persisting with the community or creation. This relation can be fractured, turned away from, temporarily forgotten, but it can never be broken: "in love I will take you forever" (2:19).

These are legitimate and hardly radical conclusions. But they should be made with an awareness of the methodology which gives them rise. Problems remain when reading the more positive aspects of the text in context, if ears are open to echoes of domestic violence patterns in which periods of violence are interrupted by the temporary absence of violence and disproportionate kindness. In this circular pattern, violent behaviors become expressions of love, and reconciliation never functions apart from the threat of punishment. It is not a genuine reconciliation, because the threat is only latent and never truly gone.

That being said, the issue one may take with this text is not primarily with the dynamics of divine judgement and love. Judgement belongs to the character of God. Christian tradition has lost much by neglecting to reflect on God's judgement as *good* judgement which is God's refusal to be indifferent to the events of this world, marked as it is by injustice, violence and oppression. In the exercise of divine purposes which seek life for creation, there is also a rejection of these same things as being anti-creation according to the values of God's reign. The truth expressed in the biblical experience of judgement is that God's people too can perpetuate those things which hinder life for all and will also be corrected for failing to live faithfully under grace. But this is good news as judgement, which is an aspect of the covenant, holding its parties to account and inviting them into the self-giving and vulnerability that love entails. The content of prophetic texts, though difficult, functions as insurance against the tendency to rush too quickly beyond judgement to comfort. At what cost might comfort and forgiveness be won in these texts, and to what extend are those just?

In Hosea's narrative arc, echoing the disproportionate power and dominance which so often escalates into violence and characterizes abusive situations, it is at Gomer's expense that this kind of positive theological point can be made. Even though the metaphor is social, entailing the self-conscious use of human relationships to articulate the relationship between God and community,[17] it is Gomer alone, or the image and figure of the female, who absorbs in her body notions of God's judgement. She then disappears from the narrative beyond the fourth chapter; a character only necessary for a time. A reader may be left with the sense that violent rhetoric is somehow justified because it ultimately seeks to make a claim that is theologically profound, but this needs serious interrogation, or it will be limitless in its potential to legitimate abuse in real terms. It is also to divorce medium and message; the metaphor makes the central affirmation of God-as-love more, not less, difficult to comprehend.

In the Interest of Battered Women

In 1985, T. Drorah Setel suggested that "the 'pornographic' nature of female objectification may demand that such texts not be declared 'the word of God' in a public setting."[18] It is difficult to conclude otherwise in Australia, where a third of women will experience physical violence, a fifth will experience sexual violence, and one in four will experience either or both by an intimate partner. It is right to question whether there

17. Graetz, "God Is to Israel as Husband Is to Wife," 129.

18. Setel, "Prophets and Pornography," 95.

is anything redeeming about this metaphor then, and whether it is of use in speaking of the God whose purposes are confessed so often in the language of liberation and justice; the One who locates themselves alongside the weak and vulnerable and who frustrates evil until it is disarmed. Does the profound concern for justice found without exception in every major and minor prophetic text, and developed in light of God's character, not include justice for women? Fortunately, hermeneutical approaches to the Bible which take seriously their subject matter will rarely be satisfied to do business with the surface of these texts alone, and particularly those which can be weaponized to oppress or subjugate.

Various contextual approaches are now interrogating patriarchal interpretative work which has for centuries remained unchallenged, making fresh and generative claims about these texts in light of both theological confession and the contemporary moment. Even if these remain marginal for the time being, the more the margins occupy the places closest to the center, the more an unjust center will be unsettled. Much has rightly been criticized about the metaphor itself but work remains to consider what theological alternatives the text may offer, which allow us to retain the prophetic truth of both God's judgement and God's claim on the community despite the experience of crisis, but does not at the same time come at too high a cost for some to pay.

At the beginning of this discussion I suggested that reading Hosea's metaphor was difficult, but necessary. That is because texts such as this have been marginalized and neglected by readers and church communities, and must be allowed to speak in some way as a text of faith and element of the canon. In working with their dominant motifs, and the social and theological meanings which have historically been dominant, one might conclude in a new moment that God is not contained by these texts, and instead look to gaps and silences for the Voice which speaks what and where She will.

For women, and their allies, it may be that God speaks most clearly not through metaphors but rather through their reactions and responses; in their sense of anger and injustice. The hermeneutical lens which questions the patriarchal assumptions of Biblical texts will always be necessary while the world holds countless women who continue to live in situations of danger, harassment, humiliation and pain. We may particularly include the category of battered and murdered women whose abusers have found a divine sanction for violence in the Biblical worldview. While these categories exist, interpreters both male and female must commit themselves to searching the Bible for counter-images which provide justification for upholding the dignity of women, and reason to argue and hope for a future characterized by bodily autonomy, safety and peace.

Bibliography

Brenner, Athalya, ed. *A Feminist Companion to the Latter Prophets*. Feminist Companion to the Bible. Feminist Companion to the Bible 8. Sheffield: Sheffield Academic, 1995.

Graetz, Naomi. "God Is to Israel as Husband Is to Wife: The Metaphorical Battering of Hosea's Wife." In *A Feminist Companion to the Latter Prophets*, edited by Athalya Brenner. Feminist Companion to the Bible 8. Sheffield: Sheffield Academic, 1995.

Kelle, Brad E. *Hosea 2: Metaphor and Rhetoric in Historical Perspective*. Academia Biblica 20. Atlanta: Society of Biblical Literature, 2005.

Mouzos, Jenny. *Femicide: An Overview of Major Findings, No. 124*. Canberra: Australian Institute of Criminology, 1999, 1–6. http://aic.gov.au/media_library/publications/tandi_pdf/tandi124.pdf.

O'Brien, Julia M. *Challenging Prophetic Metaphor: Theology and Ideology in the Prophets*. Louisville: Westminster John Knox, 2008.

Setel, T. Drorah. "Prophets and Pornography: Female Sexual Imagery in Hosea." In *Feminist Interpretation of the Bible*, edited by Letty M. Russell, 86–95. Philadelphia: Westminster, 1985.

Sherwood, Yvonne. "Boxing Gomer: Controlling the Deviant Woman in Hosea 1–3." In *A Feminist Companion to the Latter Prophets*, edited by Athalya Brenner, 101–25. Feminist Companion to the Bible 8. Sheffield: Sheffield Academic, 1995.

12

Earth Came to Help a Woman

Mythopoeic Language and Discipleship in Revelation 12:1–17

Vaitusi Nofoaiga

DISCIPLESHIP IS NOT COMMONLY associated with the Book of Revelation. The few studies on discipleship in Revelation follow the traditional interpretation of master-disciple relationship.[1] For the interpretation presented herein, I explore the vision of the woman crying out in birth pangs and Earth's attempt to help her in Rev 12:1–17. Discipleship is understood here as following Christ in any time and space in spite of suffering and pain.[2]

This essay offers a narrative-rhetorical interpretation of Rev 12:1–17 as showing the language of myths which was part of the first century Christians' defining of their Christian existence. I affirm myths because they preserve stories of how people in a particular culture view their world. Tui Atua Tupua Tamasese Taisi suggests that "Myth . . . is equated with history."[3] Barry B. Powell too considers myths important: "myths

1. An example is the book of sermons by Johnson, *Discipleship on the Edge*.

2. Fernando F. Segovia describes this general definition of discipleship: "discipleship would be understood more generally in terms of Christian existence—that is, the self-understanding of the early Christian believers as believers: what such a way of life requires, implies and entails" (Segovia, "Introduction," 2).

3. Tupua Tamasese Ta'isi, "Resident, Residence, Residency in Samoan Custom," 93. Tui Atua Tamasese Ta'isi is the former Head of State of Samoa and is one of the most

tell of the origin . . . of the universe . . . and ourselves."[4] This was one of the ways used to define being a follower or a disciple of Jesus in the first century. We use myths too to define our Christian existence in our Samoan worlds. I begin with an explanation of Christian existence as an integration of cultures, which will be used in the conclusion as a hermeneutical lens to analyze the narrative-rhetorical interpretation of Rev 12:1–17 made herein.

Integration of Cultures

Finding the meaning(s) of the visions in the book of Revelation is a challenge, including the vision of the woman crying out in birth pangs and Earth's attempt to help her (Rev 12:1–17). This vision is considered one of the blind spots of Revelation for it is not normal for Earth to act as humans do. However, Christians in the first century would have ideas of what the messages were. They were messages of survival for Christians in oppressive life situations and crises.[5]

How those messages were put together is another question. Schüssler Fiorenza elicits an answer: Revelation is a compilation of different sources—such as the Christian redactor, apocalypse and mythopoeic sources—that appealed to the author, who put together the text according to theological interests and in order to make theological arguments.[6] One of those theological arguments is discipleship.[7] Schüssler Fiorenza's view reflects the reality of how Christians make sense of the meaning and purpose of the gospel in the life they encounter within the contexts they inhabit. I pay special attention to the use of mythopoeic sources as part of defining Christian existence because this relates to our Samoan *Tala o le vavau* (Samoan myths) which help us understand and experience Christian concepts in our world.

Reflected in Schüssler Fiorenza's claim is the thought that a Christian understanding and experience of the world comes from the integration of his/her understanding of the gospel and with other cultures. Bill Ashcroft

---

recognized Samoan scholars on our indigenous references and understanding.

4. Powell, *Classical Myth*, 6.

5. For example, the situation faced by Christians in the Roman imperial rule in the first century.

6. Schüssler Fiorenza, "Composition and Structure of the Book of Revelation," 344–66.

7. See Ford, *The Revelation of John*.

explained the integration of cultures as "cultural transformation"—a process whereby cultures appropriate elements from other cultures in beneficial ways.[8] Revelation is one example which I will elaborate upon in this essay. Another example is our Christian existence in our Samoan worlds. Despite the pain and suffering we face, we consider serving (*tautua*) our families, villages, and churches, as following Jesus. I associate *tautua* in our Samoan social and cultural world to the role of discipleship. We live the life of *Kerisiano tautua faamaoni* (courageous Samoan Christian[9] servant) guided by values which we learn from the symbiotic relationship between the gospel and the Samoan culture. This relationship makes the church and Samoan culture partners in history in our Samoan Christian world and is expressed in the following common expression in our Samoan society:

> *E mamalu le Talalelei ona o le Aganuu,*
> *e mamalu foi le Aganuu ona o le Talalelei.*
> The Gospel is respected because of the support of Culture,
> so is Culture respected because of the support of the Gospel.

This expression exhibits the integration of the Gospel and the Samoan culture that defines our Christian existence in Samoan society. This is evident in the Samoan Christian understanding of the human–Earth relationship. God's creation of the human–Earth relationship (Gen 1–2) is similar to indigenous Samoan understanding of *vā-tapuia* (sacred relationship) between *tagata* (human) and *eleele* (Earth). The *vā-tapuia* (read: human–Earth) relationship is explained by three Samoan concepts: *eleele* (Earth), *tautua* (serve/servant), and *tapu* (taboo/sacred).

Eleele translates as "earth" but also as "blood." *Eleele* as blood shows that Earth is living and must be respected. *Tautua* describes the role and duty of the human and Earth in their relationship. *Tautua* means to serve (verb) and service (noun) and carries two significant meanings. First, it identifies the status and role of men and women in their families and villages. Second, it expresses serving family and Earth as a moral value. Thus, human and Earth must serve each other with respect and that respect is expressed in the concept *tapu* (sacred and taboo). *Tapu* means "to make sacred, to place under restriction" (verb). For Tamasese Taisi, "*Tapu* is taboo because it is sacred; it has a sacred essence . . . which underpins

---

8. Ashcroft, *Post-colonial Transformation*, 14–17.

9. I use "Samoan Christian" in this essay to state the integration of the two cultures of Samoa and Christianity.

man's relations with all things; with the gods, the cosmos, environment, other men and self."[10]

Tapu is a component of *tapueleele* (sacred Earth), which affirms that Earth is a sacred place and it is to be respected. Respecting Earth is the heart of *vā-tapuia*. *Vā* means space and *tapuia* is how space is to be inhabited—with respect. Thus, *vā-tapuia* refers to the sacred *(tapuia)* relationship *(vā)* between humans and all things including heaven and Earth. It is where Earth is considered as a community of interconnected living things, dependent on each other for life and survival and is evident in the Samoan proverb *Ua tagi le fatu ma le eleele* (the rock and Earth weep), which refers to a cry so deep that it hurts one's heart.

In the Samoan world, a proverb *(alagaupu)* comes from a myth; in the Savaii myth the proverb *Ua tagi le fatu ma le eleele* relates to Salevao.[11] Salevao's parents were killed by people from his village; only Salevao from his family survived. Salevao slept with tears as he could not stop crying; he could not forget the killing of his parents. A man named Vave took Salevao to the western side of Savaii looking for help to end Salevao's crying. They came to the village of Satupaitea. The people of Satupaitea felt for Salevao but they could not stop him from crying. Unable to help him, the land of Satupaitea cried with him. The cry of the land includes the cry of the dead (the ancestors) from the heart of the land. The dead feel the pain of the living, and thus emerged the saying *Ua tagi le fatu ma le eleele*. This refers to the *fatu* (heart) of people and *eleele* (Earth) crying with the boy. It is a common Samoan belief that whenever the people cry the land mourns with them. The proverb carries ecological nuances—the cries of rock and Earth.

Human and Earth feel for and with each other. Their relation *(vā)* is sacred and they serve each other with respect. Earth should be respected because it is living. It has life. Human and Earth should serve one another with respect. The integrated (Samoan culture and Gospel culture) understanding of the human-Earth relationship gives rise to the theological interests and arguments of the roles of a disciple follower of Christ—in our world, and for the sake of Earth. With this

10. Tupua Tamasese Ta'isi, "Resident, Residence, Residency in Samoan Custom," 93.

11. There are various stories of where the proverb *Ua tagi le fatu ma le eleele* came from such as "The Samoan Creation Story from Manua" and "Vaea and Apaula from Vaimauga." I privilege here the story from Satupaitea.

integrated understanding in hand, I turn to Rev 12:1–17 with the service of narrative-rhetorical criticism.[12]

Narrative Rhetorical Interpretation of Revelation 12:1–17

For Schüssler Fiorenza, any attempt to interpret Revelation must highlight the theological intentions of the author and how those intentions are shown in the integration of content and form.[13] Along this line J. M. Ford speaks of Revelation as a compilation of two Jewish apocalypses and one Christian redaction.[14] One of those sources of theological viewpoints is discipleship—a product of the first century Christians' attempt to understand their situations and contexts in light of the Gospel. For example, one of the most pervasive modern images of Christianity in the first century is that of being "born again"—which was an image of survival in difficult and painful situations. A "woman crying out with birth pangs as shown in Rev. 12:1–17 was one of the imageries"[15] considered as a symbolic representation of what a true disciple is—a disciple is prepared to bear the pain and suffering of the duties of being a follower of Christ. There are various interpretations of the woman crying out in birth pangs in Rev 12,[16] but for this essay, I consider her as a symbolic representation of the

12. See Mark Allan Powell's description of Narrative Criticism, Vernon K. Robbins' 'Sociorhetorical Criticism" and Elizabeth Struthers Malbon's description of 'Narrative Criticism' in relation to 'Rhetoric" (Powell, "Narrative Criticism," 239–255; Robbins, *Exploring the Texture of Texts*; Malbon, "Narrative Criticism," 23–49).

13. Schüssler Fiorenza, "Composition and structure of the Book of Revelation," 344.

14. According to Ford, the first apocalypse (chapters 4–11) is about the time of John the Baptist (before the arrival of Jesus). The second apocalypse (chapters 12–22) present the theological viewpoint of the disciples who envisioned the fall of Jerusalem and what would happen to those who turned away from God. The Christian redaction includes chapters 1–3 and 22:16a, 20b, 21 (Ford, *The Revelation of John*).

15. Prévost, *How to Read the Apocalypse*, 99.

16. I briefly mention these interpretations for they are significant the reading proposed in this essay. First, the woman is identified as Israel—the chosen people of God (Beasley-Murray, "Revelation," 1441; Hale, "Revelation," 980; Booker, *The Lamb and the Seven-Sealed Scroll*, 212; Osborne, *Revelation Verse by Verse*, 204). Second, the woman symbolizes Virgin Mary (Boring, *Revelation*, 152). Third, the woman is identified as Eve (Wright, *Revelation for Everyone*, 107–8). Fourth is the woman as the Church and the People of God (Boring, *Revelation*, 152; Beasley-Murray, "Revelation," 1441; Osborne, *Revelation Verse by Verse*, 204). This view is based on the setting of the Book in the time of great persecution. This view of the woman provides a concept of the Church/People of God as the body of Christ that has suffered and will suffer, but

discipleship of the church. This interpretation uses narrative-rhetorical criticism, starting with a brief exploration of the placement of the text in the book—the placement of the woman crying out in birth pang is at the middle of the book of Revelation. It will be followed by an analysis of the setting, the characters, and the use of mythopoeic language in portraying the important relationship between the woman and Earth.

The following questions guide the interpretation. If the vision of the woman crying out in pain relates to the discipleship work of the church in the first century, could the placement of that vision in the middle of Revelation be taken as a revelation emphasizing the significance of the church's discipleship work? Secondly, the role played by Earth in this revelation is critical. Earth helps by opening its mouth and swallowing the water that the serpent pours out to sweep the woman away. Is the role played by Earth in this revelation part of the church's discipleship work? The following interpretation addresses those questions, taking the text as a narrative (part of John's telling of the revelations from chapter 1 to chapter 12).

Placement of Revelation 12:1–17

There are various attempts at structuring the book of Revelation.[17] The one followed in the following interpretation is adapted from Brian Blount. Blount's structure recapitulates how John as author intends his readers to perceive the visions as they occur in the narrative.[18] I adapt Blount's structure for what I call "The discipleship work of the church":

---

eventually vindicated through a glorious resurrection. This is the view advocated in this chapter.

17. The debate on the structure of Revelation continues. See Larsen, "Neglected Considerations," 225–233; Wainwright, *Mysterious Apocalypse*; Schüssler Fiorenza, "Composition and structure of the Book of Revelation," 344–366; Beasley-Murray, *The Book of Revelation*, 30–31; Beale, *The Book of Revelation*, 144.

18. Blount, *Revelation*, 21:
Prologue (1:1–8)
Instructions to the Seven Churches (1:9–3:22)
Series of Visions (4:1–22:9)
Introductory Vision Cycle (4–11)
Visionary Flashback (12–14)
Concluding Vision Cycle (15–22:9)
Epilogue (22:10–21)

- Rev 1: Introduction—Revelation of Christ to be kept by the church on Earth

- Rev 2–3: Letters to the Seven Churches—To obey with reward

- Rev 4–5: Throne of God—Reward for the listeners

- Rev 6: Opening the first six seals—Will of God revealed

- Rev 7: Intermission—Chance to listen

- Rev 8–9: Opening the seventh seal—The seven trumpets

- Rev 10:1—11:14: Intermission—More chances to listen

- Rev 11:15–19: Blowing the seventh trumpet—Last warning

- Rev 12:1–17: Flashback—Discipleship work of the church, to give birth to repentant and new believers

- Rev 13–14: Intermission—More chances for non-listeners to turn to God

- Rev 15–16: Pouring the seven bowls—No more chances, judgment is coming

- Rev 17:1–20:3: Judgment takes place—Rome is destroyed

- Rev 20:4–22:21: Glory and everlasting life—New Heaven and New Earth for the listener

This structuring of Revelation emphasizes chapter 12 (visionary flashback) as the center of the book. It is the moment when hearers and readers pause and look back at the progress of the visions thus far. Chapter 1 introduces the book as revelations of God's love and judgment and these revelations must be heard and obeyed by both followers of Christ and those who do not know or believe the Gospel. The introduction stresses the importance of being resistant witnesses of the Gospel and the reward of remaining faithful: "Blessed is the one who reads the words of the prophecy, and blessed are those who hear and keep what is written in it; for the time is near" (v. 3). These words summarize the message for the whole book, followed by John's telling of the first revelation (1:9–17). The revelation is about the seven lampstands in the middle of which the Son of God stands holding in his right hand the seven stars. The seven lampstands are the seven churches to which the seven letters will be sent (chapters 2–3), and the seven stars are the messengers or leaders of the seven churches. Jesus as the Son of God standing in the middle of the seven lampstands (the seven churches) presents Jesus as the center of the church's discipleship work. In other words, keeping Jesus in their hearts and minds will enable them to fulfill their discipleship task.

The introduction shows the main message of the book and how that message is to be received by the intended audience. This is followed by the narration of the seven letters to the seven churches of Ephesus, Smyrna, Pergamum, Thyatira, Sardis, Philadelphia, and Laodecia (chapters 2–3). The seven letters carry the message of how to be good witnesses of God, and promise reward for being good witnesses. In other words, to be good followers or disciples of Jesus. The rewards include "permission to eat from the tree of life" (2:7); "a white stone" (2:17); "a place with me on my throne" (3:21).

The ultimate reward is a place on God's throne, and John describes the throne and the person who is worthy to open the scroll and its seven seals in chapters 4–5. That person is described as the lion of the tribe of Judah (5:5) and as a lamb standing as if it had been slaughtered (5:6, 9). The descriptions express the discipleship work of the church. The church is strong in stature but performing discipleship work with humility. The church's undertaking of its discipleship work is not easy. It is full of pain and suffering that must be endured in order to bring un-repentant and unbelievers (such as the Romans) into salvation or new life.

The vision of God's throne is followed by the opening of the seven seals (6:1–17). Opening the seventh seal is interrupted by the vision of the 144,000 of Israel. From the perspective of the church's discipleship work, the intermission shows that there are moments along the way when God gives chances to the un-repentant and the unbelievers to turn to God. This is the message in the intermission (10:1–11) and in the two witnesses (11:1–14) between the blowing of the sixth and the seventh trumpets. After the blowing of the seventh trumpet comes the vision of the woman crying out in birth pangs. The woman symbolizes the cry of the church now reaching the climax of its discipleship work. By this time, the church should be able to produce new lives—to again born lives, repentant lives, and new converted lives. The church in the beginning (chapters 2–3) was given the task of preaching and living the message of salvation. In the figure of the woman crying out in pain giving birth to a child is the imagery of the discipleship work of the church. The persuasive argument resonating for me as a reader is patient endurance and holding on to God so that new lives are begotten. The following exegesis will elaborate on this claim.

Revelation 12:1–17 as Narrative and Rhetorical Unit

Revelation 12 as a narrative and rhetorical unit divides into three parts—beginning, middle, end.[19] The three parts explain what is going on in the narrative as a whole.

- Beginning: Vv. 1–6 describe a woman in the pains of childbirth and a dragon waiting to devour her child, but the child was carried away to God and the woman fled to the wilderness on Earth.

- Middle: Vv. 7–12 describe a war breaking out in heaven between Michael and the dragon, in which the dragon was defeated and casted down to Earth.

- End: Vv. 13–17 describe the dragon's pursuit of the woman who bore a child and Earth's coming to help the woman.

The opening and the closing signs of Rev 12:1–17 as a narrative and rhetorical unit is an *inclusio*[20] that indicate the woman as one of the main characters in this vision. At the opening is a glorious vision of a woman clothed with the astrological cosmos yet writhing in pain, and it concludes with her protection and care by Earth. Schüssler Fiorenza wrote that the description of this woman uses the language of myth (showing that Revelation consists of traditional mythologies).[21] What happens at the middle of the unit is significant to show the important function of this woman character in the vision.

The literary markers that begin vv. 7 and 13 are significant in showing the progress of the unit from beginning to end. Verse 7 begins with Καὶ ἐγένετο (And then), a transitory conjunction[22] to illustrate a break in thought. Verse 13 begins similarly with Καὶ ὅτε (And when), another transitory conjunction. These breaks allow for dividing the narrative into three parts. The first is when and where the event takes place (the setting). It determines the reaction of characters involved in the story and organizes the story into different arenas and demonstrates how the

19. A rhetorical unit has a "beginning, a middle, and an end" (Kennedy, *New Testament Interpretation*, 33–34).

20. *Inclusio* is "signs of opening and closure" (Kennedy, *New Testament Interpretation*, 34, 82).

21. Schüssler Fiorenza, "Composition and structure of the Book of Revelation," 354.

22. Conjunction s has multiple functions in a sentence such as transition, continuity, and contrast (Nofoaiga, *A Samoan Reading of Discipleship in Matthew*, 57; See also Black, *Sentence Conjunctions*, 142–78).

movement of the stories from one arena to another solidifies the thoughts and ideas of the author. As suggested above, it was toward showing the woman crying out in birth pangs as an imagery of the church's discipleship work.

The setting of Rev 12:1–17 is in the mind of John the author, who sees a vision of two signs in οὐρανῷ (heaven). 1) A great portent with "a woman clothed with the sun, with the moon under her feet, and on her head a crown of twelve stars." The woman is pregnant and cries out in birth pangs. 2) Another sign appeared, not great like the first but with "a great red dragon, with seven heads and ten horns, and seven diadems on his heads." Its greatness is seen in how its tail swept across the heavens and threw down one third of the stars to Earth. It continues with the woman giving birth to a υἱὸν ἄρσεν (male child) that is to ποιμαίνειν (to tend, to shepherd, to lead to pasture, to rule over) all nations with an iron rod. The woman's description was divine yet filled with pain and agony, almost defenseless. The dragon is first portrayed as "great" and now this male child with an "iron rod" to tend, shepherd, rule the nations.

This first part ends with the woman's τὸ τέκνον (child) being ἡρπάσθη (caught up/carried away) to God and his throne while the woman was sent to the ἔρημον (wilderness), to be τρέφωσιν (feed, nourish, support, cared for) by God for 1,260 days. The setting of the story transitions from heaven to Earth, where God cares for the woman. The woman does not speak, besides writhing in pain, and she moves according to the will of God.

The ἔρημον (wilderness) is the setting for the discipleship work of the church. The wilderness was a lonely place to prepare one physically, mentally and spiritually, as well as a place in which healing took place (Matt. 4:11; Mark 1:13; Luke 4:14). The woman as a picture of the church's discipleship work returns to Earth, where God's providence and protection exists.

Both heaven and Earth are God's workstations. According to the ancient Hebrews, the heaven (sky) is the place of the stars, sun, moon and of birds (Gen. 1:20; Deut. 4:17), and Earth is the place for inhabitants, a place where the machinations of the universe begin and where new life is born. This relates to our Samoan indigenous understanding of the functions of the *lagi* (heaven) and the *eleele* (Earth). The woman crying out in pain symbolizes a new birth, anticipating the New Heaven and New Earth that come later. After she gives birth to this new life (12:5), that child is carried away to God (12:5), until the time that the new creation is to be introduced at the end times to shepherd, protect, and rule all nations with a staff of iron rod.

The ἔρημον (wilderness) has become synonymous with the place where God is found. This is seen in God's journeying with Israel in Exodus to Deuteronomy, as well as when Elijah flees/escapes the wrath of Jezebel and sought solace in the wilderness (1 Kgs 19:4ff). In those lights, the woman returned to creation to receive counsel, console, and encouragement for the aftermath of what happen in the middle of the unit. The setting of the middle part is in heaven but concludes with the dragon on Earth. It is the war between the protector of heaven in Michael and his angels, against the darkness that is the dragon, who is also called the devil. As darkness comes face to face with the divine, Michael and his angelic army subdue the dragon and casted it down to Earth. Earth is a place where the sovereignty of God will be revealed against Satan and by this time it will be carried out by God's agent from below—Earth.

The woman is in the beginning of the unit and the dragon in the middle part. The woman as the imagery of the church's discipleship work was returned to her haven, Earth, while the dragon was casted down as if to continue a battle that started in the divine realm. Earth was an agent of God from below. According to the φωνὴν μεγάλην (great voice) in heaven, the defeat of the dragon/devil is also the defeat of evil and darkness. The time of the dragon/devil on Earth was limited. This sets up in the end of the unit the important role played by Earth, in helping the woman.

The setting for the end of the unit is Earth. The event begins with the dragon wanting revenge for what God's army (Michael and the Angels) did to him. The dragon's initial focus was the woman. The dragon attempted to drown the woman with a massive flood, but Earth came to rescue and save her. The Earth's helping the woman is considered mythopoeic language describing the interconnected relationship of human and Earth.[23] The Greek word for help used here is ἐβοήθησεν from the word βοηθέω. The word speaks of helping religious needs. In the context of Earth helping this woman, what the Earth does could be interpreted as helping the woman maintain her role—religious role—as a disciple of the will of God. Earth's helping this woman with religious needs makes Earth a disciple. It shows that Earth understands what is needed by this woman in order for her to continue her discipleship role—and this has become

23. Carrignton, "Astral Mythology in the Revelation." For mythology in the Early Christian community see Gager, *Kingdom and Community.*

the discipleship work of the church. That work will be carried out in the wilderness, and there will be more pain and suffering to come.

The shift from heaven to Earth is significant. It shows the importance of the role played by Earth in fulfilling God's will of saving the world. Earth as a character is connected to the idea that Earth and Heaven are workstations or agents of God's creation. The Greek word for Earth is γῆ which is a feminine noun. It may be taken as having the characteristic of mother Earth.[24] In this sense, Earth as a mother protects its inhabitants and this interpretation corresponds to the use of the genitive case, which indicates that inhabitants of Earth do belong to Earth. Thus speaking of Earth coming to the rescue of the woman, Earth comes as mother of the woman in birth pangs. Earth participates in the story in order to assist and safeguard its children.

Conclusion

Earth helping the woman in Rev 12 is part of the mythopoeic source in the composition of Revelation. Earth is a living being acting to fulfill its role in the human-Earth relationship as emphasized in our Samoan indigenous understanding of *vā tapuia* (sacred relationship) between *tagata* (human) and *eleele* (Earth). I connect our Samoan indigenous understanding to the vision of Earth coming to help the woman crying out in pain in Rev 12.

Earth performs the role of *tautua* (servant), serving the woman. That role makes Earth a disciple. More importantly, Earth shows the dragon that the relationship between Earth and human is *tapu* (sacred and tabooed). It also shows that *eleele* (Earth) is *tapueleele* (sacred and tabooed) and must therefore be respected.

The placement of the vision of Earth helping the woman in the middle of the narrative shows important theological interests for the book of Revelation. It reveals that the visions of salvation and judgment witnessed by John are not just about the church as people and their relations with others, but also about the church as people and their relationship with Earth. It reminds the church and its members of their discipleship work. Earth's role in this vision is also an invitation that we are to assist Earth—we as church, and we as individuals.

24. See Minear, "Far as the Curse is Found."

Bibliography

Ashcroft, Bill. *Post-colonial Transformation*. London: Routledge, 2001.

Beale, G. K. *The Book of Revelation*. New International Greek Testament Commentary. Grand Rapids: Eerdmans, 1999.

Beasley-Murray, George R. "Revelation." In *New Bible Commentary*, edited by R. T. France et al. Nottingham, UK: Inter-Varsity, 1984.

——. *The Book of Revelation*. New Century Bible. Grand Rapids: Eerdmans, 1978.

Black, Stephanie. *Sentence Conjunctions in the Gospel of Matthew: καὶ, δὲ, τότε, γάρ, οὖν, and Asyndeton in Narrative Discourse*. Journal for the Study of the New Testament Supplements 216. Sheffield: Sheffield Academic, 2002.

Blount, Brian. *Revelation: A Commentary*. New Testament Library. Louisville: Westminster John Knox, 2009.

Booker, Richard. *The Lamb and the Seven-Sealed Scroll: Understanding the Book of Revelation Book 2*. USA: Destiny Image, 2012.

Boring, M. Eugene. *Revelation*. Interpretation. Louisville: John Knox, 1973.

Carrington, Philip. "Astral Mythology in the Revelation." *Anglican Theological Review* 13 (1931) 289–305.

Ford, J. M. *The Revelation of John*. Anchor Bible 38. New York: Doubleday, 1975.

Gager, J. G. *Kingdom and Community: The Social World of Early Christianity*. Englewood Cliffs, NJ: Prentice Hall, 1975.

Hale, Thomas. "Revelation." In *The Applied New Testament Commentary: Applying God's Word to Your Life*. Colorado Springs, CO: David Cook 1996.

Johnson, Darrell W. *Discipleship on the Edge: An Expository Journey of the Book of Revelation*. Vancouver, BC: Regent College, 2004.

Kennedy, George A. *New Testament Interpretation through Rhetorical Criticism*. Studies in Religion. Chapel Hill: University of North Carolina Press, 1984.

Larsen, Kevin W. "Neglected Considerations in Understanding the Structure of the Book of Revelation." *Restoration Quarterly* 59 (2017) 225–33.

Malbon, Elizabeth Struthers. "Narrative Criticism: How Does the Story Mean?" In *Mark and Method: New Approaches in Biblical Studies*, edited by Janice Capel Anderson and Stephen D. Moore, 23–49. Minneapolis: Fortress, 1992.

Minear, Paul S. "Far as the Curse Is Found: The Point of Revelation 12:15–16." *Novum Testamentum* 23 (1991) 71–77.

Nofoaiga, Vaitusi. *A Samoan Reading of Discipleship in Matthew*. Atlanta: SBL, 2017.

Osborne, Grant R. *Revelation Verse by Verse*. Osbourne New Testament Commentaries. Bellingham, WA: Lexham, 2016.

Powell, Barry B. *Classical Myth*. Translated by Herbert M. Howe. Englewood Cliffs, NJ: Prentice Hall, 2007.

Powell, Mark Allan. "Narrative Criticism." In *Hearing the New Testament: Strategies for Interpretation*, edited Joel B. Green, 239–255. Grand Rapids: Paternoster, 1995.

Prévost, Jean-Pierre. *How to Read the Apocalypse*. London: SCM, 1991.

Robbins, Vernon K. *Exploring the Texture of Texts: A Guide to the Socio-rhetorical Interpretation*. Harrisburg, PA: Trinity, 1996.

Schüssler Fiorenza, Elisabeth. "Composition and Structure of the Book of Revelation." *Catholic Biblical Quarterly* 39 (1977) 344–66.

Segovia, Fernando F. "Introduction: Call and Discipleship—Toward a Re-examination of the Shape and Character of Christian Existence in the New Testament."

In *Discipleship in the New Testament*, edited by Fernando F. Segovia, 1–23. Philadelphia: Fortress, 1985.

Tupua Tamasese Ta'isi, and Tui Atua. "Resident, Residence, Residency in Samoan Custom." In *Su'esu'e Manogi: In Search of Fragrance.* Apia: National University of Samoa, 2008.

Wainwright, Arthur W. *Mysterious Apocalypse: Interpreting the Book of Revelation.* Nashville: Abingdon, 1993.

Wright, Tom. *Revelation for Everyone.* The New Testament for Everyone Series. Louisville: Westminster John Knox, 2011.

13

Troubling Gender Scripts

Mothering and Childbearing in 1 Timothy 2:8–15

JOHNATHAN JODAMUS

THE PORTRAYAL OF CHILDBEARING as constitutive of punitive femininity in 1 Tim 2:8–15 is aligned with contemporary discourses on motherhood (often drawing on this particular text) concerned with the social, religious and political constructions of women's lives. Early feminist scholars (mostly Western) saw motherhood as the ultimate oppression—an institution that confined women's choices and was constitutive of femininity. Similarly, drawing on the lived experiences of "childless women" and weighing in on the oppressiveness of the institution of motherhood, African scholars have written extensively about the effects of sterility on women's reproductive self-determination, in contexts where men control women's reproductive capacities through religious and cultural beliefs and practices. On the other hand, some feminist scholars have drawn on the cultural value associated with motherhood in Africa and proposed the contested notion of "motherism" as providing a more plausible organizing principle for feminism to thrive in Africa.[1] This concept, however, has come under critique for its essentialist ideas drawn from a very narrow and binary understanding of gender. More recently a new turn in the literature on motherhood gives attention to the embodied and

1. Acholonu, *Motherism.*

philosophical experience of "mothering" as opposed to the conventional focus on the institution of motherhood.

In this essay I bring the notion of mothering as experience versus motherhood as a patriarchal institution to bear on an analysis of 1 Tim 2:8–15. In doing so, I answer in the affirmative Mouton's question "whether these canonised texts have the potential to reshape the memory, imagination, language and behaviour of present day Christian households (in Africa)."[2] Through a blending of sociorhetorical interpretation (SRI) and gender-critical interpretive strategies applied to the text of 1 Timothy I will demonstrate that mothering can be viewed beyond the essentialist feminine identity, and that when viewed in this way the notion of mothering as salvific in this text is not as oppressive as some feminist scholars have argued, and in fact opens up new possibilities for soteriology beyond gender confinements. This argument holds potential to queer this text beyond the feminine and masculine binary and to respond to calls from theologians advocating for more redemptive masculinities.

Three poems set the stage for what follows:

(Un)born love
In the month of July,
Our hearts met
Our bodies touched
Our souls entwined
And a love was born
That shall remain unborn

My Jemma Joy
Today I discovered you my baby
You came into being
Queerly to the point . . .
You exist
Because
Love exists
Queer love
Embodied love
Entangled messy love
I hold you my precious angel
In my body
I carry you in my heart
Your soul entwines with mine tonight

2. Mouton, "Mothering Salvation?," 2.

We are one
One being
One love
To let you go
I have to let me go
I have to let Joy go

Daddy Jo
Daddy Jo and his Joy
May never meet
But Joy knows her Daddy Jo
She knows him by heart
Don't cry Daddy Jo
Joy will come another day

The above three poems were written by my partner at a time when social norms and circumstances surrounding our love caused us to make one of the most difficult and challenging decisions of our lives—to terminate a pregnancy. We had both felt an immediate connection with the life we had created, and even gave her a name—Jemma Joy. The first two poems were written by my partner describing her own experiences of embodiment and dis-embodiment and the third she wrote for me—recognizing the pain that I felt at the thought of letting go—trying to offer comfort. At the time, the comfort felt cold. Yes she carried this life inside her body, but my body ached physically too—I too felt like something had been ripped out from inside me on the day of the termination. This was not a socially constructed dis-embodied pain of a father—no, this was a real and physical pain—a visceral pain that we are taught only mothers experience when giving birth—or indeed when birth is lost or prevented. I felt this pain.

It is this pain that is apparently what gives women salvation, according to 1 Tim 2:15 "she will be saved through childbearing."[3] The text clearly draws on Gen 3:16, "To the woman he said, 'I will surely multiply your pain in *childbearing*; in pain you shall bring forth children.'" I bring to the text of 1 Tim 2:8–15 my own range of experiences from the temporary joy I felt at the thought of childbearing to the blinding permanent pain of the loss. I dare to offer a redemptive masculine reading of this text—one that invites us to consider mothering as experiential, rather than biological and salvation as transformative rather than

---

3. Solevag, "Salvation, Gender and the Figure of Eve." See also McNeel, *Paul as Infant and Nursing*, 136–37, 144.

eschatological. I do this in a context where, as Maria Frahm-Arp has
shown, "Men are not meant to be involved in mothering but rather are
expected to be role models to their children of what it means to be dedicated Christian men and to offer them spiritual and emotional support."[4]
And yet as I have noted in a previous publication amidst ideas of such
hegemonic and dominant masculinities scholars have been calling for
redemptive masculinities.[5] For example, in their edited collected volume
of essays titled *Redemptive Masculinities: Men, HIV and Religion*, Ezra
Chitando and Sophia Chirongoma assert that they wish to "underline
the importance of religio-cultural resources in the emergence of liberating 'more peaceful and harmonious masculinities.'"[6] One such religio-
cultural resource is the bible and biblical scholar Gerald West has taken
up the challenge of using the biblical text as a resource in developing the
notion of redemptive masculinities through careful and close reading of
biblical texts with communities of faith.[7] The search for theological and
biblical resources that align with redemptive masculinities is one which I
wish to pick up here, in a text that has conventionally been interpreted as
irredeemably patriarchal.

The invitation to consider mothering as experiential rather than
biological, and salvation as transformational rather than just eschatological, opens up possibilities not only to re-read this text in this way, but to
consider the various ways in which the category of gender is rendered
unstable in Pauline texts. I proceed with this re-reading in four sections:

1. The first section reviews feminist scholarship on this passage and
   here I identify the gap in reading via the lens of motherhood (as an
   institution) rather than mothering as experiential.

2. In the second section I demonstrate how a gender-critical reading,
   via the method of socio-rhetorical interpretation (SRI), simply upholds mothering as a patriarchal institution aligned with the gender
   norms of the Ancient Mediterranean.

3. In the third section I argue that a redemptive reading of 1 Timothy
   requires us to read inter-textually with other Pauline texts specifically

---

4. Frahm-Arp, "Constructions of Mothering," 153.
5. Jodamus, "Paul, the 'Real' Man."
6. Chitando and Chirongoma, "Introduction," 1.
7. West, "The Contribution of Tamar's Story."

1 Cor 3. It is in the portrayal of Paul as a nursing mother that the argument for a redemptive masculinity is made most poignant.

4. In the fourth and final section, I expand Lopez's notion of Paul's body as a "hybridized body" that is "always negotiating (and being negotiated by) and mimicking empire,"[8] to include a reconsideration of Paul's body as a gendered hybridized body.

I conclude by noting that in contexts such as where I come from, and indeed globally, where Pauline texts are used to circumscribe and confine women in everything from matters relating to ordination to self-determination, intertextual readings provide the space to re-consider Paul, perhaps even redeem him—so that we all can be saved.

1 Timothy 2:8–15 (NRSV)

> 8 I desire, then, that in every place the men should pray, lifting up holy hands without anger or argument; 9 also that the women should dress themselves modestly and decently in suitable clothing, not with their hair braided, or with gold, pearls, or expensive clothes, 10 but with good works, as is proper for women who profess reverence for God. 11 Let a woman learn in silence with full submission. 12 I permit no woman to teach or to have authority over a man; she is to keep silent. 13 For Adam was formed first, then Eve; 14 and Adam was not deceived, but the woman was deceived and became a transgressor. 15 Yet she will be saved through childbearing, provided they continue in faith and love and holiness, with modesty.

1. Motherhood as Patriarchal Institution vs (M)othering as Transformative

Feminist scholars of the New Testament have lamented the irredeemability of 1 Tim 2:8–15 and have often argued it to be a controversial text of terror.[9] There is good reason that early feminist scholars (mostly Western) saw motherhood as the ultimate oppression—an institution

---

8. Lopez, "Visualizing Significant Otherness," 90.

9. West, "Taming Texts of Terror"; Mouton and Van Wolde, "New Life from a Pastoral Text of Terror?"; Mouton, "Mothering Salvation?" 2.

that confined women's choices and was constitutive of femininity. Similarly, drawing on the lived experiences of "childless women" and weighing in on the oppressiveness of the institution of motherhood, African scholars have written extensively about the effects of sterility on women's reproductive self-determination, in contexts where men control women's reproductive capacities through religious and cultural beliefs and practices.[10] More recently Frahm-Arp,[11] using a case study of Pentecostal Charismatic Churches in South Africa and the lens of ethnography of religions has explored motherhood as piety. These are "conservative religious ideals of motherhood,"[12] often expressed in popular media as "the nursing mother, the grooming mother, and the attentive mother."[13]

In my own previous study of this text I argued that τεκνογονίας ("childbearing") in v. 15 plays an integral part in the construction and representation of femininity in the text of 1 Tim 2:18–15.[14] The term τεκνογονίας creates a rhetographic image that functions rhetorically to construct and represent femininity. Rhetography refers to the visual imagery or pictorial narrative and scene construction contained in rhetorical depiction.[15] This "progressive, sensory-aesthetic, and/or argumentative texture of a text" allows "a hearer/reader to create a graphic image or picture in the mind that implies a certain kind of truth and/or reality."[16] Rhetology, on the other hand, refers to "the logic of rhetorical reasoning."[17] So, in my previous study I demonstrated that rhetography and rhetology as SRI analytical tools provide a very useful link for identifying the performativity of gender in the text of 1 Corinthians that functions to script and structure engendering.

Since then, my encounter with other writings on Paul and women as well as my own personal experience of a close encounter with mothering has led me to the same question that Kartzow recently asked, "what kinds of women are saved through childbirth, and secondly what does it mean

10. Oduyoye, "A Coming Home to Myself," 105–20; Dyer, et al., "Men Leave Me as I Cannot Have Children," 1663–68.

11. Frahm-Arp, "Constructions of Mothering," 145–63.

12. Frahm-Arp, "Constructions of Mothering," 156.

13. Frahm-Arp, "Constructions of Mothering," 161.

14. Jodamus, "A Socio-Rhetorical Exegesis of 1 Timothy 2:9–15," 100.

15. Robbins, "Beginnings and Developments in Socio-Rhetorical Interpretation," 17–18; Robbins, *The Invention of Christian Discourse*, 6, 16.

16. Robbins, *The Invention of Christian Discourse*, xxvii.

17. Robbins, *The Invention of Christian Discourse*, 16.

to be saved?"[18] Utilizing an intersectional lens Kartzow explores what childbearing meant for different classes and ethnicities of women such as Hagar and Mary, and further examines salvation beyond the eschatological to a more immanent idea of healing and self-preservation—and I argue perhaps even transformation.[19]

While Kartzow introduces a theoretical innovation in terms of a re-examination of this text through an intersectional lens,[20] the gender binary remains firmly intact in her analysis which restricts itself to the biological reproductive capability of women born female. If salvation is accessible to women (biologically female) through childbearing and their commitment to subservience and submission, then the opposite is true for men—men are already and always "saved" by virtue of their maleness and concomitantly through their ability to lead and dominate. Who, from this vantage point, to ask one of the central questions addressed in this collection of essays, is included and excluded, elected, rejected, and dis-elected? Kartzow examines what it means to be saved by reflecting on different meanings of σωζω, "to save, that is to deliver or protect (literally and figuratively): heal, preserve, save (self), do well, be (make) whole" and asks if childbirth "gives women access to all or some of these qualities, not only eschatological salvation in the context of worship and prayer."[21] The question I pose is what then about salvation as transformative praxis—transformation that takes into consideration positionality, power and privilege and not just a therapeutic soteriology focused on dis-embodied transcendence as opposed to embodied immanence.

Here is where the concept of mothering as opposed to motherhood is key. Contrary to the group of feminist scholars who have seen this text as irredeemably patriarchal and aligned with punitive femininity, other feminist scholars, particularly in Africa, have drawn on the cultural value associated with motherhood and have proposed the contested notion of "motherism" as providing a more plausible organizing principle for feminism to thrive in Africa.[22] Scholars like Desiree Lewis and Shireen

18. Kartzow, "Reproductive Salvation and Slavery," 9.

19. Kartzow, "Reproductive Salvation and Slavery," 90.

20. Kartzow, "Reproductive Salvation and Slavery," 103.

21. Kartzow, "Reproductive Salvation and Slavery," 90.

22. Acholonu, *Motherism*; Fester and Gouws, "Redefining the Public Space."

Hassim and Amanda Gouws have critiqued this concept for its essentialist ideas drawn from a very narrow and binary understanding of gender.[23]

More recently, a new turn can be discerned in the literature on
motherhood (and this is where I locate myself) where attention is given
to the embodied and philosophical experience of "mothering" as opposed to the conventional focus on the institution of motherhood. Moving beyond essentialist or romantic views of motherhood, Getman and
Nadar,[24] for example, drawing on Grace Jantzen's notion of natality focus
on the possibilities that mothering as experience versus motherhood
as a patriarchal institution, hold for theologizing. In this essay I argue
that 1 Tim 2:8–15 has to be read intertextually to grasp the potential of
moving beyond the gender binaries associated with mothering. This rereading, however, can only occur when we first acknowledge the ways in
which the "shape" of the text as it stands holds little potential for being
redemptive. I will demonstrate this limitation with gender-critical strategies of reading to interpret 1 Tim 2:1–15, before turning to an intertextual reading which opens up other possibilities.

2. Childbearing Rhetography as Constitutive of "Ideal" Femininity(ies) in 1 Timothy 2:8–15

One of the primary relationships that function within the household
dynamic is that of the mother as nurturer/caregiver to her offspring and
household manager.[25] Through the mapping invoked by the metaphor of
the childbearing mother, important gendered characteristics are transferred in and through the text in relation to how the text constructs and
represents femininity. From an ancient Mediterranean perspective and in
light of the dominant gender system of that epoch, engendering was also
a vital component of the "cultural intertexture" that resulted by imple-
menting these images.[26] Paul's use of τεκνογονίας ("childbearing") in v. 15
serves to re-inscribe a dominant and normalizing notion of femininity.
In so doing, it replicates and reinforces this hegemonic structuring of
gender. Kahl notes further in her analysis of Gal 4:19 that "the female is

---

23. Fester and Gouws, "Redefining the Public Space"; Lewis, "Introduction."

24. Getman and Nadar, "Natality and Motherism."

25. Malina and Neyrey, *Portraits of Paul*, 178.

26. Robbins, *Exploring the Texture of Texts*, 129.

dramatically centered in Gal. 4 as the 'mother-chapter' of Paul."[27] She fails to see, however, that this centering of the female and the procreative symbolism in the text also re-inscribes one of the archetypal constructions and representations of femininity in the ancient Mediterranean. In this way discourse serves to support the dominant structuring of femininity, ensuring that this gender performance of women primarily as baby makers is firmly established in *habitus*. Paul's use of τεχνογονίας ("childbearing") in v. 15 serves the analogous purpose of scripting femininity along these lines. By doing this it seems to jettison any alternative and possible boundary crossing construction and representation of feminine identity and serves only to further concretize strict gender normativities that primarily script female bodies to the interiority of the household with the primary purpose of household management and procreation.

The text of 1 Tim 2:8–15 with its household metaphors evokes a rhetographic image of a childbearing mother in the minds of the auditors. It is my contention that the use of this imagery also centers a particular construction and representation of femininity in the text and by doing so paradoxically buttresses dominant notions of masculinity. Ancient Mediterranean discursive thought and praxis continued to conceptualize women as mere incubators of reproduction, instead of as partners in reproductive labor.[28] Galen asks, "And what is semen? Clearly the active principal of the animal, the material principle being the menstrual blood."[29] As a result, women were rendered passive, receptive, docile, bound up with inferiority, and eventually alienable. The use of the maternal imagery in this passage furthermore constructs a rhetographic picture of femininity as being equal to motherhood and implies that to be a woman one had to fulfil the normative obligations of motherhood and the roles and duties that this encompassed within that epoch.

Paul's allusion to motherhood in the passage seems unexceptionable in relation to his cultural milieu and the ideological implications of its sex/gender system.[30] The use of maternal imagery through the use of the metaphor of the birthing mother in the text constructs and represents "motherhood–as–femininity" and re-establishes the normative and highly praised role of motherhood and childbearing held within the

---

27. Kahl, "No Longer Male," 43.

28. Galen, *On the Use of the Parts of the Body*, 14.2.299.

29. Galen, *On the Natural Faculties*, 2.3.86.

30. Robbins, *Exploring the Texture of Texts*, 58.

ancient Mediterranean. By his adoption of normative imperial Graeco-Roman gendered practices and discursive values, it seems that Paul was totally enculturated within the dominant cultural environment in which he lived. By employing this particular stereotypical gendered image in his rhetoric Paul inadvertently re-inscribes the hegemonic notion of women as docile reproductive. The notion that reproduction was the primary role of women is especially prominent in the "women as fertile soil model" and the "one-sex" model.[31] This valorizing of the maternal body in the discourse of the text serves to subordinate and marginalize women in the Ephesian community to fulfil only those roles that were suitable to the normative patriarchal cultural tradition of the first century.

At stake in this depiction is not only female shame but more importantly, from the perspective of this essay, what is at stake is gender construction and representation and their implications for understanding the text. 1 Tim 2:8–15 privileges a certain gendered normativity, one that is discursively constituted through the representation of women as child bearers. The biblical text functions as normalizing mechanism that circumscribes and regulates the possibilities for women by structuring a reductionary version of what constitutes femininity. But this comes about only if we allow the interpretive possibility to reside in the "womb." If, however, we allow for a more radical equality that dislodges mothering from the essentialist realms located only in the "womb" we free up the possibilities of seeing mothering as experience which allows for other performances that does not subscribe to strict heterosexual configurations.

The concept of redemptive masculinities as proposed by Chitando and others invite us to consider another option—mothering beyond the biological to the experiential, mothering as praxis, as opposed to motherhood as a patriarchal institution—hence the radical idea that men can mother too. This transgendering of mothering is not unique to my experience of the joys and pain of conception and termination, but is supported by an intertextual reading of Paul in 1 Cor 3:1–4, to which I now turn.

3. Intertextual Considerations: Paul the Man and Paul the Mother

McNeel in her investigation of 1 Thess 2:5–8 has convincingly shown a preponderance of mother and birth terminologies in Pauline writings but ironically, and contrary to the gender regulatory schemas of the time,

---

31. Økland, *Women in Their Place*, 40.

a dissociation of this function from femininity and instead co-opting it as a masculine task.[32] Similarly, noticing a preponderance of "mother and birth terminology" in Galatians 4 and crediting this focus in Paul's discourse to an apparent "counter-patriarchal logic" in his theology, Kahl focusses on the "mother Paul" metaphor in Gal 4:19.[33]

I argue, therefore, that constructing childbearing as punitive in 1 Timothy is a result of the immediate previous reference to the Fall, which places blame on Eve (Gen 3:16). The logic of the rhetoric which follows has to then attach childbearing to a punitive feminine task—one that is simply not in line with other Pauline writings. First Corinthians 3:1–4 where Paul portrays himself as a nursing mother in relation to the Christian community in Corinth is one example.

Scholars have attempted to make sense of this complex passage with the use of various interpretive strategies. Komaravalli makes use of blending theory as posited by Fauconnier and Turner to interpret Paul's use of complex household and building metaphors.[34] Some of the sub-metaphors that Komaravalli investigates include the mother-infants (1 Cor 3:1–4) and the father-children (1 Cor 4:14–21) relationships. These demonstrate the efficacy of understanding the everyday social and cultural *topos* of the ancient household as a complex metaphor used by Paul to validate his relationship with the Corinthian community.[35] Among the primary relationships within the household dynamic was mother as nurturer/caregiver and nurse. In 1 Cor 3:1–4 Paul, somewhat surprisingly, maps the nursing mother rhetography on to himself to explicate his relationship with the Corinthians. Through the mapping, important characteristics of the nursing mother are transferred to Paul and present him as nurturer/sustainer of the Corinthian community.

The ideology implied in the discourse of 1 Cor 3:1–4 has been a key strategy to interpret this text. Like Wanamaker,[36] Komaravalli also sees Paul's ideological dissimulation of the use of the mother-infant metaphors in 3:1–4 as a tactical ideological move by Paul.[37] He argues that the depiction of the Corinthian community as immature infants, functions

32. McNeel, *Paul as Infant and Nursing Mother.*

33. Kahl, "No Longer Male," 42.

34. Komaravalli, "Paul's Rhetorical Use of Complex Metaphors," 7, 9, 201–2; Fauconnier and Turner, *The Way We Think.*

35. Komaravalli, "Paul's Rhetorical Use of Complex Metaphors," 75.

36. Wanamaker, "A Rhetoric of Power: Ideology and 1 Corinthians 1–4," 130.

37. Komaravalli, "Paul's Rhetorical Use of Complex Metaphors," 9.

to shame them, and gives Paul ideological power, similar to the maternal power that mothers have over their infants.[38] The depiction of Paul as a nursing mother and not merely any mother, has significance as it ideologically positions him as archetypal in the lives of nursing infants. A further significance is that the nursing mother had even more significance to an infant's father at that stage of development as it was customarily the mother who fed the infant breast milk.[39] Komaravalli's analysis is useful to demonstrate the ideological function of these sub-metaphors as a tool to assert and validate Paul's power and authority within the Corinthian community and stem the tide of factionalism that was brewing. He does not, however, take into account the gendered implications of these metaphors and how this impacts the text. In so doing Komaravalli misses out on the underlying gendered script implicit in this text and so misses out on important interpretive nuances for the text.[40]

Noticing a preponderance of "mother and birth terminology" in Galatians 4 and crediting these foci in Paul's discourse to an apparent "counter-patriarchal logic" in his theology Kahl focusses on the "mother Paul" metaphor in Gal 4:19.[41] She mentions that

> she/he [Paul] is painfully trying to rebirth his/her Galatian children in the shape (μορφή) of Christ. With only a few exceptions this striking 'transgendering' Pauline self-description in terms of symbolic birth-labor has usually been ignored—it does not fit into any of the standard Pauline interpretations and stereotypes. But precisely Gal.4:19 could be a key to understanding the meaning of sex/gender-unity in Gal.3:28 and in Galatians as a whole.[42]

The text of 1 Cor 3:1–5 with its household metaphors of mother, infant, and breast milk evokes a rhetographic image of a mother breast feeding her child in the minds of the auditors. This rhetograph is used in the rhetology of the verses to place Paul in a position of absolute

---

38. Komaravalli, "Paul's Rhetorical Use of Complex Metaphors" 9. See McNeel, *Paul as Infant and Nursing Mother*, 123–54, for her discussion of Paul as infant and nursing mother in 1 Thess 2:5–8.

39. See Barrett, *A Commentary on the First Epistle to the Corinthians*, 80, who argues that the milk metaphor employed in 1 Cor 3:1–4 is used pejoratively by Paul to underscore the Corinthian congregations lack of spirituality. Other non-pejorative uses of this metaphor may be seen in 1 Pet 2:2 and Heb 5:12.

40. Komaravalli, "Paul's Rhetorical Use of Complex Metaphors," 9.

41. Kahl, "No Longer Male," 42.

42. Kahl, "No Longer Male," 42–43.

dominance over the Corinthians who are like infants in need of maternal parenting. Paul's body, however, has the potential to open up a way to see mothering differently. Mothering as experience and not mothering as patriarchal institution. The latter merely serves to re-inscribe normative notions of hegemonic masculinity. From the outset what seems first to be a diminishing of masculine virtue, when Paul takes on a role that is deemed feminine in accordance with ancient gender standards; when viewed differently in fact turns out to be a rhetorical move that opens up the gendered possibilities. These metaphors authenticate Paul's authority and dominance over the Corinthian community as well as shame the Corinthians as immature and still needing baby food.[43] Further, the metaphors construct and represent alternative gender identities.

In her analysis of 1 Cor 3:1–2 Gaventa identifies the propensity of New Testament scholars in their analyses of this text to focus on one side of the relationship between Paul and the Corinthian congregation.[44] The side that most often receives attention has been the Corinthians as infants, zooming in on what this state of spiritual immaturity means in light of Paul's teaching and preaching to them. Gaventa,[45] however, cautions that

> We cannot understand the drama presupposed in 1 Cor. 3:1–2 until we take into consideration both of the characters—not only the child who may or may not be ready to begin eating solid food but also the mother who has thus far nursed the child with milk. That is, Paul's presentation of himself as a nursing mother suggests that 1 Cor 3:1–2 illumines Paul's understanding of the nature of the apostolic task.[46]

43. Komaravalli, "Paul's Rhetorical Use of Complex Metaphors" 75–76.

44. Gaventa, "Mother's Milk and Ministry in 1 Corinthians 3," 101; Gaventa, *Our Mother Saint Paul*, 41.

45. Gaventa, "Mother's Milk and Ministry in 1 Corinthians 3," 101.

46. Paul's use of a nurturing mother image is not peculiar to 1 Cor; see for example 1 Thess 2:7–8 and Gal 4:19. Paul also uses paternal images to characterize his relationship with his correspondents as may be seen in 1 Thess 2:11–12; Gal. 4:19; and 1 Cor 4:14–21. Collins calls for a distinction between paternal and maternal images. He maintains, "The paternal image draws attention to Paul's ministry of evangelization, his having engendered children in Christ (1 Cor 4:16; Phlm 10). The maternal image evokes Paul's pastoral care, his devoted nurture of those he has evangelized (cf. 1 Thess 2:11–12)" (Collins, *First Corinthians*, 41). It is not hard to notice the blatant patriarchal and androcentric interpretive assumptions in this delineation which link the paternal imagery to active, penetrative, child producing (active male seed) evangelization and relates maternal imagery to passive, nurturing (passive female seed) pastoral care. These types of gendered assumptions are not completely dissimilar to

Gaventa investigates the imagery of Paul as nursing mother to the Corinthians to highlight the fact that Paul is not only re-establishing his authority,[47] but in his explication of his apostolic authority he is ushering in a radically different kind of authority compared to any of the other church leaders in Corinth. Her emphasis, however, is not on the gendered nature of the text in relation to how the text constructs and represents femininity. She argues that Paul's metaphorical statement that he had given the Corinthians milk to drink (4:2) foregrounds him as a nursing mother or wet nurse to the Corinthians and that this might have called into question his masculinity.[48] Given the environment of the ancient gender system, it seems reasonable, if not "natural," to imagine that "I gave you milk to drink" (γάλα ὑμᾶς ἐπότισα) would cause readers to suspect that Paul himself was not a "real man."[49] "By actively taking upon himself a role that could only be played by a woman, he effectively concedes the culturally predisposed battle for his masculinity."[50] The argument by Gaventa[51] may be summarized as follows: first, by employing maternal imagery, a focus on the ancient household family structure is centralized;[52] second, Paul's appropriation of this metaphor to himself constructs an image of masculinity that seemingly subverts normative notions of ideal masculinity and has the concomitant effect of calling

---

the dominant notions of gender from the ancient Mediterranean world. For an investigation that posits Paul as a mother to the Galatians and a transgressor of dominant gendered norms see Lopez, "Before Your Very Eyes," 154–61.

47. Gaventa, "Mother's Milk and Ministry," 101, 112; Gaventa, *Our Mother Saint Paul*, 8, 177.

48. Gaventa, "Mother's Milk and Ministry in 1 Corinthians 3." Contra Yarbrough ("Parents and Children in the Letters of Paul," 126–41) who argues that it was a male nurse (*nutritor*), rather than a nursing mother or wet nurse, who occupies the imagery in 1 Cor 3:1–2. For further discussion of this postulation, see Gaventa, *Our Mother Saint Paul*, 45–46. Cf. Bradley, "Child Care at Rome," 37–75. Even if the imagery in 1 Cor 3:1–2 refers to a male *nutritor*, Paul's association with such a role, given the first and second century Mediterranean gender standards, would nevertheless impinge on Paul's masculinity and render him effeminate.

49. Gaventa, "Mother's Milk and Ministry in 1 Corinthians 3," 109.

50. Gaventa, "Mother's Milk and Ministry in 1 Corinthians 3," 110.

51. Gaventa, "Mother's Milk and Ministry in 1 Corinthians 3," 101–2; Gaventa, *Our Mother Saint Paul*, 41–42.

52. According to Joseph H. Hellerman (*The Ancient Church as Family*, 93), the primary metaphor that Paul uses to re-establish social order in his writings is the ancient Mediterranean family. See Hellerman, *The Ancient Church as Family*, 99–108, for a discussion that traces the use of family terminology in 1 Corinthians.

into question Paul's masculinity leaves him vulnerable to derisive attacks by onlookers as weak and useless;[53] third, this metaphor serves to introduce "the later series of metaphors in which apostles are compared with farmers and builders, and prepares the way for further remarks about the nature of the apostolic task."[54]

It is my contention that the use of the maternal imagery by Paul also centers a particular construction and representation of femininity in the text and by doing so paradoxically serves to queer dominant notions of masculinity. At stake in this depiction of Paul as a nursing mother, therefore, is not only male honor or female shame. More importantly, from the perspective of this essay, however, what is at stake is gender construction and representation and what implications this has on understanding the text. It seems that the rhetographic image of Paul in the discourse of the text represents Paul as (un)masculine. This representation does not, however, subvert the dominant gendered hierarchy polarizing masculine and feminine and inadvertently only serves to further re-inscribe male domination and androcentrism.

The re-inscription and performance of dominant notions of femininity by Paul served to reproduce the dominant articulations of gender from Graeco-Roman culture and in so doing mimicked imperial power and domination in his own bodily *hexis*. Paul may suffer vituperation and ridicule in light of his association with ideal femininity, but the gendered logic that upholds this very understanding is still firmly established and left unscathed even after Paul's association with the nursing mother metaphor.[55] It does, however, offer us a glimmer to think beyond essentialized gender distinctions. The interpretive possibility that emerges in my mind is supported by Lopez who sees Paul's body as a hybridized body—a concept that transposes well into the gendered framework I have been proposing in this essay.[56]

53. See Burrus, "Mimicking," 65.

54. Gaventa, "Mother's Milk and Ministry in 1 Corinthians 3," 102.

55. Conway (*Behold the Man*, 116) argued that female metaphors in the ancient world could actually re-inscribe normative masculine ideologies. Simply because feminine imagery is employed in a metaphor does not necessitate the representation and construction of feminine identity.

56. Lopez, "Visualizing Significant Otherness," 90–91.

4. Ambivalent Engendering: Hybridized Imperial Bodies

Lopez calls for attention to the structuring and performativity of Paul's body, or what Glancy calls his "corporal vernacular."[57] Lopez asserts, "While there are numerous avenues into the discussion of (re)imag(in)ing Paul, one issue that is particularly worthy of our attention is the manner in which Paul's own body is depicted in his letters."[58] She views Paul's body as a "hybridized body" that is "always negotiating (and being negotiated by) and mimicking empire."[59] This hybridized body of Paul, as sketched by Lopez, is depicted in relation to the postcolonial notions of empire and imperialism. I am interested in Paul's hybridized body, in how it is constituted by power and the *habitus* of the ancient gendered setting. From this vantage point Paul has a hybridized or a negotiated body that constructs and represents gender in the discourse of 1 Corinthians.

This construction and representation of gender creates the rhetographic image or scenario that Paul has a negotiated body/hybridized gendered body that mimics the hegemonic gendered ideologies of Graeco-Roman culture. In associating himself with or assimilating a common feminine construction and representation of gender, he creates a rhetographic image (i.e., it creates an image in a human's mind based on social or cultural knowledge) of himself as (un)masculine or effeminate by ideal gendered standards. The mother-infant metaphors create the rhetographic image of a mother nursing her infant. This invokes a normal nurturing situation that everyone was familiar with and then asks the reader to apply that image to a different situation, namely, the relation of Paul to the Corinthian community. Assimilation of this stereotypically feminine role positions Paul as nurturer and sustainer of the Corinthian community. From a gender-critical perspective, and in light of the hegemonic engendering stereotypes, it also feminizes Paul. Paul as a nursing mother is a reversal of heteronormative and androcentric ideologies of ideal masculinity in ancient Mediterranean constructions of masculinity and renders him (un)masculine.

Paul's (un)masculine, ambivalent, gender blurring body is hardly impossible given the hegemonic "one-sex" gender model operative in the

---

57. Lopez, "Visualizing Significant Otherness," 90–101; Glancy, *Corporal Knowledge*, 12.

58. Lopez, "Visualizing Significant Otherness," 90.

59. Lopez, "Visualizing Significant Otherness," 90.

ancient world.[60] This understanding calls for a more complex structuring of Paul's gendered configuration when he assimilates the identity of a nursing mother. By doing this he re-configures his own bodily *hexis*, prioritizing ambivalence and the notion of a negotiated/hybridized body.[61] In this instance Paul's body is neither purely or only masculine, or simultaneously (un)masculine and, therefore, feminine; but also, liminal or gender blurring.

Paul's assimilation of and identification with the crucified body of Christ and his message of Christ's crucified body also carries gendered nuances. Commenting on Gal 2:19 Lopez critiques the "stability and impenetrability" of Paul's masculinity.[62] She claims that his "'manhood' is stable neither in legend nor in letter. Paul is vulnerable in a manner that he would not have been as a Roman citizen, a manly soldier and a persecutor imitating Roman hierarchical patterns, or a colonized 'other' fighting for the empire." Paul in this regard then has a "compromised masculinity that signifies vulnerability" in his construction of masculinity given hegemonic notions of masculinity in that ancient context.[63]

Conclusion

I started this essay commenting with the patriarchal irredeemability of 1 Tim 2:8–15. Bringing my own bodily *hexis* as site of contestation and conversation I have offered the possibility that mothering as experience versus mothering as biology opens up interpretive caveats that redeems masculinity from the illusion of always already being saved. Maybe mothering as experience plucks masculinity from the façade that it cannot mother, that it indeed is only other, rejected, and dis-elected. I started this essay by reading three poems written by my partner. I end with a quote by bell hooks who articulates pain as a legitimate embodied epistemology: "It is not easy to name our pain, to theorize from that location. I am grateful to the many women and men who dare to create theory from the location of pain and struggle, who courageously expose wounds

---

60. Laqueur, *Making Sex*.

61. Lopez, "Visualizing Significant Otherness," 90.

62. Lopez, "Visualizing Significant Otherness," 90.

63. Lopez, "Visualizing Significant Otherness," 91.

to give us their experience to teach and guide, as a means to chart new theoretical journeys."[64] I end with this challenge.

Bibliography

Acholonu, Catherine Obianuju. *Motherism: The Afrocentric Alternative to Feminism.* Owerri: Afa, 1995.

Barrett, C. K. *A Commentary on the First Epistle to the Corinthians.* New York: Harper & Row, 1968.

Bradley, Keith R. "Child Care at Rome: The Role of Men." In *Discovering the Roman Family: Studies in Roman Social History,* 37–75. New York: Oxford University Press, 1991.

Burrus, Virginia. "Mimicking Virgins: Colonial Ambivalence and the Ancient Romance." *Arethusa* 38 (2005) 49–88.

Chitando, Ezra, and Sophia Chirongoma. "Introduction." In *Redemptive Masculinities: Men, HIV and Religion,* edited by Ezra Chitando and Sophia Chirongoma, 1–28. EHAIA Series. Geneva: World Council of Churches Publications, 2012.

Collins, Raymond F. *First Corinthians.* Sacra Pagina 7. Collegeville, MN: Liturgical, 1999.

Conway, Colleen M. *Behold the Man: Jesus and Greco-Roman Masculinity.* Oxford: Oxford University Press, 2008.

Dyer, Silke, Naeemah Abrahams, Margaret Hoffman, and Zephne M. van der Spuy. "Men Leave Me as I Cannot Have Children: Women's Experiences with Involuntary Childlessness." *Human Reproduction* 17 (2002) 1663–68.

Fauconnier, Gilles, and Mark Turner. *The Way We Think: Conceptual Blending and the Mind's Hidden Complexities.* New York: Basic, 2003.

Fester, Shireen, and Amanda Gouws. "Redefining the Public Space: Women's Organizations, Gender Consciosness and Civil Society in South Africa." *Politikon* 25.2 (1998) 53–76.

Frahm-Arp, Maria. "Constructions of Mothering in Pentecostal Charismatic Churches in South Africa." *Neotestametica* 50.1 (2016) 145–63.

Galen. *On the Natural Faculties.* Edited and translated by Arthur J. Brock. Loeb Classical Library. Cambridge: Harvard University Press, 1979.

———. *Galen on the Usefulness of the Parts of the Body.* Edited and Translated by Margaret Tallmadge May. 2 vols. Cornell Publications in the History of Science. Ithaca, NY: Cornell University Press, 1968.

Gaventa, Beverly Roberts. "Mother's Milk and Ministry in 1 Corinthians 3." In *Theology and Ethics in Paul and His Interpreters: Essays in Honor of Victor Paul Furnish,* edited by Eugene H. Lovering and Jerry L. Sumney, 101–13. Nashville: Abingdon, 1996.

———. *Our Mother Saint Paul.* Louisville: Westminster John Knox, 2007.

Getman, Eliza, and Sarojini Nadar. "Natality and Motherism: Embodiment Within Praxis of Spiritual Leadership." *Journal for the Study of Religion* 26/2 (2013) 59–73.

Glancy, Jennifer A. *Corporal Knowledge: Early Christian Bodies.* Oxford: Oxford University Press, 2010.

---

64. hooks, *Teaching to Transgress,* 77.

Hellerman, Joseph H. *The Ancient Church as Family*. Minneapolis: Fortress, 2001.

hooks, bell. *Teaching to Transgress*. New York: Routledge, 1994.

Jodamus, Johnathan. "Paul, the 'Real' Man: Constructions and Representations of Masculinity in 1 Corinthians." *Journal of Gender and Religion in Africa* 23.2 (2017) 68–94.

———. "A Socio-Rhetorical Exegesis of 1 Timothy 2:9–15." Master's thesis, University of Cape Town, 2005.

Kahl, Brigitte. "No Longer Male: Masculinity Struggles behind Galatians 3:28?" *Journal for the Study of the New Testament* 79 (2000) 37–49.

Kartzow, Marianne Bjelland. "Reproductive Salvation and Slavery: Reading 1 Timothy 2:15 with Hagar and Mary." *Neotestamentica* 50 (2016) 89–103.

Komaravalli, Suraj K. "Paul's Rhetorical Use of Complex Metaphors in 1 Corinthians 3–4." PhD diss., University of Cape Town, 2007.

Laqueur, Thomas. *Making Sex: Body and Gender from the Greeks to Freud*. Cambridge: Harvard University Press, 1990.

Lewis, Desiree. "Introduction: African Feminisms." *Agenda* 50 (2001) 4–10.

Lopez, Davina C. "Before Your Very Eyes: Roman Imperial Ideology, Gender Constructs and Paul's Inter-Nationalism." In *Mapping Gender in Ancient Religious Discourses*, edited by Todd Penner and Caroline Vander Stichele, 115–62. Biblical Interpretation Series 84. Leiden: Brill, 2007.

———. "Visualizing Significant Otherness: Reimagining Paul(Ine Studies) through Hybrid Lenses." In *The Colonized Apostle: Paul through Postcolonial Eyes*, edited by Christopher D. Stanley, 74–94. Paul in Critical Contexts. Minneapolis: Fortress, 2011.

Malina, Bruce J., and Jerome H. Neyrey. *Portraits of Paul: An Archaeology of Ancient Personality*. Louisville: Westminster John Knox, 1996.

McNeel, Jennifer Houston. *Paul as Infant and Nursing Mother: Metaphor, Rhetoric, and Identity in 1 Thessalonians*. Early Christianity and Its Literature 12. Atlanta: SBL, 2014.

Mouton, Elna. "Mothering Salvation? Gender and Class in Early Christian Household Discourse." *Neotestamentica* 50 (2016) 1–8.

Mouton, Elna, and Ellen Van Wolde. "New Life from a Pastoral Text of Terror? Gender Perspectives on God and Humanity in 1 Timothy 2." *Scriptura* 111 (2012) 583–601.

Oduyoye, Mercy. "A Coming Home to Myself: The Childless Woman in West African Space." In *Liberating Eschatology: Essays in Honour of Letty M. Russell*, edited by Margaret A. Farley and Serene Jones, 105–20. Louisville: Westminster John Knox, 1999.

Økland, Jorunn. *Women in Their Place: Paul and the Corinthian Discourse of Gender and Sanctuary Space*. Journal for the Study of the New Testament Supplements 269. London: T. & T. Clark, 2004.

Robbins, Vernon K. "Beginnings and Developments in Socio-Rhetorical Interpretation." Unpublished paper. Emory University, 2004. http://www.religion.emory.edu/faculty/robbins/Pdfs/SRIBegDevRRA.pdf/.

———. *Exploring the Texture of Texts: A Guide to Socio-Rhetorical Interpretation*. Valley Forge, PA: Trinity, 1996.

———. *The Invention of Christian Discourse*. Rhetoric of Religious Antiquity Series 1. Blandford Forum, UK: Deo, 2009.

Solevag, Anna Rebecca. "Salvation, Gender and the Figure of Eve in 1 Timothy 2:9–15." *Lectio-Difficilior: European Electronic Journal for Feminist Exegesis* 2 (2012) 1–27.

Wanamaker, Charles A. "A Rhetoric of Power: Ideology and 1 Corinthians 1–4." In *Paul and the Corinthians: Studies on a Community in Conflict. Essays in Honour of Margaret Thrall*, edited by Trevor J. Burke and J. Keith Elliott, 115–37. Novum Testamentum Supplements 109. Leiden: Brill, 2003.

West, Gerald O. "The Contribution of Tamar's Story to the Construction of Alternative African Masculinities." In *Redemptive Masculinities: Men, HIV and Religion*, edited by Ezra Chitando and Sophia Chirongoma, 173–91. Geneva: World Council of Churches Publications, 2012.

———. "Taming Texts of Terror: Reading (against) the Gender Grain of 1 Timothy." *Scriptura* 86 (2004) 160–73.

Yarbrough, O. Larry. "Parents and Children in the Letters of Paul." In *The Social World of the First Christians: Essays in Honor of Wayne A. Meeks*, edited by Michael L White and Larry O. Yarbrough, 126–41. Minneapolis: Fortress, 1995.

14

Throwing Shade

Psalm 4 Shares the Anxieties of the Gay Community

Brent Pelton

Members of a community are constantly shaped by cultural elements as much as they are the shapers; education, religion, fashion, ethics, and other aspects uphold one's participation in a community, and at the same time commit symbolic violence[1] to keep one in check within the wider society. This communal peace keeping and acts of symbolic, and sometimes physical, violence can be seen daily in how people interact with each other as they construct their idealized community. This process has been going on since time immemorial, with early Jewish communities being no exception to this interplay between acceptability moving towards normalization and disallowance leading towards social stigmatization within society.

When one sits within the socially accepted boundaries of society—only marginally or trendily breaking social taboo—it is sometimes difficult to hear the pained voice of someone who is on society's literal and metaphorical edge. Likewise, when those with social capital transcribe the voice of the marginalized, they circumscribe the locus and the impact of that pain of those who are voiceless. As a result, the full range of expression of suffering can be cooped for socio-political gain by the already

---

1. Beilharz, *Social Theory*, 41.

powerful members of society. With this understanding in mind, how does one listen anew to the voice that lay beneath socio-political translations and interpretations, as well as cultural, linguistic, and temporal barriers? Using historical and literary analysis, one may uncover the depth of suffering expressed in Psalm 4; yet, one still does not hear the echoes of the personhood and allow the individual to resurface from the text. Using the lens of the gay community, the urgency, pain and eventual trust shared within this Psalm may be seen by those who live within boundaries of acceptability, encouraging them to hear the voice of those who do not.

Through a deeper understanding of the context from which this psalm speaks, one can transcribe the words of pain in order to gain a fresh perspective from which this psalm can speak. Although this psalm, which could be written by either male or female, contains a "lack of precise identification of either adversaries or accusations,"[2] one can use a gay lens as a placeholder in understanding marginalization. This gay framework, thus, helps readers to understand those who are struggling with the anxiety of being symbolically attacked for their behavior or beliefs and turn to God to save them from psychological harm. As a result of this perspectival placeholder, one can give a face to the marginalized and a voice to the psalmist who is desperate to find peace with God in the face of hardship.

Psalm 4, which is part of a larger collection of psalms (Psalms 3–7), has an individual seeking help and resides within the collection of Book One in the Psalter.[3] The unidentifiable individual "believes he [or she] is under attack [. . .] from people who are slandering [her or] him or bringing false accusations against him [or her]. The psalm, therefore, contains elements of a lament, but the mood throughout is rather one of quiet confidence."[4] This psalm, from an unknown time period, may "not [be] a private prayer but was probably performed for the benefit of others as well"[5]; if this was the case, it may be that the accusation had to do with the worshipping of other gods.[6] As these accusations intensify, "a psychological anxiety torments the speaker. It seems that his [or her] relationship with God, not [her or] his relationships with other people, is out of joint"[7] as a

2. Craigie, Tate and Tucker, *Psalms 1–50*, 82.

3. DeClaissé-Walford, *et al. The Book of Psalms*, 80.

4. Davidson. *The Vitality of Worship*, 22.

5. Broyles, *Psalms*, 52–3.

6. DeClaissé-Walford *et al., The Book of Psalms*, 79.

7. Charry, *Psalms 1–50*, 17.

result. For people within the gay community, these kinds of accusations are common; the Bible is often cited to control the actions and faith of a gay individual, creating psychological harm in the process. Citations, such as Gen 19 regarding the Sodomites, are often used out of context[8] to justify imbuing a faith perspective on sexuality and, thus, stating that a different belief would be counter to Christianity and one's relationship with God.

Many of those who oppose a "gay lifestyle" impose a worldview of sexuality based on the concept of natural tendencies; this concept implies that there is a "pure" state of one's body. "The ever unfinished nature of the body [is] hidden, kept secret; conception, pregnancy, childbirth, death throes,"[9] sexuality and other aspects are confined as a grotesque hindrance on the "pure" state. However, McCarthy points out that "ironically our bodies are the fundamental medium of our social world (i.e. our only world). My bodily intentions shape and are shaped by the particulars of my everyday life."[10] Owing to this, there is no "natural" expression of the body because, by its very nature, it is an expression of the owner's self-representation.

Throughout the psalm, there are three interlocutors: the accuser, the psalmist, and God. The psalmist is the one articulating the accusations of the community and the support of God to the reader. As a result, the voices and rationale of the other two interlocutors must be inferred from the text. In order to gain a fuller understanding of the interplay between the self and the community within the context of faithfulness to God, the reading of this psalm will be divided into the following sections:

> Opening plea for help (v.1)
>> Complaint about what the community has said (v. 2)
>>> Words of instruction to the community (vv. 3–5)
>> Complaint about what the community is saying (v. 6)
> Closing confession of trust (vv. 7–8).[11]

Although the placements of the *Selah* seem to indicate a three-part formation of this text (vv. 1–2, 3–4, 5–8), the concentric structure lends itself to being divided into a five-part structure as seen above. Favoring the five-part structure will also allow closer analysis and contrast with those aspects that address mainly God (v. 1, v. 8) and those parts

8. Boswell, *Same-Sex Unions*, 1994.

9. Bakhtin, *Rabelais and His World*, 29.

10. Loughlin, *Queer Theology*, 86.

11. DeClaissé-Walford, et al. *The Book of Psalms*, 80–81.

that address mainly humanity (vv. 2–7).[12] By dividing the reading of the psalm in this manner, one will be able to see the interplay of dialogue between God, the accused, and the accuser, drawing on the contemporary experiences of the gay community in order to hear afresh the hardship that this psalmist is wrestling with.

Rereading Psalm 4

Verse 1: Opening Plea for Help

> O God, my Advocate, answer me when I am calling!
> You gave me a place when I was oppressed.
> Be gentle on me, and hear my prayers again.[13]

The psalmist cries out to God with the common address—"O God"—seeking support. The Psalmist presents this psalm as a trial, as s/he invokes the word "right" (צֶדֶק) which "has a legal background and can mean acquittal, a declaration of innocence, or deliverance, as well as the more general righteousness and justice."[14] The individual is accused of a transgression for which only God can be the judge. S/he pleads the case brought before God, imploring God with three imperative verbs answer (me), עֲנֵנִי, be gracious (to me), חָנֵּנִי, and hear (my prayer), וּשְׁמַע, demonstrating the urgency of the need for deliverance. This request for aid comes as s/he introduces "a trusting recollection of past instances of such help"[15]; the psalmist remembers the God of Compassion, "the God who, as it were, gave him [or her] breathing space when life was getting on top of [her or] him, rescued him [or her] when [s/he] was being hemmed in by enemies."[16]

As this instance is similar to past experiences, one gets the sense of "psychological anxiety [that] torments the speaker."[17] This experience of torment that the psalmist speaks from mirrors many of the mental health issues that the gay community face due to external pressures of heterosexism and homophobia within a heteronormative world. Those who identify as gay, as distinct from those who are men who have sex

12. DeClaissé-Walford, et al. *The Book of Psalms*, 80–81.

13. The renderings provided here and in the following subsections are mine.

14. Davidson, *The Vitality of Worship*, 22.

15. DeClaissé-Walford, et al. *The Book of Psalms*, 83.

16. Davidson, *The Vitality of Worship*, 22.

17. Charry, *Psalms 1–50*, 17.

with men, are 14 times more suicidal,[18] fifty five percent (55%) of gay men struggle with drug addiction,[19] 1 in 4 gay men abuse alcohol,[20] and gay men are more than two hundred percent (200%) more likely to smoke.[21] Gay men across cultural, geographic, religious, and ethnic demographics are crying out in a world that does not understand them and they are feeling the mental strain of it all. Gay men know all too well the accusations of conformity that this psalmist expresses and the weight that sometimes feel impossible to bear.

Verse 2: Complaint about What the Community Said

> How long will you people throw shade on me?
> How long will you love a false god, and desire meaningless words?

In this second verse, one continues to hear that "[t]he speaker is exasperated. This untoward behavior has apparently been going on for some time."[22] The cry of "how long," often used in psalms of lament, "joins hands with the word 'why' as a natural, puzzled, and often painful response to situations in life which seem meaningless."[23] The audience of the psalm can begin to feel the yearning for understanding in the circumstances that the individual finds his or herself. Most likely, charges of idol worship and false beliefs are a part of this shaming, as both "vain words" (רִיק) and "lies" (כָזָב) can be used as metaphors for idols, "point[ing] here to the unfounded accusations, the character assassination from which the psalmist is suffering."[24] The second verse expands on the notion that the psalmist has been undergoing ongoing mental distress over false accusations with the intent of challenging the validity of his or her faith in God. These challenges would be through symbolic, and perhaps physical, violence to impose change on the psalmist. By challenging the core faith in this manner, the accusers are trying to *other* her or him by excluding the accused from the covenantal people until s/he meets the demands of those with socio-economic and political power.[25]

18. Tracy. "Homosexuality and Suicide."
19. "Drug Addiction in the LGBT Community."
20. "Addiction and Abuse in the LGBT Community."
21. "Addiction and Abuse in the LGBT Community."
22. Charry, *Psalms 1–50*, 19.
23. Davidson, *The Vitality of Worship*, 19.
24. Davidson, *The Vitality of Worship*, 23.
25. Bullock, Strauss and Walton, *Psalms*, 35.

There are possible allusions that the accusers are people of power and wealth, as the phrase בְּנֵי־אִישׁ can be understood as addressing "wealthy members of the community."[26] This assumption is further enhanced, as they are the people who are overjoyed when their land produces abundantly in v. 7,[27] hinting at their wealth from their property at the expense of the laboring poor. This "corruption of justice by those in positions of influence, particularly those too long in positions of influence, is a common occurrence" against which stern warnings were given in Exod 23:1–3.[28] This collectively shows a power differential between the accusers and the accused; their social and political capital is expended in the hopes of bringing symbolic, psychological and social harm to the psalmist.

Attacking the integrity and social standing of gay men by privileged people within the dominant heteronormative world is something that the gay community must face on a daily basis. The social and political structures that support the suppression of gay rights is not simply a feature in places like Brunei,[29] who have recently made it legal to stone gay men; it's also the indifference of Australian police towards hate crimes,[30] of Australian bishops who threaten gay workers with unemployment,[31] and of Australian politicians who link same-sex marriage to an increase in paedophilia.[32] Many in the gay community have felt the sting of these powerful people, have had to deal with the incredible harm caused, and they no longer trust those who are supposedly protecting the most marginalized of peoples. The psalmist and the gay community both know the cost of being *othered* and the pain and distress of the isolation that comes with it.

Verses 3–5: Instruction to the Community

> But know that God has reserved his covenantal partners for himself;
> God hears when this partner of his calls.
> Do not be disgusted in rage and sin;
> Think about it as you lie, and be silent.

26. DeClaissé-Walford, et al. *The Book of Psalms*, 84.

27. DeClaissé-Walford, et al. *The Book of Psalms*, 83–4.

28. Davidson, *The Vitality of Worship*, 23.

29. Haslam. "Travel Firms Shun Brunei over Law to Stone Gay People."

30. McGowan, "Police 'indifference' to Gay Hate Crimes."

31. DeBernardo, "If Marriage Equality Becomes Law."

32. Duffy, "Pauline Hanson Is 'worried.'"

> Offer the right sacrificial flesh,
> and put your faith in God.

As the lack of care or respect afforded to the psalmist continues, s/he may be "worried that [s/he] might not be among the elected faithful, yet confident that [s/he] can approach God openly, trusting that God will respond compassionately and look favorably on him [or her]."[33] The psalmist's declaration that God has set apart the faithful for Godself is as much a declaration of a known truth against accusers, as self-reassurance that s/he is amongst those who have an intimate relationship with the God of Compassion and Justice. This relationship is so integral to both, that one could translate "the faithful" (חָסִיד) as "covenant partner,"[34] emphasizing the relationality of their bond. This declaration to the accusers is followed by a statement of reassured faith that the psalmist is being heard, and, therefore, is in a right relationship with God.

Again in vv. 4 and 5, one could interpret the statement of making correct sacrifices, meditation, waiting in silence and trusting in God as both a rebuke against an accusation, as much as a reminder to oneself on how to meditate on the situation that is unfolding.[35] As these accusations have gone on for some time, and go to the core of one's identity as a people of God, the psalmist and the accusers are "in the grip of powerful emotions, often emotions which override rational conduct, such as hatred, jealousy, and bitterness."[36] These powerful emotions can take hold and the psalmist is telling the accusers, and reminding him or herself, that this level of emotive accusations cannot continue—they both need to take steps so that the sun does not set while they are still angry with one another.[37]

Verse 4 also stands within sharp contrast to v. 8, in which sleep is peaceful; here in v. 4 the psalmist is still agitated to the point of sleeplessness, needing this meditative response to the attacks on the psalmist's faith and character. There is an irony that cannot be lost on the gay community that the verb within the phrase "I will lie down" (אֶשְׁכְּבָה), in v. 8, is the same verb commanding that "you shall not lie" (תִשְׁכַּב) with a man like one does with a woman (Lev 18:22). For many in the gay community, the crux of religious conflict and questioning of identities forms around

33. Charry, *Psalms 1–50*, 19.

34. Bullock, et al. *Psalms*, 35.

35. Charry, *Psalms 1–50*, 17.

36. Davidson, *The Vitality of Worship*, 23.

37. Davidson, *The Vitality of Worship*, 24.

who one "lies" with, literally or sexually. One can see a clear contrast: if v. 4 is also a reminder to oneself, then v. 8 is a vindication that, in the end— regardless of sleepless nights, accusations of false faith and the anxieties of the world—God gives peace to God's "covenant partner."

Working towards that sense of "lying down" in safety will be a continued challenge for the gay community. The community is wrestling with ongoing challenges that hold back their ability to fully "lie" in peace. Forty percent (40%) of gay men, for example, are sexually assaulted[38] (excluding rape) and approximately sixty-five percent (65%) of all new HIV cases are gay men.[39] Gay men are being overlooked, and even sidelined, in discourse around their sexual and physical safety. Until society owns its role in providing this safety, be it physical, emotional, spiritual, or sexual, through restorative mechanisms, the gay community cannot fully "lie down and sleep in peace" (v. 8).

The final reminder to put one's faith in God (v. 4) echoes this understanding of reconciliation, as the statement asks one "not only to carry in one's heart the comforting conviction that the Lord is present to save, but carry out one's actions with a sense of responsibility to all members of the covenant community."[40] With these actions, the psalmist is encouraging a mirroring of relationship between God and God's people: a relationship of openness, trusting in compassion for one another. With this openness and trust comes the understanding that all is not lost between the accusers and the accused; instead, there is hope for reconciliation[41] that is transformative for all involved.

For many within the gay community, this need to reflect on what has been said in debates and in the heat of the moment can be a source of comfort and pain. Many have stories of being turned away from communion because they were gay, being told that gay marriage would lead to bestiality, being threatened and beaten on the streets, or arrested for simply being gay. But there are also a growing number of stories of catholic school principals standing up for their gay staff, stores sporting rainbow flags in support of a *Yes* vote, or the stories of young gay men who are entering a community more accepting than ever before. For many, these experiences bring both joy and heartache because they are so intimately

38. "NISVS: An Overview of 2010 Findings on Victimization by Sexual Orientation."
39. "HIV Statistics."
40. DeClaissé-Walford, et al. *The Book of Psalms*, 85.
41. Stuhlmueller, *Psalms 1, 1–72*, 73.

connected to the situation and it has raised their awareness of other injustices that are taking place both in and outside of Australia.

Many gay men are choosing to take the pain that they have experienced and, instead of letting it fester, used it to transform the wider
community. They have become advocates for gay rights overseas, but also
to fight for the rights of refugees or boycott Israel over its occupation of
Palestine. Although some gay men have not been able to heal from their
painful experiences imposed on them by dominant culture, many more
are not allowing the sun to set on their anger. Instead, they desire to pass
on their growing support to others who also need hope and signs that
they too are part of God's covenant community.

Verse 6: Complaint about What the Community Is Saying

> There are many who say, "O, that we might see some good!
> Let the light of your face shine on us, O Lord!"

The community of the accusers cry out, "claiming to want God, aware of
something amiss in their lives."[42] This cry is in stark contrast to their behavior towards the accused; their actions demonstrate that they are "unwilling
to take the step which would bring them into the light of God's presence
[. . .] Often good people are frightened to become God-filled people."[43] Instead, these people practice mimicry, faining the desires and appearance
of one who wants to transform their life by mirroring the open, trusting,
and compassionate nature of God. The accusers' community is unwilling
"to take the step which would convert that longing into reality, the step of
personally trusting in the Lord and thus allying themselves with, instead of
attacking, his people."[44] The accused knows their shouts for transformation
are entirely false, as the "good" (טוֹב) that they speak of is material wealth[45]
that cannot match the gladness on the psalmist's heart (v. 7) by the relational
bond shared between God and the psalmist as a member of God's people.

This false bounty that the "transformed" community speaks of is
no different from some of the social actors within the wider community
today. Brands such as Oreo and Absolut are known for branding their
merchandise with rainbow flags during Midsumma, Melbourne's Pride

---

42. Davidson, *The Vitality of Worship*, 24.
43. Davidson, *The Vitality of Worship*, 24.
44. Davidson, *The Vitality of Worship*, 24.
45. DeClaissé-Walford et al., *The Book of Psalms*, 83–84.

event, but do not create any true dialogue with the gay community and the rainbow flags disappear within days after the event. Likewise, some companies and organizations, such as the AFL and the police force, who were and are actively responsible for some of the harm in the gay community, are happy to take on the tropes of Pride, without actively taking steps to reconcile the incredible harm that they have done. These social actors have learnt that there is a large amount of social and economic capital to gain from outwardly showing support for the gay community. This outward transformation of society, like the psalmist's community, seems to have little understanding of what it means to be in communion with all of God's covenant partners. To be truly transformative, one must create real dialogue, ask for forgiveness, seek ways of making amends, and find ways of moving forward, in unison, as peoples of one community.

Verses 7–8: Closing Confession of Trust

Gayness, you have laid on my heart
more than when their profits roll in from their lands.
I will both lie down and sleep in peace;
for you alone, God, make me lie down in your trusted safety.

The psalmist concludes with words of peace, demonstrating that the anxiety and distress that was experienced before has subsided through God's peace. The psalmist is reassured, despite the words of the accusers, that "no single population should be insisted upon to the exclusion of others. The words of the psalm apply to the righteous and the wicked, the godly and the ungodly, accusers and the accused alike"[46] with regard to calling on God and the bond that God shares with humanity. As a result, one should leave aside humanity's focus of judgement, power, and privilege over each other, and reorient oneself towards God "in safety" (לָבֶטַח). This safety is not merely a safety that creates a physical sense of protection, but a realignment of thought and trust[47] in God.

This gradual shift away from the focus of judgement and power over and against others and redirecting this energy towards a higher purpose is where our wider community is finding itself today. Many barriers against equality have begun to be lifted, as gay rights groups and individuals are helping, with some coaxing, society to learn that the status quo of being

46. DeClaissé-Walford, et al. *The Book of Psalms*, 86.
47. Bullock et al., *Psalms*, 1, 35.

the arbiters of God's power has less and less sway amongst its members. As one reads this in a modern and gay Christian context, one must be reminded that the Christian faith is peacefully wrestling with us and for us within a paradox; "God [is] doing what is least expected, breaking out of an assigned role, breaking open the binary division [. . .], sensing pain, feeling fear [. . .], [and] tasting death."[48] Like the accusers within the psalm, one can be tempted to create categories of acceptability in God's sight. Yet, each time one tries to circumscribe acceptability on behalf of God, one is actually distancing themselves from the radical open embrace and paradox of God who cradles those who feel pushed to the outer edges of society.

Hearing the Psalm Anew

In the process of transmitting Psalm 4 to our modern context, some social actors from ancient times have imposed their socio-political narrative onto the text and recast it in ways that can obscure the original struggle and pain of its author. These people of power can marginalize and co-opt the narrative in a manner that expresses suffering through privileged positions as the only source of interpretation; it can, through this perspective, be interpreted as simply an attack from a "foreigner," someone who does not individually know them or care about their well-being. And yet, from the analysis of Psalm 4, it is clear that these painful accusations are not coming from external unknown sources, but rather from the powerful and political elite that see and interact with those they choose to harm on a regular basis. In reading this text as an external imposition onto "faithful" people, the cycle of exclusion, as opposed to communal and individual reconciliation with each other and with God, is allowed to perpetuate and the source of psychological pain can continue.

If one is to hear afresh the perspective of suffering from which this psalm speaks, one can utilize the lenses of the gay community as a placeholder to understanding the religious and communal harm that the psalmist addresses. In doing so, a face and an individual marginalized voice can speak from a particular context and stand in as a representative for, but not displace as the only perspective of, this hurt. It is important to stress that by allowing a gay perspective to permeate the interpretation and transmission of the text to the reader, the reader is intentionally

48. Talvacchia, Pettinger, and Larrimore, *Queer Christianities*, 59–60.

manipulating the text in order to enhance some characteristics while diminishing others. This manipulation is equally true if, in enhancing one
marginal voice, other marginal voices are not allowed to speak from the
narrative and dialogue within, beside and between the "marginality" and
the "acceptability" of voices. In recognizing the power of translation and
interpretation of a text, readers must understand that

> translation is [. . .] a transfer [. . .] [W]e leave something of our-
> selves behind as we make the border crossing, yet find a new
> dimension of ourselves on the other side [. . .] [W]e create the
> texts that create us, we ourselves are translated in the processes
> of translating texts.[49]

As a result, the reader must always faithfully be attuned to the growth
that they experience in their translation and interpretation, as much as
what is lost or diminished through the process of reading a text afresh.
The process of translation and interpretation is, by its nature, "a place
of cultural interaction"[50] that shapes one's understanding of the (pe)re-
ceived reality between the text and the interpreter.

The analysis of Psalm 4 can communicate anew to its audience in
light of this recognition for the concerns of the gay community to permeate the translation and interpretation of a text, using language appropriate
to their context and experience. In allowing this perspective to transform
a reading, words that have specific connotations for the gay community
could emerge that speak directly to a marginalized experience and create
dialogue regarding the difference in translation. Phrasing such as "God
of my right" (v. 1, NRSV) could be translated as "God, my Advocate" to
invoke the connotation for the gay community towards one who fights
for equal rights. Likewise, gay slang could enter the discourse and allow
space for their voices to literally be heard within the translation. Passages
such as "How long [. . .] shall my honor suffer shame?" (v. 2, NRSV)
could be recast as "How long [. . .] will you throw shade on me?" Lastly,
"right sacrifices" (v. 5 NRSV), could be translated as "the right sacrificial
flesh," alluding to the struggles that gay people face in redirecting the
theological conversation away from control over their bodies, and back
towards faith in God. This ability to reframe the text in new ways can
be transformative for the wider community and those that lie along the

---

49. Elliott and Boer, *Ideology, Culture, and Translation*, 1–2.
50. Elliott and Boer, *Ideology, Culture, and Translation*, 27.

spectrum of "marginality" and "acceptability," giving space for mutual integrity to a shared faith.

In addressing both the gift of cultural lenses to hear marginality from a text, as well as understand its pitfalls, this psalm can speak within the dialectal voice and experience of the gay community. In doing so, it can speak directly to the concerns that community members have while drawing out conversational partners in understanding the pain that marginalized peoples experience. Giving a gay perspective to the written expression of a psalm may be seen by some as outside the level of social appropriateness assigned to religion. Internal and external pressures affect the linguistic confidence or self-esteem, as Smalley explains,[51] and is a factor in locales that make use of particular speech patterns. These locations, thus, shape the register, formality, other linguistic and paralinguistic features, and even the language used within a specific context. Owing to this, to speak into the space of a particular habitus can offer insight for those not accustomed to the behavioral, linguistic, or social prompts given in the fresh expression of the text. Equally, it allows an invitation to those within a marginalized habitus to hear their own voice in what may have been an excluded space by the heteronormative world.

Although this piece is not an attempt to comprehensively examine how Psalm 4 speaks to marginalized communities, it is hoped that it engenders a space for how different marginal perspectives relate to the psalms beyond their gathering nature in worship. They can speak to and relay shared stories of pain and, in so doing, draw conversation with wider faith partners in the church community. In so doing, it may draw out the truth that the psalmist speaks from: God's peoples "can approach God openly, trusting that God will respond compassionately and look favorably"[52] on God's covenant partner. As we share the stories of our lived experience, we can come to God, however we appear or may have been perceived, and God will give us room so that all can "lie down and sleep in peace" (v. 8).

Bibliography

"Addiction and Abuse in the LGBT Community." *Desert Hope* (2019). https://deserthopetreatment.com/drug-abuse/lgbt-community/.

Bakhtin, M. M. *Rabelais and His World*. Translated by Helene Iswolsky. Cambridge: MIT Press, 1968.

51. Smalley, *Translation as Mission*, 142.

52. Charry, *Psalms 1–50*, 19.

Beilharz, Peter. *Social Theory: A Guide to Central Thinkers*. North Sydney: Allen & Unwin, 1992.

Boswell, John. *Same-Sex Unions in Premodern Europe*. New York: Villard, 1994.

Broyles, Craig C. *Psalms*. New International Biblical Commentary: Old Testament Series 11. Peabody, MA: Hendrickson, 2002.

Bullock, C. Hassell et al. *Psalms*. Vol. 1. 2 vols. Teach the Text Commentary. Grand Rapids: Baker, 2015.

Charry, Ellen T. *Psalms 1–50: Sighs and Songs of Israel*. Brazos Theological Commentary on the Bible. Grand Rapids: Brazos, 2015.

Craigie, Peter C., et al. *Psalms 1–50*. 2nd ed. Word Biblical Commentary 19. Grand Rapids: Zondervan, 2016.

Davidson, Robert. *The Vitality of Worship: A Commentary on the Book of Psalms*. Grand Rapids: Eerdmans, 1998.

DeBernardo, Francis. "If Marriage Equality Becomes Law, Archbishop Threatens to Fire Married Gay and Lesbian Church Workers." *New Ways Ministry* (August 22, 2017). https://www.newwaysministry.org/2017/08/22/if-marriage-equality-becomes-law-archbishop-threatens-to-fire-married-gay-and-lesbian-church-workers/.

DeClaissé-Walford, Nancy L., et al. *The Book of Psalms*. New International Commentary on the Old Testament. Grand Rapids: Eerdmans, 2014.

"Drug Addiction in the LGBT Community." *Promises Treatment Centers* (February 27, 2019). https://www.promises.com/blog/drug-addiction-in-the-lgbt-community/.

Duffy, Nick. "Pauline Hanson Is 'Worried' That Gay Marriage Will Lead to People Marrying Children." *PinkNews* (November 28, 2017). https://www.pinknews.co.uk/2017/11/28/pauline-hanson-is-worried-that-gay-marriage-will-lead-to-people-marrying-children/.

Elliott, Scott S., and Roland Boer. *Ideology, Culture, and Translation*. Semeia Studies 69. Atlanta: Society of Biblical Literature, 2012.

Haslam, Chris. "Travel Firms Shun Brunei over Law to Stone Gay People." *The Sunday Times* (World | April 07, 2019). https://www.thetimes.co.uk/edition/world/travel-firms-shun-brunei-over-law-to-stone-gay-people-k2mzp6snm.

"Hebrew OT—Transliteration—Holy Name KJV." *Read the Bible Online, Compare Translations, Post Your Comments, Search Cross-References, Strong's Concordance & Study in Hebrew-Greek*. http://www.qbible.com/hebrew-old-testament/psalms/4.html.

"HIV Statistics." Australian Federation of AIDS Organisations. https://www.afao.org.au/about-hiv/hiv-statistics/.

Loughlin, Gerard, ed. *Queer Theology: Rethinking the Western Body*. Oxford: Blackwell, 2007.

McGowan, Michael. "Police 'Indifference' to Gay Hate Crimes Led to Failures of Justice in NSW, Report Finds." *Guardian* (February 27, 2019). https://www.theguardian.com/world/2019/feb/27/police-indifference-to-gay-hate-crimes-led-to-failures-of-justice-report-finds.

Natasha, Tracy. "Homosexuality and Suicide: LGBT Suicide—A Serious Issue." *HealthyPlace* (April 12, 2013). https://www.healthyplace.com/gender/glbt-mental-health/homosexuality-and-suicide-lgbt-suicide-a-serious-issue.

"NISVS: An Overview of 2010 Findings on Victimization by Sexual Orientation." Center for Disease Control and Prevention. https://www.cdc.gov/violenceprevention/pdf/cdc_nisvs_victimization_final-a.pdf.

"Psalm 4 Interlinear Bible." *Bible Hub* (2012). https://biblehub.com/interlinear/psalms/4.htm.

Smalley, William A. *Translation as Mission: Bible Translation in the Modern Missionary Movement*. Modern Mission Era, 1792–1992. Macon, GA: Mercer University Press, 1991.

Stuhlmueller, Carroll. *Psalms 1: 1–72*. Old Testament Message 21. Wilmington, DE: Glazier, 1983.

Talvacchia, Kathleen T. et al., eds. *Queer Christianities: Lived Religion in Transgressive Forms*. New York: New York University Press, 2015.

PART 3

Ceremony

15

Ruth et alia

ELLIE ELIA AND JIONE HAVEA

[*On a stage. Lights come up on a frozen scene: Three women sit at a table with coffee and cake, and a tall lit candle. Bella holds a closed bible to her chest as if to protect it. Reggie puts her head in her hands, clearly upset. Seiko rests an open bible on her lap and looks perplexed. The three women do not notice a fourth woman at the corner—Ruth, one leg taking a step, as if to enter from another world. The three women stir when Ruth steps forward, but freeze mid action when Ruth speaks.*]

Ruth: How strange, that my name lives on. On paper. In a book. Scripturalized. And on bodies, of women. My name is re-membered.

[*Turning to the audience*]

You speak it like you own my name, like it was your very own. You even think you own me. My name. My words. My story. My body. My everything.

But . . . who cares about my roots? My heritage?

Do you know my mother's name? My father's, perhaps? Do you care if they were alive when I was first taken?

Funny that . . . You know the name of the dead man who must not
be forgotten . . . what was it again? Uh, *my god*, Eli . . . Eli who is some
kind of king? Who cares about kings, righteous or not? And please, drop
that Meleki-zedek living tradition.

Have you ever wondered how I first came to marry that foreign
man? You forget that I was once a daughter . . . named by my parents, in
honor of their roots. My name at birth was for them a reminder. But my
current name was given to me by my first husband's people.

What's in a name, anyway? A past. A future. Given. Taken . . . a
name is as fragile as the pages of history, as dry as the journals of kings.

What's in my name? Those Judahites say it has something to do with
character. Faithfulness. Devotion. Commitment. Stubborn loyalty. I did
not grow up in their language world, so I don't really know.

What's in a name? A weapon. Another's bloody bloodline.

They call my name, but I do not recognize the sounds, spoken with
an unfamiliar tongue.

My name is . . .

All women: Ruth!

> [*As they speak her name, the three women at the table look out at
> the audience, and then freeze.*]

Ruth: My name fills their lips like a forbidden kiss. Yes, these women
know me, like they know themselves.

> [*The three women unfreeze, shift position and freeze again. Ruth
> remains unnoticed to the three women. Bella unfreezes. She stands
> up, faces the audience, and shares her inner thoughts.*]

Bella: I love Ruth!

> [*Ruth comes close to Bella, and stands beside her.*]

She is so strong and brave and faithful—a role model. After all that
hardship and the endless son of blah blah blah . . . she is remembered.
She is named. She is part of God's sacred story—all the way to King David
and to our crucified Lord Jesus.

And then on my wedding day, she gave us our vows

> [*Ruth looks at Bella; Bella looks at the audience.*]

Bella and Ruth: Where you go, I will go; where you lodge, I will lodge; your people shall be my people, and your God my God. Where you die, I will die—there will I be buried.

Bella: It was so beautiful, so simple, and so perfect.

> [*Bella returns to her seat and takes her initial pose. Ruth moves in the other direction.*]

Ruth: So I'm a love story, a promise for the future, a hope of being loved and not forgotten. A sign that she and I matter to God.

> [*Reggie suddenly stands up and speaks to the audience; Ruth slowly turns towards her.*]

Reggie: It's just tragic, holding Ruth up like some sort of trophy. She's just another victim of a patriarchal world, like Hagar, Tamar, Zuleika, Zipporah, and all the way to the Samaritan woman.

In fact, we are just like her. A possession, a transaction, used, abused, bought and sold in the service of men. Sure, she challenges some social norms but in the end, in the end, that man redeems her like a raffle ticket—Boaz, the lucky winner!

I remember when I left my husband, my god, I swore I would never, ever, let anyone control me like that again. I swore. I will never let a man take me like that.

> [*Ruth reaches out to touch Reggie's shoulder, but before she does Reggie returns to her seat and takes on her initial pose.*]

Ruth: I'm a disappointment, a false idol, a broken dream, a warning that she and I must keep fighting.

> [*Seiko closes her Bible, remains seated; Seiko speaks directly to the audience with a foreign accent.*]

Seiko: Lest we forget, Ruth was a foreigner. They wanted her to act and speak like them, and they constantly remind her that she is a foreigner in their home . . .

> [*Ruth approaches and stands behind Seiko.*]

Seiko and Ruth: Your people, your God, your land, your story.

Seiko: With every mention of her name comes a reminder—she is a Moabite, and an in-law. She is outsider-times-two. I don't know if we should hate her or love her.

When I moved to this land, I tried so hard to fit in, to be like them, and to be like you. I was desperate for acceptance, I was desperate . . . and I was desired. Ruth is like me . . . she never belongs: that status is worse than being homeless, worse than not having a name.

[*Seiko closes her bible and returns to her initial pose.*]

Ruth: I'm an outsider par excellence. Someone to be feared, someone to be desired, some One to be . . . othered.

True, I came with Naomi from Moab. But no one bothers to check how my mother was a migrant to Moab. I am not fully Moabite. I come from two peoples. I have many roots.

[*Ruth moves close to Seiko, opens the bible on her lap and tucks her hair behind her ear.*]

Ruth [*speaking to Seiko*]: But I'm also unpredictable. What's in my name? A presence. A present. And an unseen gift.

[*Ruth walks towards the audience and speaks*]

I'm a survivor. I can survive anything because I raised myself. I don't even remember my mother. She was gone before I joined the way of women. Motherly blood came, but mother did not come for me. I grew up without a model for motherhood, nor for mothering. I mothered me own self.

[*The stage comes alive. Reggie slams her bible down on the table in anger. All the women unfreeze. Ruth observes.*]

Reggie: How can you call it a love story, Bella? Look what happened to her that evening. She came back tired from gleaning all day in Boaz's plot, and what did Naomi do? She sent Ruth right out, right away, to the threshing floor. What kind of mother sends her daughter to prostitute, for profit and glory?

Bella: Naomi is just trying to help, Reggie. She knows what she is doing.

Reggie: That's what makes me angry. She knows exactly what she's doing and it's dangerous. Only moments before, Naomi warned Ruth to stay in Boaz' garden so that she does not get molested. Stay with the young women, don't go to the young men. But now, now Bella, she sends Ruth to the threshing floor—where old and young men are—all dressed up and smelling sweet and ready to be taken by a blesser.

Bella: But nothing happened!

Reggie: Come on! Do you really think Naomi sent Ruth there to give Boaz a foot massage?

Seiko: Why do you assume that Ruth is not in control of her actions? Perhaps she knows exactly what she is doing, what she needs to do to survive. Maybe she is just letting Naomi feel needed.

In any case she doesn't exactly do what Naomi tells her, does she? Naomi told her to go and wait for Boaz to tell her what to do, but Ruth did not beat around the bushes. Ruth tells Boaz up front who she is, and she tells him what to do.

Reggie: I just don't think it's fair that she should have to sneak up on a man in order to survive. I haven't fought so hard all my life to watch my daughters be told that they are worthless without a husband or a son.

Seiko: Believe me, I understand. But I wonder if you are afraid that it's Ruth who used her own mind and sexuality to get the security she wanted?

Reggie: Like a mail-order bride?

Seiko: Maybe. We cannot separate the facts that she is a woman *and* a migrant. She picks up the scraps that others leave behind because that's what the new culture she has entered allows in such situations. But she does more than that, she takes the situation into her own hands, she takes the law into her own hands, she gets Boaz to marry her. You can keep seeing her as a victim, but to me, she's a model migrant. She survives with her wits.

(*Silence*)

Bella: Oh-o-ok maybe something did happen. I don't know, it's so confusing. Don't men usually make the first move?

Anyway, doesn't Boaz act honorably? I think that Boaz is a good man, who cares about her and Naomi.

Reggie: Do you think he was so honorable when he tells his workers to leave Ruth and not shame her? Don't you see, Bella—he fancied her, and had no concern for the other women in the garden? Boaz did make the first move. He sent her home from the garden with a heap of seeds. And after that next night, he sent her home with 6-times more seeds. Do you think he is honorable sending her off with payment for her services, before anyone can see her?

Seiko: I wonder why he gave her that pile of grain to take home? A huge pile, six times more than the previous day.

Bella: I think it was a sign of his promise to provide for her and Naomi?

Reggie: But that's not what he says is it, he just tells her that no one must see her. He gives her the grains, and he goes to town.

Bella: Then it must be that he wanted to show Naomi that she will be cared for . . . In the end Boaz does fulfil his promise.

Reggie: In the end Ruth is forgotten.

Bella: But she's not forgotten, is she? Her child becomes the ancestor of David. Isn't that something to remember? Ruth was kind and faithful, she patiently stood by Naomi through her endless grief and the death of her children. Ruth followed her to a different country and never stopped caring for her. Isn't that why she is remembered?

Seiko: It depends on who's telling the story and who the story is for.

Reggie: What do you mean?

Seiko: Well, in the end, does the story affirm Ruth or ultimately erases her? Is she an insider or an outsider? She gave birth to a child, but the neighborhood women took the boy and made him to be Naomi's child.

(*Silence*)

I'm not sure I like Ruth finding a home with these people where the only way to be accepted is to become like them.

Bella: She did choose to leave her home and follow Naomi, no one pressured her to make that decision.

Reggie: Why didn't she go home to her mother's house? The mother was not there, but the house was. I think that's why I get so angry. What if she was running away from something terrible, like Hagar the Egyptian, only to find herself in an even more frightening place?

> [*Silence; stage goes black, except for a spotlight on Ruth, who speaks into the distance.*]

Ruth: I remember the stars that night and how different they seemed. I could feel the heat rising from my body with fear and excitement. And the smell, an ancient sort of smell, hot flesh, sweat and tears mingled with the harvest and the illusion of hope. He woke like a lost bull desperate for water, confused, almost childlike groping in the dark looking for his mother's breast.

And in the morning, as I walked away, I felt a thousand eyes on me, and ten thousand stories followed my footsteps. But all I wanted at that point was for someone to take my name and leave the story without my presence.

All I wanted that morning was to give my name to future storyweavers, so that future stories are not Ruth-less.

> [*Silence; lights out.*]

Index